DATE			

DEVELOPMENT ALTERNATIVES
OF MEXICO

Beyond the 1980s

Robert E. Looney

PRAEGER SPECIAL STUDIES • PRAEGER SCIENTIFIC

Library of Congress Cataloging in Publication Data

Looney, Robert E.
   Development alternatives of Mexico:beyond the
1980s.

   Bibliography: p.
   1. Mexico—Economic policy—1970-
I. Title.
HC135.L6137   1982   338.972   82-11288
ISBN 0-03-060242-4

Published in 1982 by Praeger Publishers
CBS Educational and Professional Publishing
a Division of CBS Inc.
521 Fifth Avenue, New York, New York 10175, U.S.A.

© 1982 by Praeger Publishers

23456789   052   987654321

Printed in the United States of America

For Anne

It is a truism that resource based economies should safe-
guard against the future and pursue a policy of planned spending.
Yet to even the most casual observer, the OPEC states evidence
the obvious dangers of undisciplined spending behavior and
heavy reliance on an easy single income that is unlikely to last
longer than a few decades. This book is designed to illuminate
the long-run problem facing one such economy, that of Mexico.
A planning model is presented and used to examine the intertemporal investment strategies open to that country. The model
is formulated in the framework of optimal control theory, which
is the method of optimum choice over time. The variables to be
chosen pertain to different dates over the 1980-95 period. The
characteristics of the economy expressed first by means of a
macroeconomic model is subsequently invoked in the optimization
process.

As a first step in the analysis, numerical solutions are
compared with the actual policies practiced in Mexico over the
1974-79 period, and the differences between the two are examined
in detail. It turns out that the two differ markedly. The
expansion program Mexico attempted to implement after the oil
discoveries in the early 1970s was well over the limits of the
absorptive capacity of the economy. Moreover, the results
clearly indicate that the financial and exchange rate crisis faced
by the country in early 1982 were primarily the result of the
government's expenditure policy combined with its poor financial
management. One of the more interesting features of the model
is its predictive power; i.e., it projects that the expansion
pressures imposed on the country during the late 1970s will
continue to stifle growth unless proper stabilization measures
are pursued. That steady growth with minimal inflation through
the 1980s and 1990s is well within the reach of the country's
planners if more prudent expenditure policies are followed is
one of the more optimistic implications of the model's forecasts.

This study is also a follow-up of the author's first book
on Mexico, Mexico's Economy: A Policy Analysis with Forecasts
to 1990 (Boulder, Colo.: Westview Press, 1978). In reviewing
that book, Clark Reynolds noted, "at a time of post-petroleum
crisis fascination with the Mexican economy, the appearance of
this volume commands attention. While it was written before

the bonanza was fully evident, its clear and comprehensive style and optimistic conclusions should be welcome to those who are just discovering Mexico." (Journal of Economic Literature, June 1980). It has been several years since that book was written, and in the interim the significance of the oil price increases and oil discoveries in Mexico have become apparent. The purpose of this book, then, is not only to update the earlier work, but also to draw a somewhat different picture of the future based on these developments.

Altogether, the future looks very different from the way it did when the first book on Mexico was written. Perhaps the 1982 scare of impending financial collapse and internal turmoil might be summarized by noting that, if it is unfortunately true that Mexico wasted five years during which it refused to admit the limits of oil based wealth, there is now at least the possibility that future oil revenues give it something that history seldom provides: a second chance.

ACKNOWLEDGMENTS

My appreciation is due to many individuals who have assisted in helping me conceptualize the study. Discussions at the 1981 Eastern Economic Association meetings in Philadelphia with Leopoldo Solis of the Bank of Mexico, Abel Beltran del Rio of Wharton Econometric Forecasting Associates, Inc., Jeffrey Nugent of the University of Southern California, Edward Nell of the New School of Social Research, Jimmy Wheeler of the Hudson Institute, and Edgar Ortiz of the Universidad Nacional Autonoma de Mexico provided the initial stimulus. In Mexico, Barbara Griffiths and Llewellyn Pasco of the American Embassy aided in providing a wide range of up-to-date statistics on the economy.

As in the first book, discussions with Redvers Opie helped focus my attention on the economy's increased inflationary tendencies and the general limitations of government policy in controlling the overall pace of economic development.

The Mexican banking community was extremely helpful in sharing their perceptions of the country's changing financial situation. In this regard, I am especially grateful to Enrique de Bayle of Banco Nacional de Mexico and Carlos Bracho of Banco Serfin for their time and insights.

Short visits to Mexico with Eugene Mihaly, Rex Beach, and Gary Hare of Mihaly Associates International enabled me not only to gather additional information but, more importantly, to share firsthand the views of the Mexican business community.

At the Naval Postgraduate School, Peter Frederiksen aided in some of the computer analysis. My research assistant, Haruko Mimura, developed the optimal control programs from the original ones constructed by Garret Vanderplaats. I am particularly indebted to Dr. Vanderplaats for sharing his original optimal control programs.

Finally, special gratitude goes to my wife, Anne, who persevered through numerous rough drafts with patience and good cheer. Her help and encouragement made the book possible.

Special gratitude goes to the Research Foundation at the Naval Postgraduate School for its financial assistance during the spring and summer of 1981, which enabled me to complete the empirical sections of the book.

The responsibility for any errors or shortcomings is solely mine. Also, it should be noted that this study does not necessarily in any way reflect the views of the Research Foundation of the Naval Postgraduate School or the Department of National Security Affairs.

CONTENTS

DEVELOPMENT ALTERNATIVES
OF MEXICO

INTRODUCTION:
ECONOMIC STRUCTURES
AND FORCES

INTRODUCTION

Mexico is one of the world's largest countries in a number of respects. The nation's area of nearly 1 million square kilometers places it thirteenth in the world in geographic size. With over 65 million inhabitants (mid-1979), the country ranks eleventh in population, just ahead of West Germany. A gross domestic product of 121.3 billion dollars in 1979 made the country the world's eighteenth largest economy, and a per capita GNP of $1640[1] in 1979 was sufficient to place the country in the group of newly industrializing countries far ahead of the average for developing countries as a whole.[2]

Why is the Mexican experience important, and to whom? Not surprisingly, the United States, Japanese, Canadian, and European multinational companies seeking business expansion opportunities have been attracted to Mexico. Many officials of other developing countries have been scrutinizing the Mexican development model for policies and practices that they might adopt in their own national efforts to accelerate economic growth. Academic scholars, also, have been drawn to the Mexican case as a source of new insights into the process of political, social, and economic development.[3]

The Mexican case, however, has broad international importance beyond these special group interests. In a world where the supply of natural resources is becoming scarce relative to growing world demand, Mexico stands out as one of the few areas with vast potential for increasing the supply of strategic materials. It has only begun to tap its large oil deposits, and through further exploration may approach Saudi Arabia as an exporter of hydrocarbons.

Despite increased academic interest in Mexico, the press remains the principal source of information on the country for most foreigners. In the foreign press, Mexico has received both glowing eulogies and bitter criticisms. Business journals by and large have accentuated the positive features, emphasizing the business opportunities created by rapid growth and the political stability maintained by the dominant political party, the Partido Revolucionario Institutional (PRI). Other journalists, frequently joined by scholars, questioned the ethics of economic development in an environment that seems to condone high degrees of inequality and corruption.

The Mexican experience is sufficiently significant to warrant a more comprehensive analysis that allows the observer to evaluate the economic achievement against the political and social cost. Mexico's development progress gives it a chance of becoming one of the first major countries to cross the wide chasm separating the less developed and the developing countries. If it achieves this distinction while improving the economic, political, and social quality of life for its people, Mexico will be a source of encouragement and hope for billions of the world's population that still remain in poverty.

As background for the more detailed analysis in subsequent chapters, the sections that follow attempt to provide a long-term overview of Mexico's development efforts and accomplishments, examine the evolutionary patterns in key economic, social, and political sectors, identify the motive forces and sources of growth and identify the major problems the economy faces in the future.

BASIC ECONOMIC FACTS

Mexico's relevant prosperity has come fairly recently. The three decades from 1910 to 1940 were a turbulent period of revolution and reform. With real output growing (Tables 1.1, 1.2) at an average annual rate of about seven-tenths of 1 percent from 1910 to 1930, growth increased by around 2.9 percent in the 1930s, but it was the tenfold increase in GDP between 1949 and 1978 that propelled Mexico into the class of newly industrializing nations. During this period, Mexico's real output in constant prices increased at an average rate of growth of 6.2 percent per year, well ahead of the population growth rate of 3.3 percent. More specifically, between 1925 and 1939 the GNP grew at a rate of 1.5 percent per year. Then the annual growth rates

TABLE 1.1

Mexico: Population, Product, Employment, and Productivity, Selected Years, 1910-78

	1910	1921	1930	1940	1950	1960	1970	1978
Population (millions)	15.2	14.3	16.6	19.6	25.8	35.0	50.7[a]	66.8
Real GDP (billions of 1975 pesos)								
Total	74	80	85	114	223	386	761	1,105
Agriculture[b]	20	20	17	24	39	61	88	100
Industry	14	18	21	27	60	112	262	401
Services	39	41	47	63	123	211	410	604
Real GDP/Capita (1975 pesos)								
Total	4,870	5,570	5,150	5,820	8,630	11,000	15,000	16,540
Agriculture[a]	1,350	1,430	1,050	1,230	1,530	1,750	1,740	1,500
Industry	920	1,260	1,250	1,400	2,330	3,210	5,170	6,000
Services	2,600	2,880	2,850	3,190	4,770	6,040	8,090	9,040
Employment (Thousands)								
Total	5,260	4,880	5,150	5,860	8,270	11,270	13,340	17,100
Agriculture[a]	3,600	3,490	3,630	3,830	4,820	6,100	5,000	5,600
Industry	900	660	770	910	1,320	2,140	3,080	4,300
Services	760	730	750	1,120	2,130	3,030	5,260	7,200

(continued)

3

Table 1.1 (continued)

	1910	1921	1930	1940	1950	1960	1970	1978
Employment/Population Ratio (%)	34.6	34.1	31.0	29.9	32.0	32.2	26.3	25.6
Productivity (GDP/worker, 1975 pesos)								
Total	14,000	16,300	16,600	19,500	26,900	34,200	56,900	64,600
Agriculture[a]	5,700	5,870	4,790	6,280	8,190	10,100	17,700	17,900
Industry	15,400	27,300	26,800	30,200	45,500	52,500	84,800	93,300
Services	51,800	56,100	63,000	56,000	57,800	69,700	77,900	83,900

[a]Population estimates differ in various sources. The high figure shown here leads to a high growth-rate estimate for the 1960-70 period (and consequently to a somewhat low rate of growth in GDP per capita for the same period).

[b]Includes forestry and fishing.

Sources: Calvin P. Blair, "Economic Development Policy in Mexico: A New Penchant for Planning," Office of Public Sector Studies, Institute of Latin American Studies, The University of Texas at Austin, Technical Papers Series No. 26 (1980), p. 19. Nacional Financiera, Statistics on the Mexican Economy (1977), pp. 3-4, 13-15, 38-39. Banco de Mexico. Review of the Economic Situation of Mexico (September 1978), p. 350. International Financial Statistics, May 1978, p. 275, and May 1979, p. 258. Banco de Mexico, Informe Anual 1978, pp. 21-32, 50-64. Figures in 1975 pesos were calculated by the author from data given in the sources cited. Estimates for 1978 were made on the basis of preliminary and partial data. Details may not add to totals because of rounding.

TABLE 1.2

Mexico: Average Annual Growth Rates in Population, Product,
Employment, and Productivity, Selected Periods, 1910-78
(percent per year)

	1910-1921	1921-1930	1930-1940	1940-1950	1950-1960	1960-1970	1970-1978	1940-1978
Population	-0.6	1.7	1.7	2.8	3.1	3.8	3.5	3.3
Real GDP								
Total	0.7	0.8	2.9	6.9	5.6	7.0	4.8	6.2
Agriculture*	0.0	-1.8	3.3	5.1	4.6	3.7	1.6	3.8
Industry	2.3	1.6	2.9	8.1	6.5	8.8	5.5	7.4
Services	0.4	1.6	2.8	7.0	5.6	6.8	5.0	6.1
Real GDP/Capita								
Total	1.2	-0.9	1.2	4.0	2.5	3.2	1.2	2.8
Agriculture*	0.5	-3.4	1.6	2.2	1.4	0.0	-1.8	0.5
Industry	2.9	-0.1	1.1	5.2	3.2	4.9	1.9	3.9
Services	0.9	-0.1	1.1	4.1	2.4	3.0	1.4	2.8
Employment								
Total	-0.7	0.6	1.3	3.5	3.1	1.7	3.2	2.8
Agriculture*	-0.3	0.4	0.5	2.3	2.4	-1.9	1.4	1.0
Industry	-2.8	1.8	1.6	3.8	5.0	3.7	4.2	4.2
Services	-0.3	0.3	4.0	6.6	3.6	5.6	4.1	5.0
Productivity								
Total	1.4	0.2	1.6	3.3	2.4	5.2	1.6	3.2
Agriculture*	0.3	-2.2	2.7	2.7	2.1	5.8	0.1	2.8
Industry	5.3	-0.2	1.2	4.2	1.4	4.9	1.2	3.0
Services	0.7	1.3	-1.2	0.3	1.9	1.1	0.9	1.1

*Includes forestry and fishing.
Source: Table 1.1.

increased rapidly, averaging 5.8 percent between 1940 and 1954, 5.9 percent between 1955 and 1961, 7.6 percent between 1962 and 1970, and 5.4 percent between 1971 and 1977. Since 1977, the rate of growth has averaged between 7.5 and 8.0 percent.

The growth rates of the per capita GNP are also high and have been sustained over a fairly long period: 2.9 percent between 1949 and 1954, 2.7 percent between 1955 and 1961, 4 percent between 1962 and 1970, and 2 percent between 1971 and 1977. In 1980 a per capita growth rate of from 4.3 to 4.8 percent is foreseen.

From 1939 to 1978 the gross investment per inhabitant increased from 21 (in 1960 pesos) to 7,163. The volume of industrial production increased from 3.2 percent in 1940 to 273.9 in 1972 on an index with 1960 as 100. Installed electric energy capacity increased from 629,000 kilowatts in 1937 to almost 13 million in 1976. The highway system expanded from 9,929 kilometers in 1940 to 200,060 in 1977.

As might be expected, rapid increases in output have been associated with major shifts in the structure of the economy. Agriculture has expanded rapidly in absolute terms, but declined in relative importance (from 21 percent of GDP in 1940 to 9 percent in 1978), while industry as a whole (mining, manufacturing, construction, and energy) grew from 24 percent of GDP in 1940 to 36 percent in 1978. Manufacturing alone increased in relative importance from about 19 percent of total output in 1940 to 23 percent in 1978. More importantly, the composition of industry has shifted significantly away from light consumer goods (food, beverages, tobacco, textiles, clothing, shoes, and paper) toward modern high technology plants in iron and steel, petroleum refining, petrochemicals, fertilizers, electrical equipment, and transport equipment. Large-scale modern industry now accounts for more than 7 percent of GDP.

The dynamic behavior of the Mexican economy since 1977 has been centered on the sectors producing hydrocarbons and derivatives, on the construction industry, and on some branches of the manufacturing sector, especially those related to the production of machinery and equipment.

As a result of these developments, Mexico is often cited in the literature as having one of the most successful developmen models. While this point is debatable and in fact a prime concern of the chapters that follow, there is no doubt that the relationship between the public and private sectors not only is unique, but also has proven capable of adapting to changing conditions. [4]

Largely because of its resources and pragmatic approach toward development, Mexico is now among the leading ten or twenty countries in the world in size of labor force and in total use of energy, steel, cement, fertilizers, rail freight, air travel, motor vehicles, telephones, radios, television sets, and medical doctors. Recent discoveries of new oil fields guarantee the country abundant cheap energy for at least the next two decades. In addition, there are excellent long-run prospects for alternative energy sources such as solar, geothermal, and nuclear. In sum, Mexico now exhibits many of the key features of a large modern industrial nation state.

POPULATION GROWTH

As noted, by mid-1978 Mexico had a population of over 68 million people. High annual growth rates suggest at least a doubling of the country's inhabitants by 2000. Historically, the Mexican government was essentially neutral on birth control and family planning issues. However, because population grew at a yearly average of 3.4 percent in the 1960s and agriculture was increasingly unable to provide for self-sufficiency in food, the authorities began actively advocating birth control and family planning in the early 1970s. Since 1973, the government's program has had a considerable response—in fact some even credit it with a significant decline in the birth rate. The birth rate declined from 45 live births per thousand population in 1975 to about 38 in 1978. Further gains may come more slowly, however, because the most receptive group in the population has already been reached; i.e., the government's efforts at reducing the growth in population have been largely concentrated in urban areas, and, given that almost half the population is rural, it may be some time before a significant further reduction in growth occurs.[5]

Nevertheless, the government's objective is to reduce the birth rate such that population growth will have fallen to 2.5 percent by 1982 and 1 percent by 2000. These goals clearly assume both a major expansion of the population planning programs as well as a substantial increase in the number of respondents. So far, the majority of women taking active part in the program have been over 35 years old. In general, women in this age group have tended to have only one-third the fertility potential of women between the ages of 15 and 34. Since over half the population of Mexico is under the age of 15, it would seem imperative for the success of the program to solicit an increased response from the younger women in order to speak seriously about a 1 percent population growth rate by 2000.[6]

It is also possible that the recent decline in the birth rate may be somewhat deceptive. The infant mortality rate has also declined significantly since 1960, raising the proportion of the population under age 15. Other things being equal, an increase in the number of persons outside the prime childbearing age reduces the denominator in calculating the birth rate. Mathematically, the effect is to decrease the rate itself, despite the fact that women in each age group may have the fertility patterns Thus the decline in the birth rate may hold less significance for the future than would seem at first sight.

Most forecasts of the population assume some sort of change in the birth rate. But because the actual decline is highly uncertain, projections for the year 2000 range from an extremely optimistic 109.0 million people to 143.5 million. The World Bank projects 116 million people by 2000, which reflects a significant slowing in the rate of population growth.

Estimates of the average annual rate of population growth during the 1970s range from about 3.3 percent to 3.5 percent, depending on assumptions made about migration to the United States. The World Bank projection of the Mexican population in the year 2000 implies an annual growth rate of roughly 2.6 percent. However, it is likely that population growth will follow a pattern of slow decline with growth close to 3 percent during most of this decade. Without substantial improvement in agricultural output, a higher level of imports will be required to maintain per capita consumption levels.[7]

Labor Market Patterns

Historically, Mexico has had one of the lowest sustained rates of open unemployment in Latin America, despite very wide fluctuations in the country's economic activity and in the demand for labor in the economy's more productive high wage occupations It appears that rather than becoming involuntarily unemployed in slack periods, Mexican workers have tended to withdraw voluntarily from the labor markets, find low-income self-employment in the informal sector, or remain idle for large portions of the year.

For example, between 1940 and 1959 female labor participation rates doubled as jobs became more plentiful but then fell again between 1960 and 1970 as the labor market weakened. In the 1960s the growth of self-employment in urban services was substantial, as modern sectors failed to provide enough jobs for migrants from agriculture. By the mid-1970s outmigration of labor appears to have accelerated in the face of a severe domestic recession.

Since the supply of labor in Mexico tends to shift with demand at the subsistence level, the labor slack shows itself less in terms of open unemployment than in a number of other indicators:[8]

1. lagging or declining earnings of unskilled laborers
2. falling female participation rates
3. increased seasonal unemployment and underemployment
4. increased self-employment (especially in the urban informal sector)
5. slowed emigration from the rural to urban areas within Mexico
6. increased pressures for migration to the United States.

In recent years population growth has outpaced the economy's employment capacity. There are no regular or reliable statistics on unemployment in Mexico. As noted, the fraction of the labor force actually doing nothing productive is fairly low, but if one counts as underemployed those persons who earn less than the minimum wage or who work without pay in family enterprises, then the sum of unemployment plus underemployment may easily reach 40 to 50 percent of the labor force.[9]

The little information that exists on open unemployment is largely derived from sample surveys. These indicate that open unemployment rates even in the metropolitan areas, where they tend to reach their maximum levels, are not high compared to those in countries with demographic dynamics similar to Mexico's. From 1973 to 1979, for example, the open unemployment rate in the Federal District varied from a minimum of 6.1 percent in 1975-IV to a maximum of 8.6 percent in 1977-III.[10]

The structure of open unemployment by age and sex is similar to that of other countries, with significantly greater rates for people under 24 years old. Thus in 1978 the economically active population from 12 to 19 years had open unemployment rates of 18.3, 13.1, and 16.1 percent in Mexico City, Guadalajara, and Monterrey, respectively, compared with total rates of only 6.4, 5.8, and 6.2 percent, respectively. To a lesser degree there is a significant difference between the unemployment rates experienced by men and women, with women in all age groups, except between the ages of 55 and 64 in Mexico City, experiencing higher rates of unemployment.

As one might expect, there are major variations by economic sector and by geographical region. Unemployment and underemployment are heavily concentrated in agriculture, petty commerce, and the service trades, and their combined rates are highest (over 60 percent of the labor force) in the poor states in the south of Mexico. Even in the major population centers—cities of more than 200,000 inhabitants—some 20 to 45 percent of the labor force can be counted as unemployed or underemployed. Nor does Mexico's pattern of development offer great help for a rapid reduction in those rates. The fastest growing sector, manufacturing, has always had a low elasticity of employment with respect to output, and some 800,000 new jobs are needed yearly just to employ additions to the labor force.[11]

Further, the severity of the problem is not likely to diminish in the near future. Even at the government's targeted economic growth rate of 6 to 7 percent a year, a maximum of 150,000 new jobs a year can be provided. President Lopez Portillo has noted that, even with the likely expansion of oil revenues, it will take almost 20 years to create enough new jobs to defuse the unemployment crisis.[12]

Most of the problem of underemployment stems from the fact that about one-third of the Mexican population still attempts to make its living from the land, yet the agricultural sector accounts for only around 9 percent of the country's GDP. Stagnation of production in agriculture in the past decade has greatly reduced the demand for labor. At the same time, the increased availability of labor has furthered underemployment by cutting the number of days worked and consequently average incomes.

Low productivity in the agricultural sector is the primary factor in Mexican underemployment. Value added per worker in the agricultural sector has been as low as one-third of the national average. Because rural lands are overworked and overcrowded, migration of people from the rural areas into the cities has accelerated. This is most apparent in Mexico City, which now has about 14 million residents and experiences an annual influx of nearly 750,000. By the year 2000, the population of Mexico City is expected to reach 32 million, making it the world's largest metropolis (at currently projected growth rates).

Income Inequality

Income and demographic movements have produced gross inequalities not only in income distribution on a personal basis but on a geographical level as well. Average income per capita in the richest zone, the Federal District, is six times that in the poorest state of Oaxaca.[13] The average income per family for the highest 10 percent of the national population is about 31 times that of families in the poorest 10 percent. One-fifth of the families receive well over half of all income, while the poorer half of families receive less than one-fifth of all income— a situation that has changed only slightly in twenty or thirty years. The Gini coefficient for Mexico is about 0.6, indicating one of the world's most unequal income distributions,[14] and though the absolute level of real income has risen for the vast majority of Mexicans save perhaps for the poorest 10 percent, some signs indicate that inequality has worsened over the years.

As a result, about 45 percent of all Mexican families can be classified as poor; their incomes are less than half the national average. Income inequality in both rural and urban areas is among the world's worst. Figures on income reflect this. In 1975, for example, the poorest 20 percent of households received less than 2 percent of income, while the richest 20 percent received 60 percent of income. Moreover, data from previous years indicate that, contrary to the pattern exhibited by most other countries at similar stages of development, the income gap between Mexico's rich and its poor is actually worsening. Rural areas have been most affected by this growing relative inequality, particularly during the last decade. This seems to reflect the failure of the land redistribution program and the increasing duality of Mexican agriculture. Mexico's peasants continue to receive the poorer (hence less productive) lands and are consequently subject to diminishing income potential and lower real incomes. After agriculture, the most noticeable concentrations of the poor are self-employed and salaried workers in manufacturing and construction.[15]

Some 18 million underprivileged people in rural areas live in extreme misery. Forty million Mexicans have a nutritionally inadequate diet, and 30 percent of the population consume 10 percent of the food produced, while the 15 percent with the most buying power consume 50 percent. Only 35 percent of the population is covered by the social security system. Medical care represents only 2 percent of the GNP. The housing deficit is 5 million units. Forty percent of the heads of households never finished primary school.[16]

These patterns should not, however, detract from the fact that real per capita gross domestic product has risen at an annual average rate of 1.8 percent since 1970. Household budget surveys indicate that even the poor may have had a real increase in income; i.e., budget data, adjusted by the World Bank for underreporting, show that the real income of the poorest 40 percent of Mexican households increased about 35 percent or almost 4 percent a year from 1968 to 1977.[17]

The Industrial Sector

The industrial sector, broadly defined to include manufacturing, mining, petroleum and petrochemicals, construction, and the generation of electric power, accounted for over 38 percent of the GDP in 1980. Production of manufactured goods alone accounted for over 23 percent of GDP for that year, while production of hydrocarbons and construction each accounted for approximately 5 percent. In terms of the proportion of the employed labor force in 1980, manufacturing industry accounted for nearly 19 percent of the country's total, while construction is estimated to have employed around 6 percent.[18]

In general, the Mexican manufacturing sector has been characterized by a broad diversity in productive activities, firm and plant sizes, and the degree of efficiency measured at international prices. Each aspect has to a large extent been influenced over time by the nature of government policies and programs.

Mexico's industrialization received its first great stimulus with the outbreak of World War II. At this time most of the leading industrial countries began diverting substantial proportions of their productive resources toward the production of weapons for the war, through curtailing the production of consumer goods and investment goods. Shortages appeared in most of North America and European domestic markets, while at the same time their exports of industrial goods and strategic raw materials and intermediate goods became increasingly scarce. As a result, Mexico was faced with an insufficient supply of imported manufactured goods. On the other hand, given the amount of raw materials and intermediate goods the country was capable of exporting, Mexico began developing current account surpluses. Scarce supplies and rising incomes forced up the prices of imported goods and eventually made it profitable for Mexican producers to begin domestic production of a wide variety of goods formerly imported.[19]

World War II and the resulting isolation from traditional suppliers of manufacturing goods also compelled the government to begin playing an active role in the country's industrial development. Between 1941 and 1946 nearly 60 percent of all investment came from the public sector. While many of the government's programs involved building up the nation's infrastructure, a number of heavy industries such as steel, petroleum, and fertilizers also received large amounts of public capital. At the same time, the government coordinated its investment strategy with a policy of high tariffs on imported consumer goods. Ultimately, the authorities wanted to see the country producing most of its consumer necessities, and in this sense the program was quite successful. While one-third of all nondurable consumer goods were imported in 1929, only 7 percent were imported by 1950. Further, the imports to total consumption of all manufactured goods (i.e., consumer durables and capital goods) declined from 52 percent in 1929 to 31 percent in 1950.[20]

While successful in achieving its aims, the government found its initial attempts at import substitution quite costly; i.e., the authorities had found themselves placed in the position of undertaking investment because Mexican entrepreneurs were hesitant to undertake large-scale investments, and foreign firms were reluctant to invest in the country because of the nationalizations of the 1930s.

Because the country's industrial growth has been oriented toward the domestic market, manufacturing production has been concentrated in urban areas such as Mexico City and its surroundings, Monterrey, Guadalajara, Puebla, and the state of Veracruz. Although detailed information by city is not available, trends in the concentration of industry can be determined through data on industrial production by each of the Mexican states. A clear trend toward increased concentration can be found when the total geographical area is divided into three groups: (1) industrial, comprising the Federal District and the states of Mexico and Nuevo Leon, (2) semiindustrial, including the states of Coahuila, Chihuahua, Jalisco, Puebla, and Veracruz, and (3) subindustrial, comprising the rest of the country (24 states).[21]

The first group increased its share in total manufacturing output from 49 percent in 1940 to 54 percent in 1960; the second group's share also rose, from 19 percent in 1940 to 21 percent in 1960. There was also a 4.5 percent increase in the proportion of total population that concentrated in the industrial area between 1940 and 1960, while the semiindustrial and subindustrial groups' shares declined by 1.5 and 3 percent respectively during the same period.[22]

Developments in Agriculture

Agriculture and livestock accounted for less than 9 percent of Mexico's production in 1980. Despite this, it is estimated that around 28 percent of the country's working population were active in this sector. Approximately 80 percent of the agricultural work force is concentrated in seasonal crops located mainly in the nation's central and southern regions, i.e., in traditional agriculture providing grain and other basic foodstuffs.

Of major significance is the fact that the sector's real growth has decelerated an average of 5 percent per annum over the 1940-65 period, to a little over 2.3 percent between 1965 and 1974, to a little less than 2.2 percent between 1974 and 1979.

In the 1970s, average growth in the volume of agricultural output slowed to 1.8 percent per annum, well below population growth. This poor performance was recorded despite one or two years of rapid growth (e.g., 6.5 percent in 1977).

An important factor contributing to low agricultural output in recent years has been poor rainfall, combined with the limited extent of irrigation. All during the 1970s, rainfall was significantly below its historical average. In the 1978 and 1979 agricultural years, the situation was particularly bad, with rainfall 15 to 18 percent below normal.[23]

A related problem stems from the imbalance that exists between the location of the country's water resources, 40 percent of which are in the underpopulated southeast and only 10 percent in the central plateau around Mexico City, the area accommodating half of Mexico's population and the greatest concentration of small individual farms. The larger, more productive holdings are generally on irrigated land in the dry northwestern coastal plain in Sonora and Sinaloa states.

This development was particularly serious because most of Mexico's agricultural land depends exclusively on rain for moisture, with only about 15 percent under irrigation. Of the 30 million hectares of land considered suitable for cultivation in Mexico (15 percent of the surface of the country), only 11 to 13 million are actually worked, although the total harvested area is higher by some 4 million hectares because of double cropping. The amount of land under cultivation did not change significantly during the 1970s, nor did the total number of people employed in agriculture.[24]

The major problem that the agricultural sector now faces, therefore, concerns productivity. Although livestock production has increased steadily throughout the 1970s at an average of 4 percent per year, the overall contribution of agriculture to the economy has steadily declined. The expansion of production for this sector was reported at less than 1 percent for the years 1965-76, down from 6 percent per year in the period 1945-65.[25]

Research and Development

Mexico has been heavily dependent on externally developed science and technology. Despite a recent surge in the number of national research institutions and research workers, the country still spends a tiny fraction (0.22 percent) of its gross domestic product on research and development. That is a relatively low figure, even compared with countries like Argentina and India, and it represents scarcely one-tenth of the proportional amounts spent in the United States or the United Kingdom. With notable exceptions in agriculture and petroleum, research efforts are poorly coordinated, scientific journals are few, technical information services designed to link knowledge to production have barely developed, teaching and research are largely disconnected, few scientific or technological discoveries occur in Mexico, and the country remains mostly expert at importing and adapting foreign technology, often in packages that discourage the use of already existing Mexican production capacity and knowhow.[26]

Energy Development

New oil discoveries in 1974 promised to reinstate Mexico to the status it enjoyed early in the century as a major oil producer, if not a major exporter. (This status was lost because of political instability, the discovery of cheaper oil in Venezuela, and ultimately the nationalization of the Mexican oil industry in 1938.) Prior to the recent petroleum developments in the south, Mexico produced from about 4,000 wells, mostly in the northeast coast of the Gulf of Mexico. Many of these wells are, however, classed as low yield.

By mid-1974, however, 48 new wells were operating in Tobasco and Chiapas, each producing an average rate of 5,100 barrels per day, giving a daily total of 260,000 barrels. By December 1976, the number of new wells in the south had increased to about 200.

When President Lopez Portillo took office in 1976, Petroleos Mexicanos (PEMEX), the state oil monopoly, reported production of 327,285 barrels per day (bpd), exports of 34,470 bpd, and proven reserves of 6.3 billion barrels. By September 1981, the President reported that daily output had reached 2.6 million, about half of which was sold abroad. PEMEX also listed proven deposits of over 70 million barrels, probable holdings of 30 billion, and potential reserves of 300 billion. On the basis of these figures (believed by some observers to be somewhat over-optimistic), Mexico has become the world's fourth largest producer and fifth largest possessor of oil and natural gas.[27]

Under these circumstances the volumes expected from now on will fall into an entirely different order of magnitude, significantly influencing the entire scope of industrial production in Mexico and of its basic economy.

The natural gas produced in parallel from the new wells is expected to increase significantly, as will total gas production. Whereas in 1976 this production was equivalent to 18 million metric tons annually, by 1980 the production of natural gas reached a level of about 30 million tons. Mexico's production of liquified petroleum gas (LPG) totalled 20.5 million barrels per year in 1976 and reached a level of 28 million barrels in 1980. These developments reverse the trend whereby internal demand for LPG had necessitated increasing imports in recent years, especially to serve Monterrey and several other major cities in the northeast part of the country.[28]

Escalating prices combined with expanded production have raised Mexico's hydrocarbon export earnings from $311 million in 1976 to $10.4 billion in 1980, with revenues for 1981 estimated to be slightly higher. Oil wealth not only generates foreign exchange but also enhances the country's attractiveness in foreign capital markets. The availability of these resources has made the government optimistic about the nation's future. As Diaz Serrano, former director general of PEMEX, noted, "For the first time in its history Mexico enjoys sufficient wealth to make possible not only the resolution of economic problems facing the country, but also the creation of a new permanently prosperous country, a rich country where the right to work will be a reality."[29]

The government is pushing the exploration and exploitation of oil resources as fast and as far as it can. But it is also hoping to derive 25 percent of energy requirements from non-oil sources by the year 2000—including nuclear and geothermal sources (recently expanded fourfold to 270,000 kilowatt capacity). Present installed electrical capacity in Mexico is 12 million kilowatts. The government intends to invest $8.1 billion over the next five years in electrical power expansion to lay the basis for the tenfold increase in power requirement that has been projected over the next 25 years.[30]

PERFORMANCE REVIEW

Developing countries have traditionally followed three types of development models:[31]

1. the enclave or primary exporter model, with no real possibilities for industrialization (the period 1877-1910 in Mexico)

2. inward industrialization via import substitution (the Mexican strategy between 1940 and the present)

3. outward industrialization via the export of manufactured goods (the method followed by Japan and South Korea since World War II).

In pursuing the second strategy—

1. Mexico has relied extensively on government intervention

2. the government has intervened both directly, through controls on investment and trade, and indirectly, through taxes, subsidies, and other measures affecting the prices of both factor and product markets

3. reliance on direct controls appears to have been more pervasive in the 1950s than during the 1960s. The country seems to have moved gradually toward greater reliance on the market mechanism tempered by continued government intervention.

4. the aim of economic policy also appears to have gradually shifted away from one of strict import substitution, the dominant strategy from World War II through the 1960s.

In fact, given the limited possibilities for further import substitution, the opportunities that oil offers, and the likelihood of increased protectionism by the industrialized countries, Mexico is likely to develop an approach to development unique to that country.

There are many signs that a shift toward a new growth model has already begun, with industrialization shifting toward the import substitution of capital goods, development of selected manufactures for export, and increased emphasis on technology transfer and the indigenous development of scientific research and development capabilities. For sure, the country's ability to bargain access to foreign markets, together with the terms it acquires foreign technology, has been strengthened considerably by developments in the oil sector.

A major problem, however, remains in the primary and tertiary sectors, which have in general experienced below average behavior, particularly agriculture and livestock. The preliminary figures for 1979 indicate a growth of only 0.4 percent for the agriculture, livestock, forestry, and fishing sectors. This lag in agricultural production has severe implications for labor demand in the agriculture and livestock sectors and for labor supply in other sectors through a number of secondary labor migration effects.

During the 1970s three major macroeconomic trends became pronounced. First, the proportion of national income accounted for by salaries and other forms of labor remuneration increased from just over 35 percent of GDP in 1970 to slightly greater than 38 percent for the second half of the decade (Table 1.3). The proportion of income allotted to profits and interest, on the other hand, declined from about 53 percent of the GDP to around 45 percent (for the last three years of the decade). These patterns reflect not only the government's economic policies but also changes in the structure of production to activities requiring skilled labor (whose real wages thus expanded in relative terms in the 1970s).

The second trend in the national income accounts of major significance is the acceleration in the growth of real investment during the last part of the 1970s, representing a continuation of a process started at the beginning of the decade, whereby the investment programs of the federal government and of some public enterprises under its budgetary control were greatly expanded (Table 1.4). Gross fixed capital formation reached 23.2 percent of the GDP in 1979, compared to an amount somewhat below 20 percent at the beginning of the 1970s. In general this period was also characterized by the growing importance of domestically produced capital goods as a component of fixed investment.

It is reasonable to deduce that the significant increment in real investment achieved since 1977 by the Mexican economy will continue in the medium term as output, and that income will remain on a relatively high trajectory, exceeding the historic trend of 6.0 percent real growth during the period since 1950.

The third important trend has been the increased opening of the economy to international trade. This pattern clearly stemmed from the exchange rate devaluation at the end of 1976 and the availability of a growing exportable surplus of petroleum and other hydrocarbons since 1977; i.e., the joint proportion of exports and imports of goods and services had remained around 19 percent during the 1970-76 period, increasing to 23.7 percent of GDP in 1979. Traditionally, this ratio has served as an index of the proportion of the economy's production of goods and services that could be considered internationally tradable. As long as the ratio represented a greater degree of competition, increases in the ratio were indicative of improvements in the country's productive and distributive efficiency. This interpretation may no longer be correct, given the shift

TABLE 1.3

Mexico: Composition of the Gross Domestic Product, 1970-78
(thousands of millions of pesos)

	1970	1975	1977	1978	Percentage Composition* 1970	1975	1977	1978
1. Wages and salaries of employees	147.8	379.3	638.3	807.3	35.3	38.4	33.1	38.3
2. Interest and profits	221.4	456.9	755.6	948.6	52.9	46.2	45.1	45.1
3. Consumption of fixed capital	28.7	76.9	157.4	199.2	6.8	7.8	9.4	9.5
4. Indirect taxes-subsidies	20.8	75.2	123.4	149.5	5.0	7.6	7.4	7.1
5. Gross domestic product	418.7	988.3	1,674.7	2,104.6	100.0	100.0	100.0	100.0
6. Final consumption expenditures	333.4	781.0	1,296.7	1,584.9	79.6	79.0	77.4	75.3
a. Public consumption	(32.6)	(110.0)	(195.6)	(240.5)	(7.8)	(11.1)	(11.7)	(11.4)
b. Private consumption	(300.8)	(671.0)	(1,101.1)	(1,344.4)	(71.8)	(67.9)	(65.7)	(63.9)
7. Increase of inventories	11.4	17.4	40.4	60.5	2.7	1.8	2.4	2.9
8. Gross fixed capital formation	82.3	221.7	339.1	471.8	19.6	22.4	20.2	22.4
9. Exports of goods and services	34.3	75.8	176.1	228.4	8.2	7.7	10.5	10.9
10. Imports of goods and services	-42.7	-107.6	-177.6	-241.0	-10.2	-10.9	-10.6	-11.4
11. Expenditures on the gross domestic product	418.7	988.3	1,674.7	2,104.6	100.0	100.0	100.0	100.0

*The figures may not add up exactly because of rounding.
Source: Bank of Mexico.

TABLE 1.4

Mexico: Gross Fixed Investment, 1970-79
(millions of 1960 pesos)

	1970	1975	1976	1977	1978	1979
1. Construction	31,240	46,465	45,482	44,572	50,500	56,560
2. Domestic production of machinery and equipment	15,689	25,254	24,875	23,656	28,553	34,942
3. Imports of machinery and equipment	13,376	17,571	16,605	11,408	13,279	17,447
4. Others	1,300	1,392	1,129	1,086	1,119	1,323
5. Gross fixed investment	61,605	90,682	88,091	80,722	93,451	110,272
6. Gross fixed investment as a percentage of GDP	20.8	23.2	22.1	19.6	21.2	23.2
Percentage composition						
1. Construction	50.7	51.2	51.6	55.2	54.0	51.3
2. Domestic production of machinery and equipment	25.5	27.8	28.2	29.3	30.6	31.7
3. Imports of machinery and equipment	21.7	19.4	18.8	14.1	14.2	15.8
4. Others	2.1	1.5	1.3	1.3	1.2	1.2
5. Total	100.0	100.0	100.0	100.0	100.0	100.0

Source: Bank of Mexico.

toward petroleum accounting for a large proportion of exports
and the increases in effective rates of protection given domestic
firms in recent years. In this case the greater opening to international trade could represent an element of instability for the
economy.

PRELIMINARY APPRAISAL

Many of the country's basic economic trends, especially
those since 1970, can be given either an optimistic or pessimistic
interpretation, thus underlining the difficulty of ascertaining
not only the impact of government policies over the years, but
also, perhaps more importantly, in assessing the major developments that are likely to characterize the economy in the foreseeable future.

An optimistic view of Mexico's development performance to
date can be easily made, given the national identity produced
by: (1) the 1910-17 Revolution, (2) the elimination of the
military from the politics and the day-to-day running of the
country, (3) the peaceful presidential transitions of the past
50 years, and of course (4) the country's record of steady
economic growth and industrialization, modernization of communi-
cations and transport, and improvements in education and health.

While acknowledging these achievements, one may still take
a pessimistic view of Mexico's growth performance, given (1)
the lack of popular participation in the selection of political
leadership, (2) the gross inequalities that have accompanied
economic growth, (3) the low standards of education, health,
and housing among most of the citizens, (4) the backwardness
of agriculture, (5) the persistent balance of payments deficits
and indebtedness, and (6) the staggering burden on national
resources from present and anticipated population growth.

Against this economic overview, it is possible to examine
in more detail the motives, forces, policies, and potential of
the Mexican development model.

NOTES

1. All dollar references in this book are to U.S. dollars.
Mexican currency is expressed in pesos.

2. Data taken from International Bank for Reconstruction
and Development (World Bank), World Development Report, 1981
(New York: Oxford University Press, 1981).

3. Jorge Dominquez, ed., Mexico's Political Economy: Challenges at Home and Abroad (Beverly Hills, Calif.: Sage Publications, 1982), p. 10.

4. Calvin P. Blair, Economic Development Policy in Mexico: A New Penchant for Planning, Technical Papers Series no. 26 (Austin: Office for Public Sector Studies, Institute of Latin American Studies, University of Texas, 1980), p. 3.

5. Ansley Coale, "Population and Growth and Economic Development: The Case of Mexico," Foreign Affairs, January 1978, pp. 427-29.

6. An excellent survey of the country's demographic problems is given in Charles F. Gallagher, Population, Petroleum and Politics: Mexico at the Crossroads, Parts I and II, American Universities Field Staff Reports nos. 19, 42, 1980.

7. Marvin Alisky, "Population and Migration Problems in Mexico," Current History, November 1981, pp. 365-69.

8. Clark Reynolds, "Labor Market Projections for the United States and Mexico and Current Migration Controversies," Food Research Institute Studies, no. 2, 1979, p. 129.

9. James Street, "Prospects for Mexico's Industrial Development Plan in the 1980s," Texas Business Review, May-June 1980, pp. 125-27.

10. Organization of American States, General Secretariat, Short Term Economic Reports—Mexico (Washington, D.C., 1980), p. 33.

11. Ibid., pp. 34-35.

12. Arpad von Lazar, "Development Planning in Mexico: Case Study of an Oil-Rich Economy," Resources Policy, September 1979, p. 201.

13. David Felix, "Income Inequality in Mexico," Current History, March 1977, p. 111.

14. Ibid.

15. Cf. Woulter van Ginneken, Socio-economic Groups and Income Distribution in Mexico (London: Croom Helm, 1980). See Chap. 1 for an excellent survey of the income distribution situation in Mexico.

16. Salvatore Bizzarro, "Mexico's Poor." Current History, November 1981, pp. 370-73.

17. See Joel Bergsman, Income Distribution and Poverty in Mexico, World Bank Staff Working Paper no. 395 (New York: International Bank for Reconstruction and Development [World Bank], June 1980), for a discussion of this methodology.

18. Banco de Mexico, Informe Anual, 1981.

19. L. Antonio Aspra, "Import Substitution in Mexico: Past and Present," World Development, January-February 1977, pp. 112-13.

20. An excellent survey of the government's industrial policy is given in Leopoldo Solis, "Industrial Priorities in Mexico," in United Nations Industrial Development Organization, Industrial Priorities in Developing Countries (New York: United Nations, 1971), pp. 48-112.

21. A. Lamadrid, "Industrial Location Policy in Mexico," in Industrial Development Association, Industrial Location and Regional Development—Proceedings of an Interregional Seminar (New York: United Nations, 1971), pp. 563-65.

22. Ibid. See also Eliseo Mendoze-Berrueto, "Regional Implications of Mexico's Economic Growth," Weltwirtschaftliches Archiv, 1968, pp. 87-123; and A. M. Lavell, "Regional Industrialization in Mexico: Some Policy Considerations," Regional Studies, August 1972, pp. 343-63, for similar accounts.

23. von Lazar, "Development Planning in Mexico," pp. 202-03.

24. P. Lamartine Yates, Mexico's Agricultural Dilemma (Tucson: University of Arizona Press, 1981).

25. John Bailey, "Agrarian Reform in Mexico," Current History, November 1981, pp. 357-58.

26. Cf. Jack Baranson, North-South Technology Transfer: Financing and Institution Building (Mt. Airy, Md.: Lomond Publications, 1981), pp. 49-98.

27. George Grayson, "Oil and Politics in Mexico," Current History, November 1981, pp. 379-80.

28. Ibid.

29. The text of Diaz Serrano's report appears in "Petroleos Mexicanos: Activities in 1980," Comercio Exterior de Mexico, April 1981, pp. 134-42.

30. Sylvia Barkely, "Oil for Technology: Blueprint for Mexico's Development," Fusion, July 1981, pp. 25-26.

31. Rene Villarreal and Rocio de Villarreal, "Mexico's Development Strategy," in Mexico-United States Relations, ed. Susan Purcell (New York: Praeger, 1981), p. 97.

2
INDUSTRIAL ALTERNATIVES

INTRODUCTION

A number of significant changes in Mexico's industrial strategy have been introduced by the Lopez Portillo administration (1976-82).

One of the administration's initial decisions was to abandon the previous policy of strict conservation of oil resources. Both exploration and development were stepped up and the resulting increase in oil revenues used to alleviate the post-1976 recession and restore growth. A new emphasis has been placed on increased industrial efficiency to overcome the high costs characteristic of many of the country's import substitution industries. In addition SIDERMEX, the national steel enterprise, was reorganized in an effort to establish a more efficient foundation for industrial recovery.[1]

Finally, in March 1979 the Mexican government announced its National Industrial Development Plan.[2] To the surprise of many observers, the plan placed priority on the growth of basic industries rather than on labor intensive activities (which would admittedly create more employment, but were seen by the administration as economically inefficient). Although President Lopez Portillo's term expires in December 1982, the new development plan covers the period from 1979 to 1990 because a shorter period was considered insufficient to implement the plan properly.

DEVELOPMENT PLANNING

Medium- to long-term economic and social planning is relatively new in Mexico. The pace of development has typically
followed the six-year presidential cycle, and thus the economic
planning process has been aligned closely with the objectives
of the incumbent president. The realization within the president's
term of office has been paramount, leading to a planning cycle
whereby—

1. formulation of objectives and development of plans occupy
the first one or two years in office
2. execution of plans with new projects launched and resources directed towards them take the next two or three years
3. consolidation occupies the final years of a presidency.
New programs are rare during this period, presumably because
they would be perceived by the population as the work of the
following rather than incumbent administration. However, ongoing programs are monitored to assure the optimal results
during the planning period of the existing administration.

In practice, the presidential cycle appears to have influ-
enced not only government but also private expenditure decisions
giving rise to a corresponding business cycle pattern unique to
Mexico.
As noted, in 1979 the Ministry of National Property and
Industrial Development (SPyFI) published the National Industrial
Development Plan 1979-1982-1990. This was followed in 1980
by a quite separate document, the Plan Global de Desarrollo
1980-1982, published by the Secretary of Programming and
Budget (SPyP).[3]
The National Industrial Development Plan is significant for
several reasons.

1. For the first time in Mexico, serious public consideration was given to longer-term economic policy; i.e., a time
frame beyond the term of the six-year presidency was incorporated (however the PRI did elaborate a Plan Basico de Bobiero
1976-1982 in 1975).
2. Alternative growth paths were delineated. Assuming
no policy change from 1979 onwards, a real GNP growth path of
6.5 percent in the post-1982 period was considered likely. Under
different assumptions, growth of as much as 10 percent was envisaged.

3. By examining the whole economy in detail (i.e., 45 sectors including agriculture, petroleum, and the service sector, as well as manufacturing and industry) it provided an insight into the operation of the Mexican economy.

4. Distinct treatment was given to the balance of payments; distinction is made between the private, parastate, and government sector activities.

The 1979 National Industrial Development Plan was therefore an exercise in medium- to long-term indicative planning for all sectors of the economy.

In sum, the economic projections in the plan are presented as a base trajectory and a plan trajectory. The former refers to what would happen under the existing framework of economic policy if it were to continue into the future; the latter is calculated on the assumption that the policy framework is going to be different from what it has been. According to these forecasts, the rate of manufacturing output growth is expected to increase from the 1970-75 average of 5.1 percent a year to a 1980-92 average of 6.5 percent under the base projection. The plan projection for this period is for a 9.8 percent increase compared with the historical rate of growth in gross domestic product of 5.4 percent for 1970-75. The plan foresees a 6.7 percent increase for 1980-82 and hopefully a 9.4 increase during this period if the plan is successful.

The Overall Development Plan, although it covers a shorter period and is less explicit in numerical terms, is of great value in that—

1. it clearly states the reorientation of the Mexican government policy toward different sectors of the economy in general, as well as in social and political terms

2. it stresses the target of maintaining a high rate of economic growth (8 percent in real terms) in the second half of the presidential period, i.e., 1980-82, as a springboard for continuing a high rate of growth in the succeeding period, thus avoiding the normal presidential cyclical downturn one might otherwise expect in 1983

3. it clearly states that oil resource exploitation and the raising of the levels of internal savings in the public and private sectors will be used to promote growth, to create employment, to raise the living standards of the poorest strata of the population, and to proportionately lower the national debt, both internal and external.

Both plans anticipate that increased oil revenues will not only provide the economy with increased financial independence, but also will enable the state to assume the directive capacity that it previously lacked. As a starting point, a number of investment target goals have been made for various industries. Initially these are looked upon as indicative. Eventually they are to be finalized through government. At this time the goals set for business will become obligatory (although it is not clear what penalties will be imposed by the government for failure to comply with the specified investment program).

The target rates of growth for both real GDP and the industrial sector are considerably higher than Mexico has ever sustained. Clearly, however, given the country's potential, they are not infeasible, nor are they unrealistic by world standards. Since 1960, 18 of the developing nations classified by the World Bank as "middle income countries" have been able to maintain for periods of 6 to 16 years average annual rates in real gross domestic product of 8 percent or more. They include not only the well-documented experiences of Brazil, Iran, Taiwan, South Korea, Rumania, Tunisia, and Israel, but also the less-publicized success of Ecuador and the Dominican Republic. Two other countries—Saudi Arabia and Libya—classified by the World Bank as "capital surplus oil exporters" have experienced real GDP growth at sustained rates well over 15 percent per annum. Twenty-three of the World Bank's middle income countries have had periods of sustained growth exceeding 10 percent per annum. [4]

Still, the National Industrial Development Plan itself recognizes that its growth targets are simple guidelines, and that the concerted efforts of all groups—business, labor, and government—will barely suffice to meet its proposed goals.

Even with relatively modest assumptions concerning growth in the United States, Europe, and Japan, together with a slackening in world oil demand, it is still realistic to project average annual rates of real growth exceeding 8 percent per annum for the plan period. Given Mexico's prospects, the planners are certainly correct in their approach. It would make no sense at all to plan for development at a pace no higher than that realized during the past decade of unplanned expansion.

In general terms the public sector anticipates undertaking roughly one-half of the investment envisioned by the plan, the exact proportion depending on the private sector's response to the investment opportunities created by the government's programs.

Presumably the state development banks, particularly Nacional Fincerca, will step up their lending to private investors wishing to develop facilities in priority areas but unable to obtain long-term credit from Mexican commercial banks.

IMPLICATIONS FOR THE PRESENT STUDY

In terms of the chapters that follow, of particular interest is the two plans' perception of—

1. the optimal industrial strategy for the country during the 1980s and beyond
2. the most desirable geographic location of investment in the country
3. the impact increased defense expenditures may have on the economy
4. the rate of exploitation of natural resources consistent with the attainment of policy objectives
5. the best balance between public and private sectors
6. the extent of external financial requests.[5]

Also of significance but hardly mentioned in the plan was an assessment of the inflationary impact of the government's fiscal and monetary programs.

Each of these issues is discussed at length in the remainder of the study. The following sections examine the nature of the country's new industrial strategy. Monetary and external linkages are estimated and the inflation impacts associated with stepped-up expenditures are analyzed in Chapter 3.

As a prelude to forecasts of the economy, Chapter 4 examines the mechanisms of oil induced growth in Mexico. Chapter 5 provides a macro overview and the theoretical considerations underlying the forecasts, while Chapter 6 presents the strengths, weaknesses, actual forecasts, and their implications for the future through a series of optimum control exercises.

DEVELOPMENT STRATEGY

The basic development strategy of the National Industrial Development Plan involves restructuring the economy through three successive stages.[6]

The first stage involves a series of short-run stabilization measures designed to overcome the financial and commercial disorganization arising from the devaluation of the peso in 1976, and to restore confidence in the productive capacity of the country. This stage was largely completed by 1979.

The second stage is intended to concilitate the bases for self-sustained development. A major objective of this stage was to reach a platform in petroleum production of 2.25 million b/d by the end of 1980. (This target was later increased to ensure adequate export capacity.)

The third stage of the plan anticipates a period of autonomous accelerated growth intended to reduce and eventually eliminate (by 1990) the current high levels of unemployment and underemployment. As scheduled, this stage began in 1980 and is programmed to continue through the 1980s. The accelerated growth anticipated for this period is expected to be in large part financed initially with petroleum revenues. Over time, other exports are expected to play a larger role in generating foreign exchange.

As noted, the plan is exceedingly ambitious, projecting growth rates somewhat higher than those characterizing the economy in recent years and considerably above those experience by most countries at a similar level of development.

As presented, the plan outlines various industrial programs. In addition—

1. it establishes goals within a macroeconomic and sectoral framework for the medium term (1979-82) and for the long term (1982-90)

2. it identifies priority industrial activities and their capacity to contribute to the general objectives

3. it outlines priority regions in an attempt to order and redirect territorial decentralization of economic activity

4. it gives preferential treatment to medium- and small-sized firms, with the intention of balancing market structures and arresting oligopolistic tendencies in industry

5. it provides the type of joint mechanisms to be employed, the most prominent being incentives linked to sectoral and regional priorities and preferential treatment given to the medium and small-sized firm

6. it provides an institutional framework within the public sector for the application of industrial policy under general regulations that tend to eliminate needless confusion and bureaucracy

7. it provides mechanisms for the outlining of commitments with the private and social sectors.

Clearly, the success of the plan depends upon the accom-
plishment of the joint aims established for the public, social,
and private sectors. It rests, therefore, on the interlinkage
of these aims within an integral framework of global, sectoral,
and regional dimensions. To maintain such cohesion, all aims
must be considered of equal importance. In this way, it is also
the responsibility of the state to adopt the role of watchdog in
the interests of those areas of activity which may be neglected
by other sectors. These aims are expected to be revised in the
light of unforeseen circumstances.

ALLOCATING INVESTMENT TO PROVIDE JOBS

The National Industrial Development Plan realistically identifies a major problem in development spending as one of concentrating it in sectors and in places in which it will have the
maximum impact, not only in immediate job creation and wealth
distribution, but more importantly in ensuring that the jobs
created add to the real economic potential of the country. It
follows that the creation of jobs in low productivity sectors
with low potential for the creation of new wealth through improvement in the economic base or through multiplier effects are given
a relatively low priority by the plan. Although not explicitly
mentioned by the plan, the unrestricted and unselective expansion of the government payroll would fall into this category.
So would the creation of manufacturing jobs in sectors protected
by high tariffs and import restrictions, which can never hope
to become efficient in terms of achieving either any optimal scale
of output or a competitive level of technology.

In reviewing the Mexican government's published plans
from the viewpoint of their employment creation potential, it is
readily apparent that the major capital intensive sectors such
as mining, petroleum and petrochemicals, and electricity can
be excluded. These sectors employ few workers at present
and, under any realistic assumptions about future growth or
technological developments, can be expected to make only minimal
contributions to solving the country's employment problems.
The most important employment creating sectors are therefore
manufacturing, agriculture, and services.

Manufacturing

Rates of productivity growth in manufacturing during the
1970s were close to the national average for all industries at 2

to 3 percent. The plan envisages, however, significant productivity increases in the range of 3.6 to 7.3 percent.

Mexican manufacturing industry thus faces the challenge of rapidly accelerating its productivity growth, its labor force, and its output at the same time; i.e., to be consistent with plan objectives, new jobs would have to be created in the sector at a rate of 100,000 to 120,000 per year in the first half of the 1980s, rising to 140,000 to 180,000 per year in the latter part of the 1980s.

Realistically, one would have to argue that increased production simply to satisfy the growing domestic market will not be nearly sufficient to stimulate investment rates consistent with these employment targets. Expansion of manufactured exports is obviously a necessary prerequisite for making any meaningful dent in the country's unemployment level.

For manufactured exports to expand, the country's products must be price competitive, a situation that has been increasingly difficult to achieve given Mexico's high rate of inflation and the relative stability until February 1982 of the Mexican peso against the U.S. dollar. Therefore, the attainment of high output growth combined with a significant increase in employment opportunities in the manufacturing sector appears to be conditional firstly on increasing exports of manufactured goods faster than the rate of growth of output of these goods; and secondly on increasing productivity at a much more rapid rate than that of the main Mexican trading partners in order to prevent the erosion by inflation of the price competitiveness of Mexican goods.

Under the present operating conditions (i.e., a wide inflation difference between Mexico and the United States, which is being only partially compensated for by the downward float of the Mexican peso) these objectives appear most difficult to attain except on a selective basis, such as in the automotive industry. The optimal control model developed in Chapter 6, therefore, takes the attainment of an inflation parity with the United States, together with the maintenance of a stable peso-to-dollar rate, as a precondition for meeting the country's employment problems.

Agriculture

Although still accounting for around 32 percent of the Mexican work force in 1980, agriculture is unlikely to provide any more than 3 percent of the extra jobs required during the 1980s. Historically, the sector as a whole has had the lowest levels of productivity in the economy and in a related way has been one of the slowest in terms of adopting modern methods and technology. Given the magnitude of the country's unemployment problem, however, the sector must nevertheless play an important role in job creation while raising production to meet the requirements of a rapidly growing population.

It is anticipated that creating a job in agriculture will cost approximately three times the new investment behind each new worker in the manufacturing or service sectors. Nevertheless, given the degree of poverty in the sector and the linkages to industry created by a more dynamic agricultural sector, the overall cost of job creation may be justified in a number of circumstances.

Other developments in agriculture are anticipated.

1. A significant increase is expected in the proportion of agricultural workers who receive salaries. At present, salaried workers in agriculture receive considerably more compensation than the workers on ejido farms (ejidatarios) who constitute 61 percent of the agricultural work force. By 1990 the proportion of salaried workers is expected to have risen to 70 percent. This means that of the 4.5 million agricultural workers anticipated in 1990, over 1.35 million will be ejidatarios, compared with 1.72 million at present.

2. Implied in these movements is a considerable speeding up of the evolution of a predominantly wage earning labor force in agriculture. Only a small proportion of this change is expected, however, to occur during the Lopez Portillo administration. To be fully implemented by the next administration, however, current programs in agriculture will mean the end of the ejido by the early 1990s, clearly a significant development in light of this group's role in forming a cornerstone of the Revolution and postrevolutionary Mexican politics.

3. The bulk of the investment expenditure required to finance the agricultural transformation outlined above is scheduled to come directly from government funds, thus clearly identifying government policy with the changes.

4. The shift in favor of salaried agricultural labor will also have a direct impact on narrowing the income inequalities that currently preclude the rural population from mass consumer goods markets.

Construction

Construction activity has traditionally been the quickest and surest method in Mexico of converting expenditure into employment; for approximately one-fifth or one-sixth of the investment expenditure made in manufacturing, approximately the same number of new jobs can be created in the construction sector.

Another advantage of construction as a generator of new jobs is that, provided the appropriate planning measures are taken, it could eliminate the infrastructure and materials bottlenecks that currently inhibit the country's ability to generate high rates of noninflationary growth.

An obvious disadvantage of construction from the point of view of employment creation, however, is the temporary nature of these jobs. Once the infrastructure projects have been completed, the local demand for construction labor falls off rapidly, and, given that the skills of construction labor are not necessaril easy to transfer to other types of employment, many of the country's employment problems might be just postponed rather than eliminated.

Service Industries

The National Industrial Development Plan assigns to the service industries a major responsibility for creating new employment in Mexico over the next decade. From 1980 to 1985, between 390,000 and 570,000 new service industry jobs are planned each year. This figure increases to 580,000 to 1,060,000 per year in the following five years to 1990. The upper figures represent the attainment of the plan trajectory while the lower ones are associated with the base expansion path. Both targets represent two-thirds of all new jobs to be created between 1980 and 1985 and 70 percent of all requirements over the following five years.

A number of negative factors are, however, associated with the planned pattern of new job creation:

1. the low rate of productivity increase in the service industries at present (less than 1 percent per annum) and expectation that this will remain static or decline

2. the low absolute level of productivity in the service sector, which was around half that in manufacturing in 1978. It is, however, some four times better than in agriculture and about average for all economic activity in Mexico. However, in the next ten years, national productivity as well as productivity in other sectors is expected to have risen sharply, placing the service sector at a much lower relative level

3. the dominant role of the government sector in providing new service sector jobs. For example, under the plan growth trajectory, government employment is expected to increase almost fourfold from 1.6 million in 1980 to 6 million by 1990. The government's share would thus have risen from 7 percent in 1970 to 22 percent by 1990. This means that roughly one-third of all new jobs in the 1980-85 period would be created by expanding government employment (rising to 55-58 percent in 1985-90).

Thus the plan implicitly assigns to the government, through its consumption allocations, the role of the country's employer of last resort, hardly the foundation upon which to invest oil revenues as a means of creating high, self-sustaining rates of growth.

To summarize, the analysis appears to indicate that, in order to create full employment, the government is willing to dramatically expand its own payroll by adding low productivity jobs, even though dramatic improvements in productivity are not expected in this area.

If this strategy is implemented, a gap will be created between industrial workers, who will presumably have to expend considerable effort to contribute to the growth in output and in productivity, needed to offset that in the government sector. Under these circumstances, it is difficult to see what would induce a worker, everything else being equal, to enter industry, particularly given that the number of opportunities for government employment would be opening up at a more rapid rate— unless of course there was a significant wage differential in favor of industry. High wages in industry would of course mean less competitive advantage in foreign markets and thus fewer new jobs created.

These considerations form the rationale of limiting the expansion of government consumption in the optimal control forecasts presented in Chapter 7.

Finally, it appears likely that, as part of the government sector job creation program, an expansion of the armed forces is envisaged as a contingency in order to organize protection for the country's oil resources. Mexico's armed forces and defense spending are at very low levels compared with other Latin American countries.

The results of this analysis point to developments in industry as critical in ultimately determining whether the economy will become viable and dynamic or stagnant and inflation prone.

SECTORAL PRIORITIES

In terms of specific priorities, the National Industrial
Development Plan identifies seventy priority sectors of industry
based on potential markets, origin of inputs, and the sector's
macroeconomic impact on income, employment, investment, exports, and technology. Given these criteria, the export of
manufactures and the development of a capital goods industry
come out as areas receiving high priority. To the extent possible
Mexican origin of inputs counts heavily in the selection; but
even so, the plan projects the ratio of imports to total for industry as a whole as rising from 10 percent in 1978 to 12 percent
in 1982, and to nearly 15 percent by 1990.

When industries are finally ranked in terms of their potential contribution to the plan's objectives, food processing receives
the highest priority, followed by the capital goods sector. Within
the capital goods industry, food processing machinery and food
producing equipment—tractors and farm implements—are the
areas singled out for attention.

Next in terms of importance are machinery and equipment
for the petroleum and petrochemical industries: exploration and
drilling equipment, valves, pumps, blowers, compressors, pipe,
and heat exchangers. Initially much of the expanded demand
for this equipment will be imports needed to facilitate PEMEX's
planned expansion of between 18 to 23 percent per annum.
Expanded imports of machine tools, technical services, and
other specialty inputs will be required by the Mexican capital
goods sector itself.

The plan projects industrial demand at 10 percent a year
between 1978 and 1982 and 12 percent a year for the 1983-90
period. Growth is expected to be highest in: (1) secondary
petrochemicals (20 percent in 1978-82 and 18 percent in 1983-90);
(2) rubber products (13 percent during 1978-82 and 17 percent
for 1983-90), and (3) metal mechanical products (16 and 13 percent for 1978-82 and 1983-90, respectively). Nineteen new areas
are targeted for investment, including most of the products on
the export promotion list (see below) as well as transport equipment and printing. The total extra investment required over
and above that anticipated for the base trajectory is estimated
at nearly $60 billion during 1979-82. The largest increases—
other than those in such public sector activities as electricity,
steel, and petrochemicals—are to be in electrical machinery,
cement, glass, milk products, and soft fiber textiles.

Increased imports will also be required to facilitate the
expansion of most of the capital goods industries identified in

the plan as priority areas, i.e., integrated steel works, cement plants, and the manufacture of machinery and equipment—for the electrical industry (turbines, generators, and high voltage transmission equipment), for mining and metallurgy (mining machinery, pelletizing plants, foundries, and rolling mills), for the construction industry (earth moving machinery), for transport (motors, trucks, buses, locomotives, and railway cars), and for a variety of other industries (machinery tools, and laboratory and industrial control devices).

Projected annual growth rates for these capital goods activities vary from 9.5 to 20.0 percent. While import requirements are not specified for each priority industry, they are implied in the significant increase in the ratio of imports to total demand for 1982 and 1990 in the plan's projected expansion of industrial markets for metal products, industrial and electrical machinery, and transport equipment.

Other priority activities (listed as category 2 in the industrial plan) include nondurable consumer goods (e.g., textiles, shoes, soaps and detergents, containers, school and office supplies, and paper), consumer durables (e.g., appliances, furniture, auto parts, optical goods, and hand tools), and intermediate industrial goods (e.g., chemical fibers, resins, acids, alkalis, pharmaceuticals, aluminum, specialty steels, glass, plastics, and ceramics). Domestic production capacity already exists for each of these sectors. Their expansion is forecast by the plan at rates varying from 7.5 to 20 percent per annum, rates which can be expected to generate additional demand for imported equipment, parts, and components.

The encouragement of exports of nonpetroleum industrial products is one of the foremost objectives of the national plan. Manufactured products selected for export promotion were chosen on the basis of: (1) an already existing international market (such as in mining), (2) a potential for processing gains from domestic raw materials (secondary petrochemicals), (3) recent export contraction because of lack of investment competitiveness (textiles), (4) products that need economies of scale to be competitive for export (the capital goods sector), and (5) manufacturing sectors that have easy access to international markets due to their linkage with multinational enterprises (automobiles, rubber, pharmaceuticals, and chemicals).

If the plan is successful, the level of Mexican exports may increase from $4.5 billion at 1975 prices (of which $1.5 billion was in oil and petroleum products) in 1978 to $9.1 billion in 1982 ($5.6 billion in oil and petroleum products) and $15.1 billion in 1990. Manufactured exports, which accounted for half of all exports in 1978, are expected to grow at 8 percent a year between 1978 and 1982 and at 26 percent a year between 1982 and 1990, mainly by expansion in the more advanced products rather than in the traditional labor intensive consumer goods.

In sum, rapid expansion of the many priority industry sectors, the accelerated development of the oil sector, and a growing demand for food imports will result in a growing deficit in current account in the balance of payments, (projected in the plan as a cumulative $2 billion between 1979 and 1982).

Already (early 1982) this projection appears much too low. However, if the government is willing to accrue additional debt, just about any foreseeable deficit can be easily financed by external loans (because of the country's increasing capacity to service external debt out of petroleum revenues).

The plan does not reveal the means by which it projects industrial exports. Given an assumed 8 percent increase in real wages and a stable value of the peso (at an already overvalued rate), one can only assume that the authorities plan to rely on trade concessions for oil rather than price competition as the major element in their export drive.

In sum, the government thus hopes to diversify industrial exports and alleviate dependence on oil revenue. A fundamental objective of the development plan is to convert the nation's non-renewable oil resources into renewable industrial production.

IMPLEMENTATION

Industrial policy will, as in the past, be implemented through tax concessions, import protection, and various development and manufacturing programs. For those areas not included in the program, however, tariff barriers are being lowered, import embargoes lifted, and tax concessions reduced. Development programs apply to all firms in a given activity. In return for the benefits they receive under these programs, however, firms are obliged to meet certain production, price, and export and import targets. In addition, foreign firms included in the program must agree to a process of Mexicanization over a stated period of time.

In the future, foreign companies will be expected to negotiate in complete programs, including the transfer of technology in branches where national investment is insufficient or where access to international markets can be provided. The government is attempting to create an environment conducive to a fairly high long-run profit potential for foreign firms participating in the plan.

Multinational corporations in many of the high technology areas are expected to play an integral role in the plan, as are those involved in the border industry (or maquiladoras) program.

Although the industrial plan takes the form of a decree, and this is in principle legally binding, its success will clearly depend on the attitude and degree of enthusiasm shown by private business, organized labor, and the rest of the public sector.

In general the private sector has reacted favorably to the plan, largely because it provides a realistic picture of the probable economic trends and government policies in the near-to-medium future, and because it lists the main equipment requirements of the public enterprises.

Although the business distrust of government that existed during the Echeverria administration has been largely dispelled by the actions of the Lopez Portillo regime, the industrial plan provides a positive focus for support by clearly delineating the areas for state intervention.

In the past the government has used a wide variety of instruments and techniques in controlling and guiding the economy. Many of these will be strengthened in the process of implementing the National Industrial Development Plan. The government will be able to: (1) direct its current and capital expenditures toward many areas of high priority as will the large parastate enterprises and agencies, (2) use fiscal stimuli and subsidized prices for directing investment into desired areas, (3) channel credit to favored firms, (4) offer technical assistance, import protection, or export subsidies, and (5) control the licenses, permits, and dispensations needed to do business in Mexico.

The projections of the industrial plan envision a growing participation of the public sector in capital formation with heavy investments in infrastructure (required to attend to the needs of agriculture), transportation, communication, public health, social security, housing, tourism, science, education, and local government.

During the initial years of the plan (coinciding with the Lopez Portillo administration, 1977-82), fixed investment made by public enterprises is expected to grow at the highest rate, considerably above those of the private sector (although still far below the amounts accounted for by private sources). A major allocation of this investment will be made in petroleum and petrochemicals, electricity, fertilizers, and iron and steel—

industries in which public enterprises are already dominant. Between 1979 and 1982, state enterprises are expected to make two-thirds of all additional fixed investment in the industrial sector.

As will be discussed in greater detail in Chapter 6 the government's rapid and sustained rate of investment and private sector fixed capital formation are forecast at an annual rate of over 10 percent through 1990. At these rates the total amount of real private investment would greatly exceed that of the public sector. More precisely, the plan anticipates that by the first target year (1982), private enterprise will account for 61 percent of total investment while public enterprises (24 percent) and general government (15 percent) will account for the remainder. This is essentially the same pattern as that observed in the mid-1970s. By 1990, however, high growth in public sector investment brings the share of the state enterprises to 14 percent, while general government accounts for 34 percent and private enterprise for the remaining 52 percent.

By 1990, therefore, the programmed expansion of government investment would bring its level to nearly that of the private sector. Again, this pattern is expected to evolve not as a result of any particular limitations of or disinclination on the part of the private sector, but simply as a reflection of the public sector's expanded capability in financing its massive investment schemes.

Purchases of machinery and equipment by the public sector will be used to promote the capital goods industry in Mexico. Such purchases are expected to favor priority zones, determine volumes of output, and influence a number of features of the industry (including technical design, contract negotiation procedures, and terms of price and delivery). A system is being developed to include competitive bidding confined to national producers with a "buy national" margin of 15 percent over import reference prices. Public sector enterprises must now pay the established tariff duties on imports (which they formerly did not pay), and they must develop each year an approved foreign exchange outlet; both of these requirements are meant to shift demand from imports to domestically produced capital goods. To alert national firms of prospective demand, state enterprises in petroleum, electricity, fertilizers, and steel have published long lists of planned purchases for 1979-86. Additional stimuli to the capital goods industry are provided through the government's extensive system of preferential tax credits and by favored treatment of public sector credit.

In addition, preferential financing will continue to be made available for small and medium-sized industrial firms through the numerous special federal government trust funds. The activities of these often conflicting, often duplicating, trust agencies are now in the process of being coordinated through the government's program of Integral Support for Medium and Small Industry.

In terms of technical assistance, the government is expanding its aid to industry. It is upgrading its offerings of pre-investment surveys, technical and economic feasibility studies, productivity seminars, training manuals, market research, engineering design, and management consulting services—all at subsidized prices. This type of assistance is available to all companies, but preference is given to small and medium-sized firms. The government is also improving its assistance in the technology transfer process between Mexican business firms and their foreign suppliers, providing economic and technical analysis of contracts, regulations, royalties, fees, and restrictive practices. In general these programs try to increase the benefits that the Mexican firms obtain in licensing foreign technology.

While these programs of industrial assistance are expanding, import controls and export promotion continue to be the main instruments of industrial development. As in the past, the main thrust of the government's aid to industry has been in restricting competitive imports, the most common method being that of issuing import licenses or "prior import permits." This is a flexible tool and is used in a highly discretionary fashion to protect domestic industry or to favor particular areas, producers, suppliers, or products. Over the years, its flexibility and negotiability appealed to the interventionist policy orientation of many government officials. In part, continued use of import licenses has precluded Mexico from joining the General Agreement on Tariffs and Trade (GATT). However, the government began undertaking a gradual substitution of tariffs for import permits as the principal tool of import policy, and in early 1979 sent a letter of intent to GATT to open negotiations for eventually adhering to the agreement. While nothing came of this initiative (in 1980 the government turned down an offer of membership), it may be only a matter of time until the country has converted to tariffs as the prime means of protecting industry.

In fact the industrial development plan urges a continuation of the substitution of tariffs for prior import permits. The plan also proposes a tariff structure that is as simple as possible and that can be permanent, so that continuous changes will not discourage potential investment.

Export promotion by the Mexican government continues to involve a variety of elements. The foreign trade bank (Banco Nacional de Comercio Exterior) offers information and marketing and promotion services. The government also offers a wide range of tax rebates on the cost of exported goods.

A relatively new development is the growing contribution, direct and indirect, of state enterprise to the country's merchandise exports (a fact of which considerable note is taken in the industrial development plan). How much friction this development will generate with the United States and Mexico's other major trading partners is still unclear.

POTENTIAL DIFFICULTIES IN INDUSTRIAL DEVELOPMENT

A number of critical questions of revised development strategy as set out in the National Industrial Development Plan now confront the Mexican government.[7] First there is concern about how to prevent—even if the external debt is reduced—the large and rapidly expanding flow into Mexico of foreign exchange earnings from generating high rates of inflation before internal development and offsetting domestic production can take place. For sure, most Mexican officials are aware of the great dislocations uncontrolled expenditures of oil revenues had on the Iranian and Venezuelan economies. They are determined to prevent that occurrence in Mexico. As a step in this direction, various methods of "sterilizing" (temporarily setting aside and gradually directing the revenues into productive investments) are under discussion.

Second is the problem of alleviating the high rates of unemployment and underemployment within the country. The expansion of the petroleum industry is likely to create relatively few jobs, and the high rate of population growth will continue to add to the labor force. Indications are, however, that by 1982, even with the plan on schedule, the economy will be creating only 600,000 new jobs a year, while an estimated 800,000 new workers a year will be entering the labor force.

Third, both the first and second problems above reduce somewhat the scope for government action. For example, a logical means of reducing short-run inflationary pressures would be to utilize some of the country's surplus foreign exchange earnings for increased imports of consumer goods (as done in Iran, Venezuela, Saudi Arabia, and several of the other major oil exporting countries). Given the inefficiency of many of Mexico's import substitution industries, however, this approach might result in a decline in domestic production and hence displacement of industrial workers.

POSSIBLE ALTERNATIVES

There is still considerable debate within the government about the overall economic strategy to be adopted for the remainder of the 1980s. Many monetary and financial authorities are in favor of a more open economy, a position resisted to some extent by the Ministry of Industry. Many economists in the Bank of Mexico feel the oil money should be used to support the balance of payments, reduce the external debt, and finance the increased importation of consumer goods in order to rationalize inefficient elements in Mexican industry. While reducing inflationary pressures, this position also stresses the desirability of joining GATT. In general, therefore, the monetary view stresses the desirability of relatively free markets and in part a desire to control inflationary pressures without increasing taxes.

Domestically Oriented Approaches

In contrast, many Mexican planners feel that the plan places excessive emphasis on manufacturing modernization to the neglect of agriculture. The result, they fear, would be insufficient job creation and an increasingly inequitable income distribution (since the benefits of the oil boom and rapid growth will most likely be confined to the upper segments of Mexican society). This group, therefore, advocates a broader and more welfare oriented development strategy.

Finally the position of organized labor has been one of stressing expansion of public sector welfare and production activities (in order to assure real income redistribution and job creation). Labor is on record as opposed to joining GATT on the ground that it would reduce employment and the nation's industrial strength. This is also the position of the Colegio Nacional de Economistas (the professional association of economists in Mexico) and by organizations representing small businesses.

An attractive alternative under consideration is increased investment in the rural sector. Agricultural productivity, which attained impressive rates in the 1950s and 1960s, has been allowed to decline. When agriculture was expanding, a number of processing industries generated significant local incomes. The result was not only a better balance of payments position for the country as a whole, but also a dynamic domestic market for the import substitution consumer goods industries. If import substitution industrialization is to remain part of a balanced national development program, the government will undoubtedly find it advantageous to use its prospective financial resources to accelerate this type of internal development. Such a program will require the promotion of domestic scientific and technological activity on a wide scale.

The basis for this strategy has been outlined in the National Indicative Plan for Science and Technology. This plan, formulated by the Mexican National Council for Science and Technology in November 1976, indicates that sustained agricultural development as well as the continued growth of other economic sectors will require large investments in human capital in order to take advantage of the new financial resources made possible by increased oil revenues.

The original 1976 plan called for a comprehensive, integrated program for all scientific and higher educational institutions, with a common budget and a centrally established set of priorities related to the needs of national growth. The National Program for Science and Technology finally proposed in 1978, however, only provided a fiscal framework for financing uncoordinated research projects and scholarships. The plan contains no clearly defined priorities, nor any guidelines or provisions for systematic institution building. Since it took nearly twenty years of concentrated domestic research and education effort for what is now the International Center for the Improvement of Wheat and Maize to modernize Mexican agricultural production, a failure to widen the scientific infrastructure along similar lines in other fields could ultimately allow severe constraints on the country's growth to develop over time.

Export Oriented Approaches

Finally, the government has the option of further expanding the border industries program. This was initiated in 1965 to stimulate investment by firms operating on the basis of international subcontracting and engaged in assembly work at labor intensive stages in the production process. The tax arrangements under which the border or maquila industries operate allow the temporary duty-free importation of all the machinery and materials used in the manufacture of products (that are exported in their entirety). Given the structure of U.S. customs regulations, Mexican maquila firms need pay duties only on that portion of their value that was added in Mexico (while the portion corresponding to the costs of the inputs and machinery imported from the United States is exempt).

The duty-free zone in which U.S. firms could initially establish in-bond plants in Mexico was a strip 12 miles wide along the northern border. Most plants are still located in the border zone, but the restriction on location was lifted in 1967 to allow in-bond plants in the interior of Mexico.

Several restrictions are still imposed on foreign owned companies operating in Mexico. The constitution of 1917 prohibits foreign ownership of real estate within 62.5 miles of the U.S. border and 13.25 miles of the sea coast. Therefore, most border plants and the land they are located on are owned by Mexican interests and are normally leased to U.S. firms. A small proportion of firms have gained more permanent control of their plants through trust agreements sanctioned by the Secretariat of External Relations.

Industrial parks have developed on the Mexican side of the border and have facilitated the growth of the industrialization program. Tenants rent existing building space or have plants constructed to their own specifications. Manufacturers are allowed to furnish plants with their own equipment.

At least 90 percent of the labor force employed at border plants is required to be Mexican nationals. This causes no problems since the only foreign worker at most plants is the manager.

Lower wage rates spurred many labor intensive industries to participate in the twin plant program. Electric and electronic products account for about two-thirds of the total value added in the border plants. Next in order of relative importance are: shoes and apparel, nonelectrical machinery, furniture and wood products, services, and food products. Nearly 10 percent of total value added is accounted for by various other industries.

By the end of 1965, 12 plants employing over 3,000 workers were operating in the Mexican border area. Investment in maquila firms continued to grow rapidly during the late 1960s and early 1970s, reaching a peak of 455 plants and almost 76,000 workers in 1974 (value added totalling nearly $316 million).

With the recovery of the U.S. economy from recession, total employment in the border plants rose to more than 78,000 in 1977. The increase, however, occurred mainly at plants that were not affected substantially by the recession. The total number of in-bond plants fell to 443.

The decline in the number of border plants from 1975 through 1977 indicated that the rising rate of inflation in Mexico provided little incentive for new firms to enter the program. Consumer prices in Mexico rose at an annual rate of 11 percent in 1973, or double the rate of a year before. The rise in price doubled again to a 23 percent rate in 1974 (before declining to 17 percent in 1975).

The rapid rise in consumer prices prompted commensurate increases in factory wages. For example, average gross monthly earnings in manufacturing rose from $176 in 1973 to $273 in 1975. That sharp increase raised the average labor costs in Mexican factories from about one-fourth of the comparable cost in U.S. manufacturing in 1973 to one-third of the U.S. equivalent in 1975. [8]

As the relative cost of Mexican labor has begun to increase, competitive advantage tilted to countries with lower wage rates. Competition for U.S. investment in manufacturing facilities has come chiefly from Caribbean and Far Eastern localities—such as the Dominican Republic, Puerto Rico, Hong Kong, South Korea, Singapore, and Taiwan—where increases in labor costs developed less rapidly in the period 1972-75. In addition, average wage rates in manufacturing in many competing countries were only about 10 percent of the U.S. equivalent. Apparently, the saving obtained in employing the much cheaper labor in these countries more than offset the higher transportation and inventory costs.

By 1978 economic conditions had changed sharply again and Mexico had regained its comparative advantage. Total employment in the border industry was estimated at more than 90,000, and value added was over $400 million. But more important, the number of plants along the border was increasing, reaching a total of 445 by July 1978.

The devaluation of the peso in August 1976 from 8 cents to 5 cents immediately reduced the cost of Mexican goods and services by 37.5 percent. A further depreciation occurred in October 1976, and the value of the peso subsequently fell to around 4 cents. As a result, payroll costs were halved for U.S. manufacturers operating twin plants. However, workers in Mexico demanded and were granted wage increases that partially offset the sharp reduction in payroll costs. Moreover, the value of the peso began drifting upward in 1977 and is now (June 1982) about 2.2 cents, while the gap between wage rates in the United States and Mexico has continued to widen.

Average hourly earnings in U.S. manufacturing have increased sharply in recent years. From 1975 to 1978, U.S. hourly wages rose by 28 percent, partially reflecting the cost of living increases (resulting from the accelerated pace of inflation and the legislated rise in the minimum wage). Both the peso devaluation and the increase in U.S. wage rates have caused Mexican wage rates to decline from one-third of the U.S. wage equivalent in 1975 to about one-fourth by 1978, a proportion about the same as that prevailing in the first ten years of the border industrialization program.

Another factor leading U.S. firms to reconsider setting up manufacturing plants in Mexico was the faster rise in recent years of factory wages in the Far East. While the average factory wage rate in South Korea in 1978 was 17 percent of the U.S. equivalent, it had doubled since 1970. Similarly, while manufacturing wages in Taiwan were 14 percent of the U.S. equivalent in 1978, but up sharply from over 7 percent five years earlier, by 1978 the average factory pay in Hong Kong was 15 percent of the U.S. equivalent (up from 9 percent in 1970). In general, firms preferring to locate in the Far East have had an extremely large share of labor input in their production processes and do not have to supply large volume of materials or components to overseas location (or firms that plan to sell their output fairly close to where it is processed).

In contrast to the Far East, the average factory wage in Caribbean countries has not changed much in recent years relative to the U.S. equivalent. Manufacturing wages in Puerto Rico in 1976 for example were about 53 percent of the U.S. equivalent and that had barely changed from 52 percent in 1969. The average factory wage in the Dominican Republic has also held at about 11 percent of that paid in the United States. Despite their relatively low wage costs, many of the Caribbean sites are still not able to offset their higher transport costs and thus increase their attractiveness to foreign investors. [9]

The success of maquila industries has demonstrated the benefits Mexico can derive from utilizing its comparative advantage. It has an abundant work force that can be efficiently utilized in a wide range of activities or at certain stages of production (not necessarily for the entire production of a given product). On the other hand, the relative success of these firms points out the high social costs imposed upon the country by the incentives associated with the government's import substitution industrialization program. The export bias associated with this strategy has created a condition whereby, to increase manufactured exports, it has been necessary to develop an entirely new group of firms maintained in isolation from domestic firms, many of which are unable or unwilling to export even though experiencing excess capacity. Apparently, the major

factor contributing to the profitability of the border industries
(together with their generation of jobs and foreign exchange)
is that the social price of foreign exchange is higher than the
official price and the social price of labor less than the market
price.

The major limitations of the border industries is their acute
reliance on the U.S. market and thus dependence on cyclical
fluctuations in economic activity in that country. For example
in 1974-75, the U.S. recession was undoubtedly responsible
for the cutback in 35,000 jobs by the maquila industries. The
competition of other countries offering equal or better incentives
to attract subcontracting industries of the maquila type is another
factor adding to the vulnerability of these industries.

The future of the border industries will undoubtedly depend
in large part on the rate of expansion of the U.S. economy and
the relative rates of inflation in Mexico and the United States.
In the past five years, consumer prices in Mexico have risen at
rates considerably above those in the United States. A continuation of this pattern could lead to higher labor costs in Mexico
as wage rates rise to reflect the increased cost of living (again
discouraging participation in the border industry by U.S. firms).

Because the border industry is a major economic program
of the Mexican government, it is not likely the monetary authorities would allow the relative cost of labor to rise so far that
investment in twin plants would be discouraged (as in the 1973-
75 period). When the peso was devalued in 1976, the exchange
rate was moved from a fixed rate to a floating rate. Therefore,
if the rise in consumer prices in Mexico persists relative to
inflation in the United States, Mexican authorities would likely
permit the peso to decline against the dollar, thus maintaining
the favorable cost of labor relationship.

In a longer view, development and sale of Mexico's large
oil reserves and natural gas could put upward pressure on the
value of the peso and undermine the twin plant program by
increasing relative wage rates. However, substantial exports
of Mexican oil and gas will not likely take place before the mid-
1980s, and it is not clear at this time how much effect such sales
will have on the value of the peso.

Other tax incentive schemes are applied to certain industrial
branches including the automotive industry, and more recently
the publishing industry, as part of the special schemes for
supporting these activities. The export incentives for these
special sectors are similar to those provided for by the general
systems described and are essentially special procedures for
granting them.

Currently, the country is using additional export incentives in the form of—

1. import and investment licensing Standard Industrial Code (SIC) favoring export activities. Requests for import licenses are more likely to be granted and are sometimes granted more quickly if the need for the import is justified by a need to compete in export markets.
2. various promotional activities such as those of IMCE
3. financing by the Bank of Mexico increasingly directed to export oriented firms.

As a result of industrial protectionism, activities involving the export of goods and services became less attractive, since exporters had to use national inputs of steadily rising cost while the price of exports remained set by the world market.

The pronounced antiexport bias can be seen in an effective implicit protection rate of -5 percent for export activities in marked contrast to a rate of 39 percent for import substitution industries. As noted, it is not surprising that exports of manufactured goods account for less than 4 percent of domestic manufacturing, an extremely low proportion in terms of the degree of industrial development achieved, when compared with other developing countries.

The rate of inflation in Mexico, which is higher than in the United States, has helped to increase the overvaluation of the exchange rate, thus adding one more disincentive to export.

Mexico's present system of protection through licensing, which provides a potentially very high rate of protection to many manufactured products and less to others, is probably the most important element inhibiting exports. The system insulates Mexican producers from motivation to cut production costs to increase quality. This allows considerable inefficiency in domestic production, most of which could be eliminated if motivation were greater. The greatest part of the inefficiency shows up as higher costs and/or lower quality of products, a condition that would be quickly corrected if the protected firms had to compete with imports or if export incentives were modified to make foreign markets more attractive. To induce greater efficiency, Mexico should increase access to imported products where domestic costs are unreasonably high, and also increase the profitability of exports. This would permit more Mexican producers to increase volume and profits through successful competition and international markets. Increases in competition as well as more efficient specialization would no doubt induce faster overall growth.

CONCLUSIONS

The National Industrial Development Plan is an ambitious yet realistic program using the country's increased foreign exchange earnings. The thrust of the plan in moving industrialization into the domestic production of capital goods and export of intermediate goods seems realistic in light of the country's stage of industrialization and development requirements. The plan is also realistic in that it aims to strengthen long-term trends rather than to propose a radical change in the direction in the economy. The decision to support the private sector, but to expand state intervention as a substitute if no private response is forthcoming, is quite consistent with the tradition of Mexican economic policy since the Revolution.[10]

Of course, the success of Mexico's industrial development will not hinge completely on the plan. The attitudes of foreign firms and U.S. policymakers will also be critical in shaping the country's pattern of growth.

In addition, the parity of the peso and the real wage rate will be crucial for the development of manufactured exports. Clearly, the relative rise of both the value of the peso and the wage rate would depress the profitability of labor intensive exports. Unfortunately, this has been a common occurrence among oil exporters. Finally, the scope of Mexico's manufactured exports will depend in large part upon the farsightedness of the U.S. government and the U.S. capacity to restructure its economy away from traditionally labor intensive items such as textiles and automobile parts, or resource intensive items such as steel and cement, towards technologically advanced branches of industry. There is little indication, however, that U.S. policymakers are capable of implementing a policy along these lines.

NOTES

1. James Street, "Prospects for Mexico's Industrial Development Plan in the 1980s," Texas Business Review, May-June 1980, p. 127.

2. Estados Unidos Mexicanos, Secretaria de Patrimonio y Fomento Industrial, Plan Nacional de Desarrollo Industrial, 1979-82 (Mexico, D.F., March 1979).

3. Estados Unidos Mexicanos, Poder Ejecutivo Federal, Secretaria de Programacion y Presupuesto, Plan Global de Desarrollo, 1980-82 (Mexico, D.F., 1980).

4. Calvin Blair, Economic Development Policy in Mexico: A New Penchant for Planning, Technical Papers Series no. 26 (Austin: Office for Public Sector Studies, Institute of Latin American Studies, University of Texas, 1980).

5. Mexico: National Industrial Development Plan, volume 1 (London: Graham & Trotman, 1979), p. 17.

6. Ibid., pp. 6-7.

7. E. V. K. Fitzgerald, "Oil and Mexico's Industrial Development Plan," Texas Business Review, May-June 1980. See also Fitzgerald's "Mexico: A New Direction in Economic Policy?" Bank of London and South American Review, 1978, pp. 528-38 for an elaboration of the conflicts within the Mexican bureaucracy over the direction policy should take in the 1980s.

8. Edward McClelland, "U.S.-Mexico Border Industry Back on Fast Growth Track," Voice of the Federal Reserve Bank of Dallas, July 1979, pp. 3-5.

9. Ibid., pp. 6-7.

10. Ernesto Marcos, "Design of a Development Policy for Mexico: Industry and Oil," in Public and Private Enterprise in a Mixed Economy, ed. William Baumol (New York: St. Martin's Press, 1980), p. 62.

3

MONETARY AND
EXTERNAL SOURCES OF INFLATION

INTRODUCTION

When analyzing Mexico's recent inflationary experience,
most observers have tended to concentrate almost exclusively
on developments within the country. Most likely, this orientation
is biased toward identifying the structural or cost factors associated with price increases and a picture of inflation as largely
a nonmonetary phenomenon. Viewed from a broader perspective,
the country's inflationary experience takes on a much different
appearance. At least in the early part of the 1970s, developments similar to those taking place in Mexico were, to a large
extent, experienced by a wide number of developing countries.
As with Mexico, inflation in most of these countries was beginning
to be significant in 1971-72, becoming rapid and synchronized
in 1973 (Table 3.1). Furthermore, almost all countries experienced a rate of inflation in 1973-74 that either was close to their
historical peaks or set new record highs.

EXTERNAL LINKS

It is this universal and synchronous pattern of worldwide
inflation in the 1970s that makes this period unique. Explanations[1] of the worldwide pattern of price increases range from
crop failures and the oil shock to excessive monetary demand,
generalized wage-push and disputes over the division of income.
Four channels have been identified through which inflation may
have been transmitted internationally during this period.

TABLE 3.1

Rate of Change in the Consumer Price Index, Thirty Developing Countries, 1956-76 (percent)

| Country | Annual Average* | | | Peak, | Annual Average* | | | | | Acceleration in 1972 over |
	1956-60	1961-65	1966-70	1956-70	1971-72	1972	1973	1973-74	1975-76	1966-70
Argentina	41.8	23.2	n.a.	111.1	46.8	58.5	60.7	46.1	313.2	n.a.
Bolivia	65.8	5.2	6.0	11.2	5.1	6.6	31.5	47.8	6.3	0.6
Brazil	25.6	63.0	n.a.	87.0	18.3	16.4	12.7	20.2	35.3	n.a.
Chile	29.4	28.6	26.8	46.0	49.2	79.1	351.9	428.7	293.2	52.3
Colombia	9.5	12.9	10.2	32.2	11.7	14.3	22.8	23.6	21.5	4.1
Dominican Republic	0.1	2.8	1.3	9.2	6.1	7.9	15.1	14.1	11.1	6.6
Ecuador	-0.1	3.9	4.7	6.5	8.2	7.9	13.0	18.1	n.a.	3.2
Egypt	1.4	3.4	4.2	14.9	2.6	2.1	4.3	7.6	10.0	-2.1
El Salvador	0.4	0.2	1.1	5.7	1.0	1.5	6.4	11.6	15.1	0.4
Ghana	1.7	11.0	4.1	25.4	8.0	13.5	10.2	17.2	46.9	9.4
Guatemala	-0.2	0.1	1.5	2.4	0.1	0.6	13.8	15.1	11.9	-0.9
India	5.2	6.0	6.9	13.8	4.4	5.8	17.4	22.4	-1.0	-1.1

Indonesia	20.1	83.8	n.a.	n.a.	9.1	12.7	31.5	36.0	19.4	n.a.
Iran	6.9	2.0	1.4	11.2	5.3	6.4	9.8	11.9	12.1	5.0
Iraq	2.1	1.1	3.5	6.5	4.4	5.2	4.9	6.6	9.9	1.7
Korea, Re-public of	11.2	15.2	11.4	27.9	12.1	11.7	3.0	13.4	28.4	-0.2
Malaysia	0.4	0.5	1.4	4.6	2.4	3.2	10.6	14.0	3.6	2.8
Mexico	5.9	1.9	3.7	12.2	5.4	5.0	11.4	16.9	16.5	1.3
Morocco	3.6	4.0	0.6	6.1	3.9	3.7	4.2	10.9	8.2	3.1
Nigeria	4.1	2.8	5.9	13.9	9.4	2.8	6.0	9.2	27.6	0.1
Pakistan	4.1	2.0	4.5	11.3	7.2	5.1	23.1	24.9	14.0	0.6
Peru	8.5	9.0	9.8	19.0	7.0	7.1	9.5	13.2	28.6	-2.7
Philippines	2.2	4.7	6.1	14.4	12.4	10.2	11.0	22.7	7.1	4.1
Sri Lanka	0.6	1.7	4.2	7.4	4.5	6.3	9.6	10.9	4.0	2.1
Sudan	1.0	3.3	3.9	12.6	6.2	10.9	17.9	22.0	12.8	7.0
Syria	4.3	0.6	3.3	14.7	3.0	1.0	19.8	17.4	15.6	-2.0
Taiwan	11.2	2.4	4.4	n.a.	2.8	2.9	8.2	27.8	3.9	-1.5
Thailand	2.4	1.5	2.6	6.2	3.0	3.9	11.7	17.5	4.1	1.3
Tunisia	2.7	2.7	2.9	13.5	3.9	2.1	4.6	4.4	7.4	-0.8
Venezuela	2.4	0.4	1.6	5.0	3.1	2.9	4.1	6.2	8.9	1.0

*Single years refer to price rises over the previous year's level, two or more years to an average over those years.

Note: n.a. Not available.

Source: International Financial Statistics, various issues.

1. External demand, operating through the trade account, may have bid up the prices of domestic goods (assuming either that there was full employment or that the elasticity of supply of exportable goods was low).

2. External price movements may have brought the prices of domestic goods in line with those of traded goods.

3. Excess liquidity may have been created by increased external reserves (which encouraged spending on goods whose prices rose until the equilibrium level of real balances was restored).

4. Indirect stimuli, such as more aggressive international trade union activity, increased social gains, and international inflationary expectations, may have been increasingly active at this time.

In contrast to the real factors examined in the previous chapter, trade, price, and reserve channels of transmission of inflation to Mexico are examined in the sections below.[2] Considerable evidence was presented in the last chapter supportive of the argument that at least part of the country's inflationary patterns was caused by demand pressures (as measured for example by higher rates of real income growth or by deviations on real gross domestic product from its trend). The extent to which monetary factors have contributed to the country's recent acceleration in prices is the chief concern of this chapter.

As noted, Mexico's current inflation began in 1973, and in many regards this is the most productive period to examine in detail. For one thing, causation is much more difficult to establish once inflation has been under way for some time. For another, movements in factors usually listed as major contributors to the inflationary process were experiencing particularly wide fluctuations in the late 1960s and early 1970s, thus making their impact easier to identify through standard regression techniques.

INFLATIONARY PRESSURES 1973-74

One of the most popular explanations of the 1973-74 worldwide inflation (and Mexico's as well) is the OPEC price increases. Ironically, this is the easiest source of inflationary pressure to dispose of. In terms of timing, the OPEC price increases did not take place until late in 1973 (November). It is clear, however, that prices around the world were increasing well in advance of the OPEC action (some of the effects of the higher oil prices are contained in the 1973 inflation rates, of course).

The worldwide bad weather of 1972-73 and subsequent poor food harvests were undoubtedly contributory factors to the country's subsequent inflation, but weather and food prices cannot explain the duration of the inflation. The expansion of excess liquidity (especially before 1973) would appear more logical in this regard.

In contrast to the pattern of inflation that began to develop in 1973, there was a large growth in the money supply in 1972 (Table 3.2). Of the 26 sample countries whose past inflation rates can be regarded as normal (Argentina, Brazil, Chile, and Indonesia are excluded from the normal group because they have suffered hyperinflation in the past), 8 showed much higher rates of growth in the money supply during 1972 than at any other time between 1956 and 1970. In addition, only 1 country showed a higher rate of inflation between 1956 and 1970 than in 1973.[3]

Not only were the 1972 rates of growth in the money supply high in most countries (compared with past rates), but the jump from historical levels seems to have occurred almost simultaneously. The average growth in the money supply for the group of normal (nonhyperinflation) countries ranged from 8.6 percent to 12.5 percent during 1961-69. It increased to 14.6 percent in 1970, expanding to 17.7 percent in 1972. Significantly, the average growth in consumer prices did not increase above its 1961-72 range of 2.3 percent to 5.8 percent until 1973.

These patterns were unprecedented. In normal times, the acceleration in the rate of growth of the money supply and prices over their historical increases would be expected to be zero. And indeed, this was the case in 1972, with the acceleration in prices (over the 1966-70 average) ranging for the above sample of countries from -0.8 to 0.7. In 1973, however, prices accelerated by 5.9 percent, increasing again in 1974. In contrast the acceleration of money supply during 1968-71 had a range of 3.0 to 2.6 for the sample countries, increasing to 6.1 in 1973 and even further to 7.4 percent in 1974.[4]

In sum, there is no question that, at least for the 1970-72 period, the acceleration in the money supply preceded the acceleration in prices. Causation would thus seem to be from money to prices, rather than, as often hypothesized by Keynesians, from prices to money.[5] More precisely, increases in the money supply were not the result of an accommodating monetary policy, and, more importantly, the acceleration in the money supply in 1972 (and in prices in 1973-74) was worldwide.

As can be seen in the comparative tables, movements in prices and money in Mexico closely followed these worldwide

TABLE 3.2

Rate of Growth of the Money Supply, Thirty Developing Countries, 1956-76[a]
(percent)

Country	Annual Average			Peak, 1956-70	Annual Average[b]				Acceleration in 1972 over 1966-70
	1956-60	1961-65	1966-70		1971-72	1972	1973-74	1975-76	
Argentina	53.8	18.6	10.2	23.0	17.2	22.4	39.2	20.6	12.2
Bolivia	53.8	18.6	10.2	23.0	17.2	22.4	39.2	20.6	12.2
Brazil	29.1	65.8	n.a.	87.4	32.8	34.6	39.9	37.4	n.a.
Chile	23.3	37.8	n.a.	104.5	103.8	105.7	296.7	265.2	n.a.
Colombia	n.a.	18.4	19.8	24.0	15.4	20.6	27.1	21.9	0.8
Dominican Republic	n.a.	4.9	6.8	15.7	11.9	12.6	23.6	9.0	9.8
Ecuador	6.3	9.9	15.5	25.1	18.0	17.6	38.8	22.2	2.1
Egypt	n.a.	10.4	4.0	20.2	9.4	13.0	24.0	23.4	9.0
El Salvador	1.5	3.8	3.9	12.4	9.3	11.3	25.1	22.4	7.4
Ghana	6.2	16.8	4.7	26.1	19.0	38.8	22.8	42.5	34.1
Guatemala	5.6	6.3	4.5	14.3	10.3	14.6	23.7	23.1	10.1
India	6.5	9.0	9.5	11.9	12.7	12.5	15.3	11.4	3.0
Indonesia	29.9	n.a.	n.a.	n.a.	30.0	33.8	41.0	30.5	n.a.
Iran	17.5	12.1	10.5	26.6	23.7	32.6	26.6	41.5	22.1

Iraq	17.5	6.1	9.3	44.8	7.0	11.8	27.0	31.1	2.5
Korea, Republic of	18.3	22.9	35.9	45.7	26.6	32.6	38.8	27.0	-3.3
Malaysia	6.8	4.9	6.2	15.9	10.7	14.5	27.2	11.8	8.3
Mexico	10.6	11.5	11.2	11.1	10.9	14.2	21.6	22.1	3.0
Morocco	n.a.	7.3	8.2	23.8	12.5	16.6	20.1	19.3	8.4
Nigeria	n.a.	9.6	16.1	51.9	10.7	7.8	30.6	69.8	-8.3
Pakistan	7.4	7.4	9.2	16.9	18.7	20.2	8.9	17.4	11.0
Peru	n.a.	17.3	19.4	43.7	23.4	22.2	30.1	24.3	2.8
Philippines	n.a.	8.7	11.0	27.5	16.6	18.7	23.0	15.3	7.7
Sri Lanka	3.7	6.9	3.7	10.9	6.8	6.9	15.2	12.9	3.2
Sudan	11.5	11.8	13.0	20.5	6.6	7.0	27.9	18.0	-6.0
Syria	9.6	9.4	13.9	19.3	13.1	17.3	35.5	24.1	3.4
Taiwan	15.2	21.7	17.7	36.4	24.1	20.4	29.8	19.9	2.7
Thailand	6.9	6.2	7.1	12.2	11.5	12.7	17.7	10.5	5.6
Tunisia	n.a.	9.5	2.9	21.2	19.5	21.0	17.5	15.1	18.1
Venezuela	8.7	7.2	6.6	27.9	16.1	20.7	27.5	37.7	14.1

[a]Money supply refers to cash and demand deposits.
[b]Single year refers to price rises over previous year's level, two or more years to an average over those years.

Note: n.a. Not available.
Source: International Financial Statistics, various issues.

patterns. If there is any doubt that the initial inflationary pressures were monetary, it should be noted that in 1972 and 1973 the deviations of real GDP in Mexico did not lie appreciably above the long-run trend. Neither growth rates nor their deviation from the trend can explain the extraordinary increase in money supply in 1972. Furthermore, similar periods of expansion have occurred before without a corresponding acceleration in consumer prices.

DOMESTIC CAUSES OF EXPANSION
OF THE MONEY SUPPLY

Little evidence has been found so far that purely domestic causes were responsible for the acceleration of money supply in Mexico in 1970-72. Crop failures and lagging food supply, which have been assigned a prominent position in the structuralist list of causes of inflation, however, could have played an important role at this time.

In terms of food production on a per capita basis, Mexico's performance was substandard, declining by 3.6 in 1972 and 1.9 in 1973 (with 1961-65 = 100, the index of per capita food production was 110 in 1971).

Whether this was sufficient to induce an increase in the domestic money supply is much more uncertain. The structuralists' argument that lagging agricultural supply causes inflation is based on three assumptions that food prices are flexible, that nonfood prices are relatively fixed, and that imports are not used extensively to maintain a stable price level.[6] If foreign exchange shortages dictate a policy of permitting only essential imports, a food shortage can, by inducing an increase in the relative price of food, initiate a period of inflation; i.e., to avoid a severe decline in output when prices in the nonfarm sector are sticky, an increase in the relative price of food would most likely have to be financed by an increase in nominal money, thus leading to inflation.

On the surface this argument seems to have some merit in the Mexican case. In terms of the pattern of food prices, Mexico's relative food prices actually declined from a base of 1970 = 1.00 to 0.93 in 1972. Thereafter, they rose to 1.09 in 1973, 1.47 in 1974, and 1.21 in 1975. A closer examination of quantitative data, however, reveals that, while food prices began to rise in mid-1973, the money supply had been increasing at an accelerated pace all through 1972. Food shortages may therefore have had a limited role in causing the money supply growth of 1972, with

the food decline at most exacerbating the acceleration of the
money supply. On the other hand, the decline in food production and increased prices of food imports cannot be completely
ruled out as having played a significant role in the overall
1973-74 price acceleration.

Wage increases were not excessive (Table 3.3) and are
easily disposed of as a major contributory factor to the money
supply increases.

Clearly, the government budget is the logical place to
begin any analysis of the expansion in the money supply. Although Mexico's financial markets are relatively developed by
Latin American standards, they are not developed to the extent
that large-scale noninflationary financing of the government
deficit is possible through the issuance of public bonds. In
the final analysis, if the government cannot mobilize domestic
savings, the budget deficits must be financed by creating money.

Budget deficits as a percentage of gross national product
increased from 0.81 percent in 1970 to 2.04 percent in 1972,
3.06 in 1973, and 3.61 in 1974, largely (Table 3.4) as a result
of a higher rate of expenditures relative to revenues.

The deficits in turn created a number of dilemmas for the
Bank of Mexico.[7] First, the bank had to decide the source of
funds to draw upon to finance the government deficit. This
process entailed a series of steps. First, the bank had to estimate the amount of credit that would be available from foreign
sources. After this was determined, the levels to be financed
with domestic credit were set. If the amounts of domestic funds
needed were impossible to raise, the bank often attempted to
attract more foreign savings into the Mexican banking system
(through increasing the interest differential vis à vis international financial centers). The interest rate differential
together with the reputation for political and economic stability
that Mexico had earned in the 1960s acted as an incentive for
large amounts of savings.

Therefore, besides helping to finance the current account
deficit of the balance of payments, foreign savings were used
to finance the government's budget deficits. To facilitate this
process, banks were obliged to invest their required reserves
in government bonds or in selected sectors of the economy. In
essence, since these legal reserves were imposed on all the
funds, the banks received the funds for government financing
regardless of their origin.[8]

If the total amount of available funds (foreign plus domestic)
was sufficient to finance the government deficit, the Bank of
Mexico would be in a neutral position, neither expanding nor

TABLE 3.3

Mexico: Selected Growth Rates, 1968-80
(average annual rates of growth)

Year	Wholesale Prices Mexico City 1954 = 100	Consumer Prices Nation-wide 1978 = 100	Implicit Deflator of GDP 1960 = 100	GDP 1960 Prices	Total Money Supply	Currency and Coin	Demand Deposits	Urban Minimum Wages	Real Manufacturing Wages	Total Reserves Minus Gold	Foreign Assets Bank of Mexico
1968	2.0	0.8	2.4	8.1	12.9	13.0	12.9	0.0	0.0	17.1	7.1
1969	2.6	3.4	3.9	6.3	11.6	11.3	11.9	0.0	2.6	0.2	5.0
1970	6.0	5.3	4.5	6.9	10.5	10.4	10.5	16.3	0.9	15.2	3.5
1971	3.7	5.3	4.5	3.4	8.3	8.3	8.2	0.0	2.4	32.4	24.5
1972	2.8	5.0	5.6	7.3	21.2	22.8	20.1	18.3	2.4	29.8	30.6
1973	15.7	12.0	12.4	7.6	24.2	27.6	21.7	5.2	0.3	18.9	7.0
1974	22.5	23.8	24.0	5.9	22.0	25.1	19.9	35.9	4.0	6.7	1.1
1975	10.5	15.2	16.7	4.1	21.3	22.4	20.5	16.0	4.8	11.7	10.8
1976	22.2	15.8	21.7	2.1	30.9	52.8	13.5	29.3	9.0	-14.1	39.8
1977	41.2	28.9	32.0	3.3	26.6	11.0	43.3	27.9	2.0	38.8	5.0
1978	15.8	17.5	18.1	7.3	32.6	29.5	35.2	13.5	-3.1	11.7	17.0
1979	18.3	18.2	20.7	8.0	33.1	30.3	35.6	16.8	n.a.	10.4	33.3
1980	24.5	26.3	30.0	7.4	33.7	32.0	34.9	17.8	n.a.	39.3	31.8

Note: n.a. = not available.
Source: Compiled from data in Bank of Mexico, Informe Anual, various issues, Bank of Mexico, Indicadores Economicos, various issues.

TABLE 3.4

Mexico: Public Sector Expenditure, Borrowing[a] and GDP, 1972-80 (billions current pesos)

Year	GDP (1)	Increase Percent (2)	Expenditure (3)	Ratio Percent (3)/(1)	Gross Borrowing (4)	Ratio Percent (4)/(1)	IPD[b] (5)
1972	512.3	13.2	147.3	28.7	37.5	7.3	5.6
1973	619.6	20.9	204.0	32.9	62.3	10.1	12.4
1974	813.7	31.3	276.5	34.0	76.5	9.4	24.0
1975	988.3	21.5	400.7	40.5	137.1	13.9	16.7
1976	1228.0	24.3	530.2	43.2	157.4	12.8	21.7
1977	1674.7	36.4	730.6	44.6	250.0	14.9	32.1
1978	2104.6	25.7	938.6	44.6	317.4	15.1	17.4
1979	2704.4[c]	28.5	1124.3	41.6	487.7	18.0	19.5
1980	3650.9[c]	35.0	1683.4	46.1	465.8	27.6	25.3

[a]The actual total gross borrowing is given, except in 1979, when it is the estimated actual, and in 1980, when it is the budgeted.

[b]IPD is the implicit price deflator of GDP.

[c]Estimated, as explained in the text.

Source: Constructed by the author from Bank of Mexico annual reports and budget tables, 1972-80.

reducing its holdings of international reserves. On the other
hand, if all of these funds were not enough to finance the gover
ment deficit, the bank would have to consider direct credit to
the Treasury, even at the risk of overstimulating total demand. [9]

If the threat of excess aggregate demand became very
serious, the Bank of Mexico would have to take compensatory
action on private credit (so that the nation's overall economic
goals would not be endangered). In this case, the bank would
most likely reduce bank credit to allow Mexico's stock of international reserves to remain unchanged (thus assuring the goals
of maintenance of a stable exchange rate together with free convertibility).

Summing up, one could conclude that government expenditures are the main exogenous variable in the short term. The
Bank of Mexico authorities were quite clearly in 1972 left in the
rather compromising situation of either reducing the amount of
funds available to the private sector or losing foreign exchange.

Quantitatively the Bank of Mexico's reserve money (BMRM)
is clearly a function of its largest component, commercial bank
reserves (CBR), although these reserves by themselves account
for only about 75 percent of the variation in BMRM (Table 3.5).
Clearly, the government deficit (GDEF) is a significant variable
(equation 5, Table 3.5). On the other hand, reserve assets of
the bank (BMFA) were related to nominal exports (EXPTNA)
and imports (Z). For reasons outlined below in the discussion
of the reserve flow mechanism, real income proved significant
in each regression in which it was introduced.

Bank of Mexico credit to the government was found to be
explained simply by total government expenditures (GENAN)
and the government deficit.

$$BMGC = 1.73 \text{ GENAN} + 2.22 \text{ GDEF} - 14.56$$
$$(5.98) \qquad (3.52) \qquad (-5.14)$$

$$r^2 = 0.989; \ F = 1109.07$$
$$DW = 1.72$$

One implication of these linkages is the inherent tendency
toward disequilibrium that began building up in the late 1960s. [1]
Price stabilization and development objectives were to a certain
degree becoming increasingly incompatible, especially during
times when one goal was pursued more vigorously than the
other. Given the policy framework at the time, the development
goal required that output grow at the highest annual rate possible. Government expenditures were, therefore, promoted to
the extent possible on the assumption that increased total deman
would, through increasing private profitability, further induce

TABLE 3.5

Mexico: Estimated Structural Equations—Bank of Mexico Block (1951-79)

Bank of Mexico Reserve Money (BMRM)

(1) BMRM = 2.31 CBRL - 0.39 BMGC - 1.76 E + 1.06 GENAN + 18.84
$\quad$ (16.64) $\quad$ (-1.63) $\quad\quad$ (-4.57) $\quad$ (6.95) $\quad\quad$ (2.86)

$r^2 = 0.989$; F = 509.54; DW = 0.98

(2) BMRM = 3.24 CBR - 571.98 DUMEX + 577.39 DUMDV + 1.80 DUMTDV + 0.36
$\quad$ (12.47) $\quad$ (-7.75) $\quad\quad\quad$ (8.14) $\quad\quad\quad$ (0.078) $\quad$ (0.016)

$r^2 = 0.945$; F = 98.29; DW = 3.19

(3) BMRM = 1.97 CBRL + 3.54 ΔEX - 0.76 EX - 1.11 GDEFL + 129.54
$\quad$ (12.23) $\quad$ (1.24) $\quad\quad$ (-4.23) $\quad$ (-3.89) $\quad\quad$ (4.55)

$r^2 = 0.976$; F = 278.94; DW = 1.24

(4) BMRM = 2.28 CBRL - 0.76 BMGC + 1.49 CPI + 0.29 INFD - 49.79
$\quad$ (9.79) $\quad$ (-2.45) $\quad\quad$ (2.67) $\quad\quad$ (0.28) $\quad$ (-1.95)

$r^2 = 0.968$; F = 205.68; DW = 0.91

(5) BMRM = 1.44 CBR - 3.34 GDEF - 2.23 BMGC - 20.72
$\quad$ (2.63) $\quad$ (-3.80) $\quad\quad$ (-2.62) $\quad$ (-1.60)

$r^2 = 0.873$; F = 54.81; DW = 2.14

(6) BMRM = 0.64 BMGC - 1.28 CBR + 2.64 CBRL + 8.81
$\quad$ (7.08) $\quad$ (-9.55) $\quad\quad$ (24.87) $\quad$ (3.53)

$r^2 = 0.993$; F = 1042.12; DW = 1.58

Reserve Assets (BMFA)

(7) BMFA = 0.20 EXPTNA + 0.0056 GDPNP + 0.21
$\quad$ (37.61) $\quad\quad$ (4.48) $\quad\quad\quad$ (0.33)

$r^2 = 0.994$; F = 1975.56; DW = 1.16

(8) BMFA = 0.22 EXPTNA + 0.12 Z + 0.015 GDPNP + 1.66
$\quad$ (5.70) $\quad\quad$ (2.96) $\quad$ (5.43) $\quad\quad$ (4.89)

$r^2 = 0.994$; F = 1567.05; DW = 1.15

(9) BMFA = 0.16 EXPTNA - 11.11 DUMEX + 1.60 EX + 5.15 DUMDV - 3.75 DUMTDV - 12.91
$\quad$ (9.12) $\quad\quad$ (-2.50) $\quad\quad\quad$ (2.93) $\quad$ (7.97) $\quad\quad$ (-1.61) $\quad\quad$ (-2.72)

$r^2 = 0.992$; F = 678.99; DW = 1.64

(10) BMFA = 0.21 EXPTNA + 2.56
$\quad$ (47.60) $\quad\quad$ (6.01)

$r^2 = 0.989$; F = 2265.76; DW = 0.727

(11) BMFA = 0.26 EXPTNA - 0.08 GBMGC - 0.087 GDEF
$\quad$ (7.63) $\quad\quad$ (-4.02) $\quad\quad$ (-2.29)

DW = 1.05

Source: Compiled by the author.

65

private sector investment. Under Keynesian conditions of genera unemployment, demand stimulations might have been expected to result in increased real output at relatively constant prices. Given the structural nature of much of Mexico's unemployment, however, price stability and high rates of growth became conflicting goals.[12] The bank was thus placed in the position whereby, in order to finance the increased level of government expenditures, it had either to create new money or to reduce the amount of credit available to the private sector. Clearly, whenever new money was created in excess of the prevailing trend, additional pressure was exerted on prices.[13]

INTERNATIONAL CAUSES OF EXPANSION
OF THE MONEY SUPPLY

External factors were perhaps nearly as responsible during this period for the monetary acceleration as the government deficits. External reserves increased at an unusually high rate in both 1971 and 1972 (and, as shown below, these increases were systematically related to money supply changes).

During 1966-70, the country maintained a ratio of reserves to imports of around 0.32. In 1970 the ratio was still 0.32, but increased to 0.40 and 0.41 in 1971 and 1972, respectively. Since the government attempted to maintain reserves in a relatively fixed relation to imports, the 1971 and 1972 deviations from the 1960s average is indicative of the extent to which the country suddenly acquired excess reserves.

Another indicator of the degree to which the 1971-72 reserve accumulation was excessive is the increase in reserves in 1971 and 1972 compared with the long-run degree of fluctuation (both positive and negative) in the country's reserves. For the base period 1965-69, typical reserve fluctuations were calculated as the average absolute value of the annual percentage reserve change. By this measure the country had a 0.0 average annual rate of change. In 1970, however, reserves increased by 12.4, and in 1972 by 22.3, but were down to 3.0 in 1974.

These measures strongly support the conclusion that there was an unusual increase in the country's international liquidity in 1971-72. In order to identify the channels of transmission of external inflation, however, it is necessary to determine whether the increase was due to changes in the trade balance (which primarily would reflect commodity prices and movements in real activity) or to capital flows (which are the result of monetary factors).

Both the level and the change of the trade balance are relevant for the analysis of the changes in reserves. Because the country had negative trade balances and thus used borrowing to cover trade deficits, an unanticipated improvement in the trade balance might have led to an increase in reserves (if capital flows including borrowing were kept at planned levels). Neither the size of the trade deficit nor the change over the previous year, however, suggests a partial role for trade in expanding reserve changes, since the country's trade balance deteriorated from $888 million in 1970 to $893 in 1972, to $1,515 million in 1973, and to $2,792 million in 1974.

It appears therefore that a greater part of the expansion of reserve changes in the early 1970s lies in the behavior of the capital markets than in the trade balance. Moreover, it is likely that the reserve growth caused the money supply growth. Again, because the country lacked developed financial institutions (to the extent that open market operations could be conducted on a large scale), reserve changes were likely to have a direct and immediate effect on the domestic liquidity; i.e., since capital inflows and reserve increases generally are not sterilized in Mexico,[14] their expansion thus results in a corresponding increase in the domestic money supply.

Changes in the country's money supply and reserves during the period of fixed exchange rates during 1956-72 indicates that the money multiplier associated with a change in reserves was 1.6; i.e.,

$$GM1 = 3.72 + 1.61 \; GR$$
$$(3.6) \qquad r^2 = 0.712$$

where GM1 = annual growth in M1 money; GR = annual growth in reserves.

These results suggest the importance of reserve changes in influencing movements in the money supply. More elaborate estimates of the money supply function (Table 3.6) show it to be very stable, either as a function of the reserves (CBR) of the commercial banks with the Bank of Mexico, or as a lagged function of Bank of Mexico reserve money (BMRM, BMRML, BMRML2).

Combined with the information on reserve growth, these results suggest that the Bank of Mexico's monetary policies were influenced to a considerable degree by external events and in particular by changes in the level of reserve assets. The precise role of sterilization policies cannot, however, be determined directly from the estimated equations since monetary

TABLE 3.6

Mexico: Estimated Structural Equations—Money Supply Block
(1951-79)

Narrow Money Supply (M1)

(1) M1 = 0.17 CBR + 0.12 GDPN + 17.57 DUMDV - 14.22 DUMEX - 0.26
         (5.45)   (43.09)   (2.92)   (-2.77)   (-0.34)

$r^2 = 0.999$; F = 12891.7; DW = 1.14

(2) M1 = 0.18 CBR + 0.12 GDPN + 13.62 DUMDV - 11.55 DUMEX - 0.68 EXL + 7.39
         (5.81)   (39.34)   (2.19)   (-2.23)   (-1.69)   (1.61)

$r^2 = 0.999$; F = 11187.3; DW = 1.17

(3) M1 = 1.35 CBR - 96.52 DUMEX + 177.43 DUMDV + 26.65
         (8.60)   (-2.24)   (4.15)   (6.48)

$r^2 = 0.992$; F = 703.87; DW = 1.28

(4) M1 = 0.90 CBR - 83.86 DUMEX + 125.03 DUMDV + 17.92 MI - 4.29 MID - 108.66
         (11.93)   (-3.92)   (6.66)   (10.86)   (-3.48)   (-6.68)

$r^2 = 0.994$; F = 849.15; DW = 1.48

(5) M1 = 0.28 CBR + 31.47 DUMDV - 17.38 DUMEX + 4.23 MI + 0.93 M1L - 32.77
         (4.25)   (2.60)   (-1.52)   (3.23)   (12.66)   (-3.24)

$r^2 = 0.999$; F = 4671.22; DW = 2.82

(6) M1 = 0.67 BMRM + 27.53
         (10.46)   (3.11)

$r^2 = 0.814$; F = 109.49; DW = 1.49

(7) M1 = 0.49 BMRM + 0.38 BMRL + 22.56
         (5.52)   (2.79)   (2.80)

$r^2 = 0.859$; F = 73.43; DW = 1.18

(8) M1 = 0.38 BMRM + 0.38 BMRML2 + 2.48
         (9.13)   (6.24)   (0.60)

$r^2 = 0.969$; F = 272.83; DW = 1.41

(9) M1 = 0.35 BMRM + 0.33 BMRML2 + 37.09 DUMEX + 7.15
         (8.50)   (5.15)   (1.96)   (1.55)

$r^2 = 0.977$; F = 230.78; DW = 1.84

(10) M1 = 0.28 BMRM + 0.35 BMRML2 + 69.50 DUMEX - 78.93 DUMDV + 8.61
          (13.44)   (11.50)   (10.68)   (-8.63)   (3.88)

$r^2 = 0.995$; F = 816.6; DW = 0.51

(11) M1 = 0.26 BMRM + 0.34 BMRML + 0.67 BMRML2 + 93.13 DUMEX - 86.75 DUMDV - 3.97 MID + 29.73
          (15.54)   (14.44)   (14.09)   (10.15)   (-12.33)   (-4.25)   (5.68)

$r^2 = 0.997$, F = 1237.12; DW = 1.07

(12) $M1 = 0.029$ BMRM $+ 0.26$ GDPN $+ 0.049$ ΔGDPN $- 1.56$
$\quad\quad\quad$ (2.35) $\quad\quad$ (16.05) $\quad\quad\quad$ (1.86) $\quad\quad\quad$ (-1.20)
$\quad\quad\quad\quad\quad\quad\quad\quad\quad\quad\quad\quad\quad\quad\quad\quad\quad\quad\quad\quad\quad\quad$ $r^2 = 0.999$; $F = 7364.45$; DW $= 1.13$

(13) $M1 = 0.075$ CBR $+ 0.028$ CBRL $+ 0.13$ GDPN $- 1.05$
$\quad\quad\quad$ (3.57) $\quad\quad\quad$ (2.03) $\quad\quad$ (13.97) $\quad\quad$ (-1.37)
$\quad\quad\quad\quad\quad\quad\quad\quad\quad\quad\quad\quad\quad\quad\quad\quad\quad\quad\quad\quad\quad\quad$ $r^2 = 0.998$; $F = 4971.8$; DW $= 1.97$

Broad Money (M2) Supply

(14) $M2 = 1.24$ BMRM $+ 0.75$ BMRML $+ 16.58$
$\quad\quad\quad$ (5.54) $\quad\quad\quad$ (2.17) $\quad\quad\quad$ (0.81)
$\quad\quad\quad\quad\quad\quad\quad\quad\quad\quad\quad\quad\quad\quad\quad\quad\quad\quad\quad\quad\quad\quad$ $r^2 = 0.842$; $F = 64.05$; DW $= 1.46$

(15) $M2 = 1.03$ BMRM $+ 0.76$ BMRML $+ 1.69$ BMRML2 $- 21.88$
$\quad\quad\quad$ (5.89) $\quad\quad\quad$ (2.91) $\quad\quad\quad$ (4.40) $\quad\quad\quad$ (-1.23)
$\quad\quad\quad\quad\quad\quad\quad\quad\quad\quad\quad\quad\quad\quad\quad\quad\quad\quad\quad\quad\quad\quad$ $r^2 = 0.914$; $F = 81.84$; DW $= 1.33$

(16) $M2 = 0.53$ BMRM $+ 0.45$ BMRML $+ 0.24$ BMRML2 $- 334.97$ DUMDV $+ 395.18$ DUMEX $- 6.17$ MID $+ 5.58$ MI $+ 1.41$
$\quad\quad\quad$ (19.42) $\quad\quad\quad$ (8.49) $\quad\quad\quad$ (1.51) $\quad\quad\quad$ (-25.02) $\quad\quad\quad$ (30.22) $\quad\quad$ (-5.07) $\quad$ (1.33) $\quad$ (0.041)
$\quad\quad\quad\quad\quad\quad\quad\quad\quad\quad\quad\quad\quad\quad\quad\quad\quad\quad\quad\quad\quad\quad$ $r^2 = 0.999$; $F = 3618.31$; DW $= 1.01$

(17) $M2 = 0.55$ BMRM $+ 0.51$ BMRML $+ 0.43$ BMRML2 $- 347.97$ DUMDV $+ 402.29$ DUMEX $- 6.09$ MID $+ 45.44$
$\quad\quad\quad$ (24.93) $\quad\quad\quad$ (16.49) $\quad\quad\quad$ (6.79) $\quad\quad\quad$ (-37.34) $\quad\quad\quad$ (33.09) $\quad\quad$ (-4.92) $\quad$ (0.55)
$\quad\quad\quad\quad\quad\quad\quad\quad\quad\quad\quad\quad\quad\quad\quad\quad\quad\quad\quad\quad\quad\quad$ $r^2 = 0.999$; $F = 4064.67$; DW $= 1.04$

(18) $M2 = 1.47$ CBR $+ 0.14$ CBRL $+ 0.13$ GDPN $- 0.24$
$\quad\quad\quad$ (17.67) $\quad\quad\quad$ (1.57) $\quad\quad$ (14.34) $\quad\quad$ (-0.076)
$\quad\quad\quad\quad\quad\quad\quad\quad\quad\quad\quad\quad\quad\quad\quad\quad\quad\quad\quad\quad\quad\quad$ $r^2 = 0.998$; $F = 4882.2$; DW $= 1.91$

Note: See Appendix for definition of symbols. Ordinary least squares estimates; TSP estimation program.
Source: Compiled by the author.

69

expansion might have occurred in the absence of reserve change
The result above does indicate, however, that changes in domestic money supply were strongly correlated with changes in reserves during this period. Since there was an unusual expansio
of reserves in the country in 1971 and 1972, that connection
implies that the acceleration of money supply in 1972 and 1973
was strongly influenced by international as well as domestic
factors.

One index that might be used to determine the external or
imported contribution to money supply growth is the ratio of
reserve changes to the previous year's money stock. Trends
in this ratio should be indicative of the relative importance of
external and internal factors responsible for money expansion.

As a basis for comparison, the ratio was 1.1 in 1966, rose
to 2.1 in 1970, to 4.6 in 1972, and fell to 3.5 in 1973 and to 1.7
in 1975. Therefore, 1972 represents the greatest external contribution to the growth in the money supply.

THE ROLE OF PUBLIC POLICY

Many of the patterns noted above were reinforced by a
series of ill-timed government policies.[15]

1. In 1970 the current account deficit of the balance of
payments turned out to be almost twice as great as in the previous year. To reduce the current account deficit, a drastic cut
in government spending was budgeted for 1971. Actual spending
however, was even lower than budgeted, so the end result was
that the government's deficit as a percentage of GDP was reduced from 1.5 in 1970 to 1.05 in 1971.

2. Considerable banking system resources, only partially
utilized by the private sector, were freed by the sharp decline
in government expenditures. Although the increase in the
financial sector's real credit extended was at normal levels,
financial institutions accumulated 2.7 billion pesos in excess
reserves. The result was the severe economic slump in 1971
with real output growing at only 3.4 percent.

3. When the slippage of the growth rate became known and
the existence of bank's excess reserves was disclosed, the government attempted to restore the traditional growth rate through
increased expenditures. The budget deficit as a proportion of
GDP more than trebled from 1971 to 1972.

4. Not only was public spending stepped up, but private
investment increased substantially as well. Reserve require-

ments for commercial banks and investment banks (financieras) were lowered in May 1972 when the recovery of output was in full swing.

5. Monetary ease came three months after the rate of change in industrial production had already increased above its long-run growth trend.

6. Excess reserves were quickly exhausted, and the Bank of Mexico, under the stress of a low rate of economic growth, abandoned its long-run tradition of yearly changes of monetary targets (in line with long-run trends) and attempted fine tuning by expanding domestic credit.

7. As noted above, prices reacted with a lag. It was not until the second semester of 1972 that the wholesale price index started rising gradually. In January 1973 the annual rate of change of this index was already 7.3 percent; by December of that year it had increased to 25.5 percent.

8. At the end of May 1973, much too late, and in the face of accelerating inflation, the Bank of Mexico reversed its policy of monetary ease by raising reserve requirements for financieras and banks. Interest rates were also increased later that year. By that time, however, these measures were largely symbolic.

9. The government's deficit as a proportion of GDP increased by 35 percent in 1973, and the money supply grew at a rate of 24.1 percent. The rate of inflation turned out to be 15.7 percent for that year, and for the first time since the 1950s real interest rates on financial savings became negative. This trend continued until 1976.

Suffice it to say from the analysis in the sections above that there is adequate evidence to warrant a more detailed examination of the monetarist explanation of the country's balance of payments-money supply-inflation process.

THE MONETARY MODEL AND ITS ASSUMPTIONS

The monetary model[16] tested for Mexico simply assumes that, if the government wishes to maintain a relatively fixed exchange rate, then the balance of payments through its effect on the quantity of money will be the main channel for attaining and maintaining monetary equilibrium; i.e., when the domestic money supply exceeds the demand for money, people must readjust their portfolios by purchasing in the goods or assets markets in order to achieve portfolio equilibrium.[17]

The fundamental element in the monetary theory of the balance of payments is the existence of a stable demand for money function (estimated in Appendix, Chapter 3). Usually this demand is considered to be a function of the level of real income and the opportunity cost of holding money. If each of these determinants remains constant, the monetary approach can be regarded as a theory of the rate of inflation whereby the price level will adjust to ensure that, whatever the stock of nominal money, the level of money in real terms will be equal to the amount of money demanded; i.e., the nominal money supply determines the price level. [18]

These assumptions imply a three-equation model that includes the demand for money, the supply of money, and money market equilibrium conditions.

(1) $Md = kPy^{a1}e^V u^{a2}$

(2) $Ms = a(R + D)$

(3) $Md = Ms$

Differentiating equations (1) and (3) logarithmically with respect to time yields:

$$gM = INF + a1gyn - a2gi + v$$

for the money demand equation and

$$(\frac{R}{B}) gR = INF + a1gyn - a2gi - ga - (\frac{D}{B}) gD + u$$

for the reserve flow equation, with gyn the growth in nominal GDP. The coefficient (a1) is the income inelasticity of demand for nominal money. From studies in other countries and for theoretical reasons, a value of around 1.0 would be expected. [19]

For a given interest rate, price level money multiplier (a) and domestic credit (D), the growth in income (gy_n) should be associated with reserve inflows just sufficient to result in a 1 percent increase in the nominal and real stock of money.

Increases in the interest rate (ai) should result in reserve outflows. Other things being equal, a given increase in the interest rate would depress the demand for money, creating an excess demand for it, and consequently would result in reserve outflows. Again, work in other developing countries suggests that a2, the interest elasticity of demand for money, should be a positive number.

Mexican interest rates were used in the empirical estimations. Clearly, however, if changes in the actual Mexican rate during this time was dominated by changes relative to the rest of of the world, estimates of a2 could very well be positive; i.e., increases in the rest-of-world rates relative to Mexican rates should attract capital and generate reserve inflows (and vice versa). If no money illusion existed during this period, the price coefficient, as noted above, should be around 1.0. Similarly, the theory predicts the coefficients of ga and $(\frac{D}{B})$ gD should each be -1.0.

Finally, the money multiplier (ga) and the domestic credit creation $(\frac{D}{B})$ gD were both policy variables of the central bank during this period. An increase in either or both would tend to increase the money supply and, ceteris paribus, should lead to an outflow of reserves sufficient to restore money to its previous level.[20]

In summary, income and prices (INF) should be positively related to reserve flows while domestic credit, money multiplier, and the interest rate would be negatively related to reserve flows. Most of these implications are in disagreement with the Keynesian theory of the balance of payments.

EMPIRICAL RESULTS

The estimates of the various formulations of the reserve flow equation (Table 3.7) confirm the relevance of the monetary model for Mexico.

In the first difference formulation, the change in reserves is strongly related to the change in Bank of Mexico domestic credit, changes in the gross domestic product, and changes in the interest rate (MI). The signs are correct, and over 99 percent of the variation in the change in reserves is accounted for by these variables.

The results of the growth formulations of the model (Table 3.8) are acceptable but not as striking as in the first difference form. The coefficient of the weighted growth in domestic credit, though correct in sign, is somewhat below 1.0 (usually 0.4 to 0.5).

Also the overall r^2 values are in the range of 0.5 to 0.6. Still, the signs are all correct, with the growth in nominal income (gyn), real income (gy), inflation (INF), and the nominal interest rate all significant.

TABLE 3.7

Mexico: Reserve Flow Estimations—Growth Formulation (1951-80)

Dependent Variable	Equation	Independent Variables						RHO	Inter-cept	r²	F	DW
		$\frac{D}{B}$ GD	GYM	DUMDV	GY	INF	MI					
Weighted growth in reserves (R/B) gR	(1)	-0.31 (2.85)	0.42 (2.94)	-12.15 (-2.41)				0.04 (0.22)	1.65 (0.78)	0.621	11.45	1.93
	(2)	-0.40 (3.15)			0.42 (1.63)	0.30 (2.12)		-0.12 (-0.63)	1.18 (0.43)	0.539	8.19	2.05
	(3)	-0.44 (3.53)			0.42 (1.61)		0.75 (1.89)	-0.07 (-0.38)	-4.73 (-0.97)	0.525	7.75	2.01
	(4)	-0.50 (4.41)						0.11 (0.57)	6.07 (4.49)	0.438	19.45	1.93
	(5)	-0.38 (3.52)	0.35 (2.58)					-0.11 (-2.05)	1.72 (0.85)	0.539	14.08	2.05

Note: DUMDV = dummy variable for 1976 evaluation; INF = the rate of change in the implicit GDP deflator; MI = nominal interest rate. See text for definition of other symbols.

Source: Compiled by the author.

74

TABLE 3.8

Mexico: Reserve Flow Estimations—First Difference Formulation (1951-80)

Dependent Variable	Equation	ΔD	$\Delta GDPN$	$\Delta MR1$	ΔWPI	ΔMI	RHO	Inter-cept	r^2	F	DW
Change in Reserves (ΔR)	(1)	-1.05 (54.53)	0.01 (2.94)	-0.11 (-2.36)			0.22 (1.19)	0.45 (0.75)	0.998	4539.52	1.73
	(2)	-1.05 (46.41)	0.01 (2.57)				0.05 (0.24)	0.40 (0.77)	0.998	7619.27	1.92
	(3)	-1.03 (46.54)	0.02 (3.30)			0.35 (1.83)	0.19 (0.68)	0.03 (0.05)	0.999	4663.87	1.84
	(4)	-1.02 (44.37)	0.01 (0.68)		0.26 (3.03)		0.04 (0.24)	-0.06 (-0.13)	0.999	6237.81	1.95

Note: ΔD = Change in Bank of Mexico domestic credit; $\Delta GDPN$ = change in normal gross domestic product; $\Delta MR1$ = change in real interest rate; ΔWPI = change in wholesale price index; ΔMI = change in nominal interest rate.

Source: Compiled by the author.

Looking at the balance of payments in the monetarist reserve flow form has the added advantage that the individual components of the country's external accounts do not have to be estimated separately.

In fact, attempts to estimate the various subcomponents of the balance of payments, particularly short-term and long-term capital movements, encountered a number of difficulties. In terms of the individual components of the balance of payments, estimates indicated that exports (BOPE) are largely affected by U.S. economic conditions (equations 2 and 3, Table 3.9) where USGDP (nominal U.S. gross domestic product) and USYP (real U.S. gross domestic product), together with the U.S.-Mexican exchange rate (EX), accounted for around 90 percent of the fluctuations in exports. Imports (BOPZ) were largely determined by the level of exports (BOPE) together with the exchange rate (EX), and a dummy variable to reflect the 1976 devaluation (DUMDV).

The inclusion of domestic investment (TIN) in the import formulation (equation 9, Table 3.9) is consistent with the increasing practice in Mexico during this period of imposing import controls on all but nonessential items.

As noted, short-term capital movements (BOPST) were more difficult to estimate, perhaps because of the lack of a relevant short-run interest rate series. Best results were obtained with the government deficit (GDEF = government expenditures - government revenue). The external gap (EGAP = imports - exports) and the change in the peso-U.S. dollar exchange rate (ΔEX) where higher values indicate devaluation.

This formulation is consistent with the notion that an increasing share of the government's deficits and the trade gap were financed with external loans and that devaluation of the currency induced capital flight (errors and omissions are included in short-run capital).

As noted, long-term capital movements were difficult to estimate, again perhaps because of lack of an interest rate series adequately reflecting the rates pertinent to this variable. In short, the reserve flow equation's main advantage, in addition to its theoretical implications, is the avoidance of separate estimates for the components of the balance of payments.

THE MONETARIST MODEL OF INFLATION

The monetarist theory of inflation differs from alternative explanations of inflation largely in the basic assumptions from which it starts; instead of assuming for example that wage changes provoke price changes and conversely through institutionally given (and therefore arbitrary) reaction coefficients, it assumes that during an inflationary period individuals would become accustomed to the expectation of continued inflation, so that the processes of determining wages and prices would become fundamentally real processes (and not arbitrary processes determined exogenously).

The monetarist approach is a logical one to use in examining Mexico's price movements since: (1) although the economy is large by most standards, it is still relatively small in the sense that the prices of such important items as capital goods are largely determined in world markets, and (2) even though Mexico is considered a less developed country, it does have a relatively advanced financial sector, headed by a central bank, which over most of the period under examination was responsible for influencing the external balance (the balance of payments) as well as domestic credit conditions.

Thus Mexico provides not only the conditions necessary for testing a monetary model but also some interesting insights into the model's policy implications, especially with regard to the nature and causes of inflation experienced by the country.

The monetary approach to inflation in Mexico is similar to that outlined above in connection with the balance of payments; i.e., it starts with the fundamental proposition that inflation is merely an interaction of market supply and demand for money. Put differently, price movements are viewed by this model as systematically dependent upon current and immediate past evolutions of the interaction between supply and demand conditions, and, as noted in the preceding chapter, with movements (Table 3.10) in the U.S. or world rate of inflation.[21]

The starting point of this analysis is the basic monetarist model derived from the equation of exchange.[22] More specifically, assume a simple money demand function of the following form:

(1) $M/PY = Y^a C^b$

where M is the (exogenously determined) nominal stock of money; P is the price, Y is a measure of real income; and C is the expected cost of holding real balances. Equation (1) is solved for P and expressed in terms of growth rates (or depicted by G prefixing the variable):

(2) $INF = GM - (1 - a)GY - bGC$

TABLE 3.9

Mexico: Estimated Structural Equations—Balance of Payments Block (1951-79)

Balance of Payments—Exports (BOPE)

(1) BOPE = 2.60 BOPC + 2.83 BOPST + 889.40
      (13.79)   (5.53)   (2.81)
$r^2 = 0.888$; F = 95.38; DW = 1.20

(2) BOPE = 3.94 USGDP + 237.98 EX - 35.87
      (4.84)   (2.86)   (-5.17)
$r^2 = 0.918$; F = 138.18; DW = 2.70

(3) BOPE = 3.76 USYP + 423.79 EX - 7298.59
      (3.42)   (6.36)   (-7.93)
$r^2 = 0.892$; F = 98.83; DW = 2.39

(4) BOPE = 0.48 BOPC + 0.58 BOPST - 139.59 ΔDFGDP + 6.02 PENAN + 521.36
      (3.57)   (2.99)   (-0.34)   (16.34)   (5.41)
$r^2 = 0.992$; F = 695.97; DW = 1.94

(5) BOPE = -0.78 BOPEL + 6.53 PENAN + 80.50 ICEUV - 1804.35
      (-5.20)   (6.38)   (4.05)   (-2.46)
$r^2 = 0.973$; F = 325.17; DW = 1.89

(6) BOPE = 7.31 PENAN - 0.49 BOPEL + 0.90 BOPC + 0.77 BOPST + 1013.45
      (8.06)   (-3.46)   (4.64)   (2.47)   (5.37)
$r^2 = 0.980$; F = 275.7; DW = 2.18

(7) BOPE = 4.69 PENAN + 0.97 BOPC + 1.20 BOPST + 574.51
      (7.79)   (4.22)   (3.51)   (3.41)
$r^2 = 0.969$; F = 249.78; DW = 2.72

Balance of Payments—Imports (BOPZ)

(8) BOPZ = 0.95 BOPE + 1.05 BOPC + 1.13 BOPST + 733.26 DUMDV + 39.92
      (65.90)   (26.09)   (14.41)   (3.52)   (1.55)
$r^2 = 0.999$; F = 18906.1; DW = 1.84

(9) BOPZ = 1.42 BOPE - 181.34 EX + 3.17 TIN + 1595.51 DUMDV + 1758.48
      (19.36)   (-4.74)   (1.62)   (4.08)   (4.02)
$r^2 = 0.995$; F = 1205.31; DW = 1.38

(10) BOPZ = 1.47 BOPE - 2009.86 DUMEX + 2271.36 DUMDV - 184.84 DUMTDV - 325.77
      (39.35)   (-3.91)   (5.30)   (-0.53)   (-0.96)
$r^2 = 0.996$; F = 1313.31; DW = 1.60

(11) BOPZ = 1.18 BOPE - 427.84 EX + 53.76 INFW + 2.94 GDPN + 243.47 DUMEX + 1264.69 DUMDV + 973.39 DUMTDV + 3576.77
      (11.52)   (-2.37)   (2.46)   (3.01)   (0.19)   (1.84)   (1.50)   (2.16)
$r^2 = 0.997$; F = 967.70; DW = 1.10

Balance of Payments—Short Term Capital (BOPST)

(12) $BOPST = -241.73\ \Delta EX + 0.88\ EGAP + 41.79$
$\qquad\qquad\quad (-6.97)\qquad\quad (2.19)\qquad (0.53)$

$\qquad\qquad\qquad\qquad\qquad\qquad\qquad\qquad\qquad\qquad r^2 = 0.669;\ F = 24.31;\ DW = 2.37$

(13) $BOPST = -7.76\ MRI + 18.81\ TIN + 41.34\ GDEF - 219.46\ \Delta EX - 23.35$
$\qquad\qquad\quad (-0.82)\qquad\ (2.98)\qquad\ (2.83)\qquad\quad (-6.12)\qquad (-0.29)$

$\qquad\qquad\qquad\qquad\qquad\qquad\qquad\qquad\qquad\qquad r^2 = 0.807;\ F = 23.06;\ DW = 2.44$

(14) $BOPST = 16.69\ GDEF - 219.33\ \Delta EX + 7.92\ EGAP - 24.59$
$\qquad\qquad\quad (3.26)\qquad\quad (-7.90)\qquad\ (3.70)\qquad (-0.40)$

$\qquad\qquad\qquad\qquad\qquad\qquad\qquad\qquad\qquad\qquad r^2 = 0.831;\ F = 37.57;\ DW = 2.11$

(15) $BOPST = -227.67\ EX - 17.12\ TIN + 23.76\ EGAP + 2448.87$
$\qquad\qquad\quad (-7.27)\qquad (-4.97)\qquad\ (6.65)\qquad\quad (6.92)$

$\qquad\qquad\qquad\qquad\qquad\qquad\qquad\qquad\qquad\qquad r^2 = 0.755;\ F = 23.69;\ DW = 1.72$

Balance of Payments—Long Term Capital (BOPC)

(16) $BOPC = 23.19\ \Delta K - 20.78\ \Delta GDPN + 257.95\ \Delta CPI + 155.59$
$\qquad\qquad\ (2.35)\qquad (-2.02)\qquad\qquad (2.80)\qquad\quad (0.83)$

$\qquad\qquad\qquad\qquad\qquad\qquad\qquad\qquad\qquad\qquad r^2 = 0.753;\ F = 24.44;\ DW = 1.15$

(17) $BOPC = -48.07\ TIN - 129.71\ GDEF + 1876.36\ DUMDV - 131.78\ MI + 1600.25$
$\qquad\qquad\ (-3.80)\qquad (-3.98)\qquad\qquad (3.53)\qquad\qquad\quad (0.79)\qquad\quad (1.12)$

$\qquad\qquad\qquad\qquad\qquad\qquad\qquad\qquad\qquad\qquad r^2 = 0.925;\ F = 71.03;\ DW = 1.34$

(18) $BOPC = 67.27\ MI - 55.40\ TIN - 141.03\ GDEF$
$\qquad\qquad\ (4.05)\qquad (-5.14)\qquad (-5.79)$

$\qquad\qquad\qquad\qquad\qquad\qquad\qquad\qquad\qquad\qquad DW = 1.85$

Balance of Payments—Change in Reserves (BOPR)

(19) $BOPR = 0.90\ BOP + 0.91\ BOPC + 0.93\ BOPST + 13.43$
$\qquad\qquad\ (9.60)\qquad (10.32)\qquad\ (12.08)\qquad\ (0.94)$

$\qquad\qquad\qquad\qquad\qquad\qquad\qquad\qquad\qquad\qquad r^2 = 0.893;\ F = 66.55;\ DW = 1.98$

(20) $BOPR = 0.77\ BOP + 0.78\ BOPST + 0.76\ BOPC + 8.95\ EX - 10.85\ \Delta EX - 83.11$
$\qquad\qquad\ (6.24)\qquad (6.94)\qquad\quad (6.04)\qquad\ (1.80)\qquad (-0.93)\qquad (-1.49)$

$\qquad\qquad\qquad\qquad\qquad\qquad\qquad\qquad\qquad\qquad r^2 = 0.906;\ F = 42.63;\ DW = 1.83$

(21) $BOPR = 0.84\ BOPE - 0.83\ BOPZ + 0.83\ BOPST + 0.80\ BOPC + 1.17$
$\qquad\qquad\ (8.04)\qquad\ (-7.51)\qquad\ (7.65)\qquad\quad (6.63)\qquad\ (0.069)$

$\qquad\qquad\qquad\qquad\qquad\qquad\qquad\qquad\qquad\qquad r^2 = 0.900;\ F = 51.79;\ DW = 2.08$

(22) $BOPR = 0.74\ BOP + 0.73\ BOPST + 0.79\ BOPST + 0.75\ \Delta USGDP - 5.86$
$\qquad\qquad\ (5.06)\qquad (4.67)\qquad\quad (6.09)\qquad\quad (1.40)\qquad\qquad (-0.30)$

$\qquad\qquad\qquad\qquad\qquad\qquad\qquad\qquad\qquad\qquad r^2 = 0.901;\ F = 52.42;\ DW = 1.77$

(23) $BOPR = -0.048\ BOP + 0.19\ BOPST + 1.52\ \Delta USYP$
$\qquad\qquad\ (-2.81)\qquad\quad (4.29)\qquad\ (1.52)$

$\qquad\qquad\qquad\qquad\qquad\qquad\qquad\qquad\qquad\qquad DW = 1.46$

Note: See Appendix for definition of symbols. Ordinary least squares estimates; TSP estimation program.
Source: Compiled by the author.

79

TABLE 3.10

Changes in Money and Real Wages in Mexico and the United States, 1968-80 (1968 = 100)

| | Mexican Average Urban Minimum Wage | | | | Average Real Manufacturing Wages | | | |
| | Money Wage | | Real Wage[a] | | Mexico | | United States[b] | |
	Index	Annual % Change	Index	Annual % Change	Index	Annual % Change	Index	Annual % Change
1968	100	—	100	—	100	—	100	—
1969	100	0.0	96.6	-3.4	102.6	2.6	103.2	3.2
1970	116.3	16.3	107.0	10.8	103.5	0.9	103.8	0.7
1971	116.3	0.0	101.5	-5.1	106.0	2.4	106.5	2.6
1972	137.6	18.3	114.4	12.7	108.5	2.4	109.7	3.0
1973	144.7	5.2	107.3	-6.2	108.8	0.3	109.7	0.0
1974	196.7	35.9	117.9	9.9	113.2	4.0	106.7	-2.7
1975	228.2	16.0	119.0	0.9	118.6	4.8	105.9	-0.7
1976	295.0	29.3	132.8	11.6	129.3	9.0	107.3	1.3
1977	377.3	27.9	131.6	-0.9	131.9	2.0	108.4	1.0
1978	428.1	13.5	127.1	-3.4	127.8	-3.1	109.0	0.6
1979	500.0	16.8	125.6	-1.2	n.a.d	—	105.6	-3.1
1980[c]	589.0	17.8	141.1	12.3	n.a.d	—	102.5	-5.5

80

aIndex of money wage increases corrected for inflation by dividing by the national consumer price index for each country.

bIndex of hourly earnings in private non-agricultural industries (constructed from US Economic Indicators, February 1980). For statistical convenience, I took this measure of wage increases rather than manufacturing wages. From 1970 to January 1980, manufacturing gross hourly earnings in current dollars were at a higher level than total non-agricultural, and in those ten years, manufacturing rose by 4.3% more than total non-agricultural.

cFor Mexico, the January figure is the annual increase for 1980, which will be eroded by inflation as the year goes by. For the United States, it is the percentage change from January 1979.

dn.a. = not available.

Source: Bank of Mexico, Precios, Cuaderno Mensual, Febrero 1980, constructed from Tables 7 to 11; and US data from Economic Indicators, February 1980, Washington, D.C.

Equation (2) incorporates the basic elements of the monetarist approach to inflation: money, real income, and the expected cost of holding real balances. In addition, this formulation captures the basic methodological bias of the monetarist school; i.e., the equation has a limited number of variables, and the nature of relationships is clear and straightforward. The growth of money relative to output and cost of holding real balances will generate an increase in the rate of inflation. The growth of real income will cause decreases in the rate of inflation (via absorbing money in the increased demand for real balances). Similarly, the rate of inflation is assumed to be inversely related to the expected cost of holding real balances.

Equation (2) assumes instantaneous adjustment of monetary changes and no money illusion. Therefore, the tested form of the monetarist equation is

$$INFW = a + a1GM + a2GML + GML2 - GGDPNP + INFWE$$

where GGDPNP is the growth of real gross domestic product; GML is the growth of the money supply (either M1 or M2) lagged one year; GML2 is the growth in the money supply lagged two years; and INFWE is some measure of inflationary expectations (using the wholesale price index). Here INFWE is the current rate of inflation minus last year's rate.[23]

The basic monetarist contention is: (1) that the causal relation runs from money to prices and output, (2) that any persistent increase in money relative to output is a sufficient condition for inflation, (3) that magnitude and length of inflation are dependent on the magnitude and persistence of monetary growth, (4) that the occurrence of inflation is independent of the level of employment in the economy, and (5) that it is the increasing growth rate of money that yields inflationary pressures.

The results of the monetary regressions on the rate of increase in the wholesale price index indicate that the monetarist model performs extremely well. The growth in both M1 and M2 were used, with M1 performing slightly better.

GM1 is highly significant, explaining nearly 73 percent of the observed rate of inflation (equation 1, Table 3.11). Similar results (Table 3.12) were obtained for the rate of increase in the gap deflator (INF) and the rate of increase in the currency price index (INFC). When combined with other variables in the wholesale equations, GM1 is still significant, rising to over 89 percent explanation of the variance in INFW when combined with GM2L, the expected inflation (INFWE) and the U.S. inflation

TABLE 3.11

Mexico: Monetary Determinants of Inflation (1951-80)

Dependent Variable	Equation	Independent Variables								RHO	Intercept	r^2	F	DW
		GM1	GM1L	1NFWE	US1NFC	GM2	GM2L	ZA	GGDPNP					
Rate of Inflation (Wholesale price index)	(1)	0.97 (8.11)								-0.03 (-0.17)	-5.98 (-3.25)	0.725	65.91	1.89
	(2)	0.71 (4.32)	0.37 (2.15)							0.04 (0.22)	-7.28 (-3.70)	0.744	34.95	1.83
	(3)	0.43 (3.48)	0.54 (4.53)	0.45 (5.50)						0.40 (2.24)	-5.99 (-2.93)	0.813	30.56	1.89
	(4)	0.33 (2.65)	0.45 (3.65)	0.45 (6.06)	0.43 (1.68)					0.17 (2.89)	-5.41 (-2.45)	0.822	23.09	1.29
	(5)	0.49 (3.50)	0.61 (3.92)	0.45 (4.46)	0.26 (1.03)			1.08 (2.36)	-0.42 (-1.55)	—	16.47 (-3.98)	0.891	25.88	1.66
	(6)					0.56 (7.06)	0.15 (1.80)			0.26 (1.39)	-3.17 (-2.00)	0.762	38.43	1.67
	(7)			0.43 (3.54)	0.50 (2.66)	0.28 (3.13)	0.29 (3.18)			—	-3.56 (-3.62)	0.899	46.78	1.89
	(8)			0.43 (3.12)		0.32 (3.18)	0.35 (3.54)			—	-3.08 (-2.83)	0.846	47.03	1.83
	(9)				0.34 (3.77)	0.58 (10.65)			0.33 (2.73)					

Note: See text for definition of symbols.
Source: Compiled by the author.

TABLE 3.12

Mexico: Estimated Structural Equations—Inflation Block
(1951-79)

Inflation—Gross Domestic Product Deflator Measure (INF)

(1) INF = 0.66 GM1 + 0.46 GM1L - 8.83
          (2.87)   (2.48)   (-4.30)

r^2 = 0.733; F = 31.56; DW = 1.28

(2) INF = 0.84 GM1 - 0.636 GDPNP - 0.51
          (7.10)   (-3.44)   (-0.20)

r^2 = 0.776; F = 39.95; DW = 1.66

(3) INF = 0.616 M1 + 0.286 M1L + 0.34 GM1L2 - 9.99
          (3.75)   (1.43)   (2.01)   (-4.97)

r^2 = 0.774; F = 25.17; DW = 1.18

(4) INF = 0.57 GM1 + 0.45 GM1L - 0.62 GGDPNP - 2.58
          (4.16)   (3.12)   (-4.00)   (-1.15)

r^2 = 0.845; F = 40.08; DW = 1.60

(5) INF = 0.51 GM1 + 0.32 GM1L + 0.28 WINF - 0.56 GGDPNP - 1.84
          (4.07)   (2.23)   (2.32)   (3.88)   (-0.89)

r^2 = 0.877; F = 37.38; DW = 1.67

(6) INF = 0.54 GM1 + 0.47 GM1L - 0.77 GGDPNP + 0.03 INFE - 1.63
          (4.18)   (3.42)   (-4.53)   (1.99)   (-0.74)

r^2 = 0.866; F = 33.89; DW = 1.74

Inflation—Consumer Price Index Measure (INFC)

(7) INFC = 0.30 GM2 + 0.24 GM2L + 0.31 INFCE + 0.38 WINF - 59.71 ZB - 8.36
           (2.83)   (2.08)   (2.32)   (2.66)   (-1.66)   (-1.96)

r^2 = 0.828; F = 19.29; DW = 1.36

(8) INFC = 0.27 GM2 + 0.29 GM2L + 0.34 WINF + 0.35 INFCE - 1.64
           (2.53)   (2.53)   (2.30)   (2.54)   (-1.14)

r^2 = 0.804; F = 21.61; DW = 1.08

Source: Compiled by the author.

84

(USINFC), the ratio of imports to GDP (ZA), and the growth in real GDP (GGDPNP). In general the growth of U.S. prices gives somewhat better results than world inflation lagged one year.

The positive sign on the inflationary expectations term (INFWE, INFCE), as proxied by this year's rate of price increase minus last year's, is of interest and has certain implications for monetary policy. The positive sign (equations 6, 7, and 8 of Table 3.12; equations 3, 4, 5, 7, and 8 of Table 3.11) indicates that, with increased inflation, individuals may have actually increased their holdings of money, an apparently irrational move since inflation was eroding the value of these holdings at the time. This, however, can to some extent be explained by the financial structure of the country, which can be characterized by—

1. greater reliance of firms on internal financing than on the issuance of new securities
2. only limited activity in the domestic stock exchange, with new securities being purchased mainly by the financial institutions rather than the nonbank private sector
3. deposits with the monetary system constituting the major portion of the public's claims on the financial intermediaries.[24]

Given the relative lack of alternative assets and financial instruments, increased money holdings during periods of inflation are not as irrational as might at first appear.

GOVERNMENT PERCEPTION OF THE
INFLATIONARY PROCESS

From the above monetary analysis, the impact of openness, deviations from the trend, and reserve movements, it is clear that any meaningful framework for the analysis of Mexican inflation must systematically take into account the role of money in the economy.

Unfortunately, President Echeverria never publicly acknowledged the role of government deficits and monetary expansion in the country's inflationary process.

President Lopez Portillo, although taking a more realistic approach toward the economy, has also tended to minimize the role of money or government actions in affecting price change. For example, in his 1979 Annual Report (Informe) inflation was attributed largely to the time consuming process of production, "the natural lack of synchronization with the consequent waiting period between investment and output of the final product;" oil subsidies to consumers were viewed as reducing private expenditure thus moderating inflation, and a considerable part of the inflation was attributed to the rising prices of imports.[25]

The president noted that there is not a certain cure for inflation "for the world has been struggling to eradicate it for six years." He also declared that Mexico was doing its best to control domestic inflation, but since it was suffering from many shortages, "it would be unfair to fight inflation by preventing these from being converted into demand. . . ." The remedy was to improve supply "by increasing the flow of basic consumer goods," and if this could not be done through the "existing structure," the government must step in.[26] In other words, the president believed that Mexican inflation was mainly if not entirely a supply phenomenon. But the shortages to which he refers are always present in some degree in every country. Converting them into demand gives no assurance that insufficiencies in supply will disappear; on the contrary, if the money supply is increased to create the demand, the analysis above shows that the likely result will under present conditions be largely one of increased prices with little increase in real output.

CONCLUSIONS

In an exhaustive analysis of presidential attitudes toward inflation, Dr. Redvers Opie has noted that eight fundamental errors continually crop up, six directly related to the problem of stopping inflation and two indirectly related but with much more far-reaching significance for economic policy in general.[27]

1. The first and perhaps the most fundamental error is the belief that more growth and employment can be created by continuing inflation than by stopping it. A look at the record shows that overall during the 1960-79 period, economic growth was greater under conditions of price stability than under those of inflation (Table 3.13).

2. The second error is the belief that government action to stop inflation will cause massive and prolonged unemployment, and that over a relatively short period average growth will be less than it will be if inflation is continued.

3. It is also an error to believe that inflation can be stopped gradually.

TABLE 3.13

Mexico: Economic Progress 1950-79
(percentages)

	1950-59	1960-70	1971-79
Real Wages			
Total increase (%)	31.7	91.5	23.3
Annual average increase	2.8	6.7	2.4
Consumer Prices			
Total increase (%)	85.2	31.4	243.7
Annual average increase	5.4	3.5	14.7
GDP Per Capita			
Annual average increase	2.5	3.1	1.0*
Money Wages			
Total increase (%)	142.7	151.9	324.7
Annual average increase	9.3	8.8	17.4
Annual Average Inflation			
Mexico	5.4	3.5	14.7
United States	2.4	2.8	6.4
Industrial countries	2.5	4.2	7.3

*1970-77.
Source: Antonio Ortiz Mena, President of the Inter-American
Development Bank, speech before the Fifth Hemispheric Trade
Union Conference on Economic Affairs, Washington, D.C.,
November 13, 1979, tables at pp. 2 and 7 of the Statistical Annex.

4. A less serious error perhaps is to blame external forces
rather than those domestically created for the differentially
higher rate of inflation in Mexico. Government policies in every
country are virtually the exclusive cause of its having a higher
rather than a lower rate of inflation than that of other countries.

5. The most poignant error is the refusal to accept as a
fact that the suffering of the vast majority of the Mexican people
from prolonged inflation outweighs the short-term so-called
cost of stopping it.

6. An important source of error is that of failing to take
into account the difference between adjustmental and inflationary
increases in prices. This distinction is similar to that sometimes

made in economic literature between the nonmonetary and the
monetary causes of price increases. In the Mexican context it
is preferable to emphasize the distinction between the adjustmental causes and the continuing causes of rises in the price
level, because of the supreme importance of the distinction for
policy making. The adjustmental causes include such factors
as the increases that occur when controlled prices are moved
upwards when goods are disappearing from the market in order
to restore production. From the point of view of economically
rational policy making, it is highly desirable that such price
adjustments should be encouraged rather than resisted.

7. The first of the errors indirectly related to the analysis
of inflation is the belief that job creation can rationally be made
a direct objective of economic policy rather than a derived objective from optimizing real economic growth.

8. Finally, experience in post-World War II international
trade and investment demonstrates that it is an error and a
delusion to believe that Mexico can "do it alone," that the country
can gain more from retaining its "freedom to act" in relative
economic isolation than from gearing the economy (however
slowly) into the world cost price structure based on the international division of productive processes, in accordance with
comparative cost advantages.

NOTES

1. Robert Looney, The Economic Consequences of World
Inflation on Semi-Dependent Countries (Washington, D.C.:
University Press of America, 1979); see also Lawrence Krause
and Walter Salant, eds., Worldwide Inflation: Theory and Recent
Experience (Washington, D.C.: Brookings Institution, 1977);
David Meiselman and Arthur Laffer, eds., The Phenomenon of
Worldwide Inflation (Washington, D.C.: American Enterprise
Institute for Public Policy Research, 1975); and Michael Parkin
and George Zis, eds., Inflation in Open Economies (Manchester:
Manchester University Press, 1976).

2. These channels may be incorporated in the monetary
theory of the balance of payments. Cf. Harry Johnson, "The
Monetary Approach to the Balance of Payments Theory," in
Further Essays in Monetary Economics, ed. H. Johnson (Cam-
bridge, Mass.: Harvard University Press, 1973), Chap. 9; and
Michael Parkin, "A Monetarist Analysis of the Generation and
Transmission of World Inflation: 1958-1971," American Economic
Review, February 1977, pp. 164-71.

3. Surjit Bhalla, "The Transmission of Inflation into Developing Economies," in World Inflation and the Developing Countries, ed. William Cline (Washington, D.C.: Brookings Institution, 1981), p. 54.

4. Ibid.

5. See N. Kaldor, "Inflation and Recession in the World Economy," Economic Journal, December 1976, pp. 703-14, for an exposition of the prices-money causal mechanism for this period.

6. Susan Wacher, Latin American Inflation (Lexington, Mass.: Lexington Books, 1976), pp. 11-12.

7. Gilberto Escobedo, "The Response of the Mexican Economy to Policy Actions," Federal Reserve Bank of St. Louis Review, June 1973, p. 19; see also Gilberto Escobedo, "Formulating a Model of the Mexican Economy," Federal Reserve Bank of St. Louis Review, July 1973, pp. 8-19 for an excellent summary of the applicability of various macroeconomic models to the Mexican economy.

8. Escobedo, "The Response of the Mexican Economy to Policy Actions," p. 20.

9. Ibid.

10. For an alternative and quite different interpretation, see E. V. K. Fitzgerald, "Capital Accumulation in Mexico," Development and Change, July 1980, pp. 391-414. Fitzgerald criticizes this orthodox approach. His own interpretation is, however, subject to a number of errors. Cf. Robert Looney, "Mexico's Fiscal Crisis: A Critique of the Fitzgerald Thesis," paper presented at the Eastern Economic Association Meetings, Philadelphia, April 9-11, 1981.

11. For a detailed analysis of this period, see Robert Looney, Mexico's Economy: A Policy Analysis with Forecasts to 1990 (Boulder, Colo.: Westview Press, 1978), Chap. 5.

12. The classic statement of this problem is given in A. Navarette, "El Sector Publico en el Desarrollo Economica," Investigacion Economica, 1957, pp. 43-61.

13. Leopoldo Solis, Economic Policy Reform in Mexico (Elmsford, N.Y.: Pergamon Press, 1981), pp. 19-24.

14. Brian Griffiths, Mexican Monetary Policy and Economic Development (New York: Praeger, 1972), pp. 78-79.

15. Summarized from Guillermo Ortiz and Leopoldo Solis, "Financial Structure and Exchange Rate Experience," Journal of Development Economics, December 1979, pp. 515-48.

16. Developed in Jacob Frenkel and Harry Johnson, "The Money Approach to the Balance of Payments: Essential Concepts and Historical Origins," in The Monetary Approach to the Balance

of Payments, ed. Jacob Frenkel and Harry Johnson (London: George Allen & Unwin, 1976), pp. 22-45.

17. Earlier studies have confirmed the general applicability of this approach to Mexico. In particular see the analysis of D. Sykes Wilford in Monetary Policy and the Open Economy: Mexico's Experience (New York: Praeger, 1977), Chap. 3; Bluford Putnam and D. Sykes Wilford, The Monetary Approach to International Adjustment (New York: Praeger, 1978); and D. Sykes Wilford and J. Richard Zecher, "Monetary Policy and the Balance of Payments in Mexico, 1955-1975," Journal of Money, Credit and Banking, August 1979, pp. 340-48.

18. M. Mussa, "A Monetary Approach to Balance of Payments Analysis," Journal of Money, Credit and Banking (August 1974), p. 338.

19. Putnam and Wilford, p. 74.

20. Increased oil revenues should not in and of themselves affect this result, as evidenced by the results of Robert McNown and Myles Wallace, "International Reserve Flows to OPEC States: A Monetary Approach," The Journal of Energy and Development, Spring 1977, pp. 267-78.

21. As formed here and by D. Sykes Wilford, "Price Levels, Interest Rates, Open Economies and a Fixed Exchange: The Mexican Case 1954-1974," Review of Business and Economic Research, Spring 1977, pp. 52-65. See, however, Francis W. Ahking, "Mexico: The Open Economy—A Note," Review of Business and Economic Research (Fall 1978), pp. 103-07, for a discussion of the statistical limitations in drawing conclusions as to the validity of the unified goods market for Mexico and the United States.

22. The formulation used follows that of Harberger. Cf. Arnold Harberger, "The Dynamics of Inflation in Chile," in Measurement in Economics, ed. C. Christ (Stanford, Calif.: Stanford University Press, 1963), and R. Vogel, "The Dynamics of Inflation in Latin America, 1950-1969," American Economic Review, March 1974, pp. 102-14.

23. In the original Harberger formulation, inflationary expectations were approximated by the rate of inflation last year minus the rate two years prior. The formulation used here gave slightly better results.

24. Francis Lees and Maximo Eng, International Financial Markets: Development of the Present System and Future Prospects (New York: Praeger, 1975), Chap. 18.

25. As reported in Comercio Exterior de Mexico (September 1979), pp. 312-15.

26. Ibid.

27. See Redvers Opie, The Overall Development Plan 1980-1982: An Appraisal (Mexico, D.F.: ECANAL, 1980); and Mexican Industrialization and Petroleum (Mexico, D.F.: ECANAL, 1979).

APPENDIX TO CHAPTER 3: EMPIRICAL ESTIMATES

Various forms of the demand for real balances were estimated. In general an adjustment relationship

$$MP = MPL + x(MP^d - MPL)$$

was assumed where MP = either M1P or M2P measure of money deflated by the gross domestic product deflator; MPL = real balances lagged one year; MP^d = the desired level of real balances; and X a measure of the speed of adjustment between the actual (MPL) balances and their desired levels (MP^d).

The speed of adjustment in expectation depends primarily on the costs the individual incurs (or anticipates incurring) in altering his portfolio and his attitude towards risk.[1] A priori it would seem that one could hypothesize this lag to be either long or short in Mexico; i.e., at times uncertainties and risks are high, leading to a rapid adjustment in asset holdings.

On the other hand one could just as logically argue the opposite position; i.e., that the presence of high risks and uncertainties would cause risk averters in Mexico to be conservative (i.e., accasioning a long lag) in adjusting their portfolios.[2]

The rationale of this approach is simply to take into account the fact that while it is costly for individuals to be out of equilibrium, it is also costly for them to make adjustments in their portfolios to restore equilibrium. Clearly, a deficiency in money holdings must imply excessive holdings of other assets and vice versa. The costs associated with restoration of an individual's optimum portfolio must depend among other things on the liquidity and convertibility of assets available to him. If the speed of adjustment depends on adjustment costs, it would take, for example, longer for individuals to adjust their money holdings (i.e., smaller x) when their other assets are dominated by real assets.

An expectation lag was also assumed to be present in Mexico at this time.[3] This lag reflects the adjustments individuals make about future developments in light of new information they receive; i.e., an individual making a forecast of a certain variable would most likely base that forecast on the forecast value of the previous period plus a portion of the error made in his previous forecast. In other words, in each period it is likely that his expectation is revised in proportion to the size of error committed in the forecast for the previous period. A proportionality factor (z) can be used to depict the speed of the change in expectation.

With the two adjustment lags defined in the above manner, it can be shown that both the adjustments can be incorporated into an empirically testable equation of the form

$$MP = [(1-x) + (1-z)MPL - (1-x)(1-x)MPL2] + xzb1Y - xzb2CR - xzb3INFE$$

where MPL2 is the measure of money lagged two years; Y = real gross domestic product; CR - a measure of credit restraint, and INFE is a measure of expected inflation.

The magnitude and statistical significance of the coefficient of the lagged money (one- and two-year periods) in a demand for money function can therefore be used to evaluate the existence and the length of either the expectation lag or the demand adjustment lag.

The credit restraint term is defined as either: (1) private credit (PC) divided by gross domestic product GDPN = CR; or (2) private credit (PC) divided by total private expenditure (PENAN) = CRP. Presumably as credit becomes tight, the opportunity cost of holding money goes up, and holdings of real balances are reduced.

The estimates (Table 3.14) show that both the adjustment and the expectations lags may be present (as evidenced by the statistical significance of the M1PL and M1PL2 terms in equation 7, Table 3.14, and the M2PL and M2PL2 terms in equation 17, Table 3.14. Current inflation (INF) seems to be the best proxy for expected inflation or the opportunity cost of holding money, as current inflation minus last year's rate of inflation (INFE or INFW) both had positive signs. The same is true when first differences in the various price indices (ΔCPI, ΔWPI) were used as a proxy for the opportunity cost of money. As noted in the discussion of the inflation results, the underdevelopment of the financial markets may explain the positive sign to inflation expectations.

The lack of developed markets where borrowers and lenders could interact directly, together with a lack of confidence in the stability of the country's financial markets and the inadequacy of government regulations for dealing with fraud in the stock markets, apparently made broad money (M2) the most desirable asset to hold during this period. The reason for the desirability of money despite rapidly rising prices at the time must have been that individuals perceived it as a relatively risk-less asset in the short run.

The sign was incorrect for the real interest rate (MRI), casting some doubt on the accuracy of this variable to depict an alternative rate of return for portfolio adjustment purposes.

The proxy for credit restraint (CR and CRP) had a positive sign, contrary to expectations. Perhaps, during periods of easy credit in Mexico, individuals hold more money than usual because of lower returns on alternative assets.

While the issues surrounding the credit restraint, interest rate, and cost of holding money are interesting and could lead to a number of further tests, it is clear that their inclusion in the regression equations is marginal at best, with real GDP alone yielding an r^2 of 0.992 (equation 10, Table 3.14) for M1. For M2 real gross domestic product accounted for 81.2 percent of the observed variation.

In sum, the demand for real balances appears stable and adequately explained by a limited number of variables. Thus the Mexican data seem to meet the conditions posed by the monetarists for the validity of the quantity theory.

A demand for money function was also specified in the general (semi) log-linear form as:

(1) $LMP = a_1 LGDPNP - a_2 INFWE - a_3 MRI$

where LMP denotes the national logarithm of real money balances (either M1 or M2 deflated by the GDP deflator); LGDPNP equals the natural logarithm of real gross domestic product; INFWE denotes the expected rate of inflation (i.e., this year's inflation minus the last year's); and MRI is the real rate of interest in Mexico. [4]

Equation (1) is an equilibrium relationship. As found above, however, during this period real monetary balances adjusted with a delay to changes in income, the expected rate of inflation, and perhaps credit conditions. A modification of the above analysis is to assume a partial adjustment mechanism for the change in real money balances. In this framework the actual stock of real money balances adjusts proportionately to the difference between the demand in the same period and the actual stock in the previous period, or

(2) $\Delta logMP = x[logMP - logMPL]$

TABLE 3.14

Mexico: Estimated Structural Equations—Demand for Money Block
(1951-79)

Demand for Real Balances—Narrow Money (M1P)

(1) M1P = 0.13 GDPNP + 0.20 ΔCPI - 6.05 r^2 = 0.994; F = 1857.95; DW = 1.05
         (37.52)   (1.77)   (-3.25)

(2) M1P = 0.14 GDPNP + 0.027 INFE - 8.73 r^2 = 0.994; F = 1814.95; DW = 1.04
         (58.03)   (1.59)   (5.08)

(3) M1P = 0.074 GDPNP + 0.50 M1PL - 3.45 r^2 = 0.993; F = 1880.99; DW = 1.29
         (2.10)   (1.86)   (-1.23)

(4) M1P = 0.13 GDPNP + 67.03 CRP - 8.39 r^2 = 0.996; F = 2925.61; DW = 1.33
         (51.72)   (4.25)   (-6.56)

(5) M1P = 0.13 GDPNP - 0.15 ΔCPI + 115.61 CR - 11.11 r^2 = 0.996; F = 2035.0; DW = 1.37
         (47.87)   (-1.21)   (3.96)   (-5.74)

(6) M1P = 0.13 GDPNP + 1.60 ΔWP1 - 6.00 r^2 = 0.994; F = 1945.48; DW = 1.01
         (41.88)   (2.10)   (-3.40)

(7) M1P = 0.13 GDPNP + 0.51 M1PL - 0.48 M1PL2 - 9.18 r^2 = 0.985; F = 1465.43; DW = 1.46
         (3.15)   (2.06)   (-2.20)   (2.50)

(8) M1P = 0.12 GDPNP + 71.96 CRP - 7.70 r^2 = 0.996; F = 2926.52; DW = 1.21
         (52.42)   (4.48)   (-6.14)

(9) M1P = 0.13 GDPNP + 101.96 CR - 6.28 ΔDFGDP - 10.45 r^2 = 0.997; F = 2253.41; DW = 1.50
         (51.41)   (5.06)   (-1.94)

(10) M1P = 0.14 GDPNP - 6.65 r^2 = 0.9922; F = 3310.72; DW = 0.78
          (57.53)   (-4.06)

(11) M1P = 0.032 GDPNP + 0.81 M1PL - 0.049 INF   DW = 1.54
          (1.71)   (5.16)   (-2.71)

(12) M1P = 0.14 GDPNP - 0.035 INF - 8.01 r^2 = 0.993; F = 1841.31; DW = 0.97
          (55.61)   (-1.94)   (-4.70)

96

(13) M1P = 0.069 GDPNP - 0.048 INF + 0.54 M1PL - 3.48
      (3.21)   (-2.70)   (3.15)   (-2.15)
$r^2 = 0.995$; F = 1590.38; DW = 1.35

Demand for Real Balances (M2P)

(14) M2P = 0.13 GDPNP + 7.89 ΔCPI + 3.12 MR1 - 17.62
      (6.78)   (9.35)   (4.08)   (-1.75)
$r^2 = 0.961$; F = 212.25; DW = 1.12

(15) M2P = 0.15 GDPNP + 6.81 ΔWPI + 4.95 MRI - 29.71
      (10.32)   (12.28)   (7.02)   (-3.75)
$r^2 = 0.978$; F = 338.06; DW = 1.27

(16) M2P = 0.049 GDPNP + 4.09 ΔWPI + 2.18 MRI + 0.59 M2PL - 5.75
      (3.03)   (8.42)   (3.97)   (7.24)   (-1.04)
$r^2 = 0.993$; F = 833.62; DW = 1.22

(17) M2P = 0.072 GDPNP + 4.30 ΔWPI + 2.48 MRI + 0.69 M2PL - 0.24 M2PL2 - 9.70
      (3.97)   (9.41)   (4.75)   (7.86)   (-2.22)   (-1.81)
$r^2 = 0.995$; F = 787.60; DW = 1.26

(18) M2P = 0.15 GDPNP + 22.87 INFW + 16.46 MR1 - 157.45
      (4.06)   (3.76)   (3.33)   (-4.30)
$r^2 = 0.896$; F = 66.13; DW = 1.12

(19) M2P = 0.16 GDPNP + 1.18 ΔWPI + 1283.19 CR - 68.44
      (21.14)   (4.69)   (15.41)   (-12.83)
$r^2 = 0.994$; F = 1238.99; DW = 1.66

(20) M2P = 0.15 GDPNP + 1.05 ΔWPI + 990.58 CRP - 56.06
      (22.17)   (4.64)   (17.48)   (-13.05)
$r^2 = 0.995$; F = 1564.63; DW = 1.80

(21) M2P = 0.15 GDPNP + 2.29 ΔWPI + 1.27 MRI + 824.19 CRP - 53.02
      (24.70)   (4.76)   (2.81)   (10.69)   (-13.54)
$r^2 = 0.996$; F = 1530.06; DW = 2.19

(22) M2P = 0.13 GDPNP + 7.89 ΔCPI + 3.12 MR1 - 17.62
      (6.78)   (9.36)   (4.08)   (-1.75)
$r^2 = 0.965$; F = 212.25; DW = 1.12

(23) M2P = 0.24 GDPNP + 2.99 INFW - 45.98
      (7.39)   (2.11)   (-2.61)
$r^2 = 0.846$; F = 65.96; DW = 1.37

(24) M2P = 0.28 GDPNP - 45.36
      (10.86)   (-2.64)
$r^2 = 0.812$; F = 118.02; DW = 0.32

Note: See Appendix for definition of symbols. Ordinary least squares estimates; TSP estimation program.
Source: Compiled by the author.

where (x) can assume a value between zero and one and is the coefficient of adjustment. Substituting (1) into (2) yields

(3) $LMP = xa_1 LGDPNP - xa_2 INFWE + (1-z)LMPL + xa_3 MRI$

The short-run impact effects are measured by the coefficients xa_1, xa_2 and xa_3. The corresponding long-run elasticities are

$a_1 = xa_1/1 - (1 - x)$

$a_2 = xa_2/1 - (1 - x)$ and

$a_3 = xa_3/1 - (1 - x)$

For M1P, the estimates (Table 3.15) yielded

$(1 - x) = 0.81$

yielding a value of 0.10. The short-run elasticities for

INCOME = 0.17

INFWE = 0.002

USINFC = -0.005

While the long run elasticities were

INCOME = (0.12)(0.19) = 0.89

INFWE = (0.002)(0.19) = 0.011

USINFC = (-0.005)(0.19) = -0.026

In the estimated forms omitting the lagged money term, the income elasticity for M1P is around 1.0 (equations 1, 3, Table 3.15), while for M2P the corresponding income elasticity equals 1.24 (equation 7, Table 3.15).

The negative sign on expected inflation (INFWE) is not consistent with the theoretical assumptions underlying the model which leads to the impression that the U.S. inflation rate may be a better proxy for this particular variable. The income elasticity of around unity for M1P is more or less consistent with the findings of others. While the elasticity of 1.25 for M2P can be explained by the fact that, in a financially under-developed country such as Mexico the demand for money may well rise faster than income because of the lack of opportunities open to economize on cash balances and the limited amounts of other financial assets in which to hold savings.

TABLE 3.15

Mexico: Demand for Real Balances, 1951-80
(logarithmic form)

Dependent Variable	Equation	Independent Variables					RHO	Inter-cept	r^2	F	DW
		LGDPNP	LM1PL	1NFWE	USINFC	MR1					
LM1P	(1)	0.99 (24.34)					0.60 (3.92)	-2.03 (-7.73)	0.958	592.27	1.59
LM1P	(2)	0.17 (1.22)	0.81 (6.02)				0.03 (0.16)	-0.20 (-0.60)	0.996	2920.66	1.93
LM1P	(3)	1.02 (26.26)		0.002 (2.20)			0.58 (3.81)	-2.25 (-8.91)	0.967	361.31	1.73
LM1P	(4)	1.12 (22.49)		0.003 (3.48)	-0.01 (-2.17)	0.003 (1.90)	0.68 (3.20)	-2.89 (-9.35)	0.976	211.68	1.84
LM1P	(5)	0.20 (1.43)	0.80 (5.92)		-0.055 (-1.22)		-0.05 (0.26)	-0.34 (-0.97)	0.995	1980.85	1.90
LM1P	(6)	1.05 (30.10)		0.003 (2.16)		0.004 (3.10)	0.51 (3.17)	-2.47 (-10.85)	0.997	48.00	1.61
LM2P	(7)	1.24 (7.00)					0.81 (7.21)	-3.29 (-2.75)	0.653	48.99	1.31
LM2P	(8)	1.58 (7.47)		0.003 (2.32)	-0.02 (-1.27)		0.78 (6.68)	-5.46 (-3.98)	0.763	25.87	1.45
LM2P	(9)	1.40 (9.20)		0.003 (2.10)			0.76 (6.25)	-4.36 (-4.28)	0.782	42.97	1.32

Note: See text for definition of symbols.
Source: Compiled by the author.

99

The hypothesis that the long-run response of M2P to chang in real income is greater than for the narrower M1P is also borne out by the results.

Private Sector Credit

Private credit was estimated in both nominal (PC) and real (PCP) terms (Table 3.16). The sign on government deficit (GDEF) (defined as government revenues minus government expenditures) is positive, indicating (because of the negative sign of the GDEF series) that the deficits do not appear to reduc credit to the private sector as has been often hypothesized in the literature. The positive sign for the change in money suppl (ΔM1) indicates that a good deal of private sector credit perhaps comes from the monetization of the government deficits.

The positive sign on manufacturing output (MANP) may indicate that a large percentage of private sector credit is being utilized to expand plant and capacity.

The Interest Rate

Estimates of the rate of interest were not entirely satisfactory. Solis has noted that, at least during the latter part of the 1950s through the 1960s, the Bank of Mexico attempted to keep rates in line with those in New York.

Some link was found with the Mexican nominal rate, MI, and the U.S. treasury bill rate, but the relationship was fairly weak (equations 25, 29 and 31, Table 3.17). Other factors that would logically affect the nominal rate would be some measure of excess money supply. Here the ratio of M1 to real gross domestic product (EXCESSA) and M2 to real gross domestic product (EXCESSB) were used. These were also significant and of the right sign (equations 14, 15, 16, 19, 26, and 27, Table 3.17). In fact, when the lagged nominal rate (MIL) and EXCESSB were used, over 91 percent of the variation in MI was accounted for.

The government deficit (GDEF), defined as government revenue minus government expenditures, is a logical inclusion in the equations, as was its lagged value (GDEFL), on the presumption that higher deficits could be financed only at the cost of some pressure on interest rates. This variable was significan and had the right sign in those equations where it was included (equations 15, 23, 28, and 32, Table 3.17).

TABLE 3.16

Mexico: Estimated Structural Equations—Private Sector Credit Block (1951-79)

Nominal Private Credit (PC)

(1) PC = 1.97 GDEF + 1.19 PCL + 4.41 ΔM1 + 0.83 PCN + 11.32 MI - 98.10 r^2 = 0.996; F = 1213.2; DW = 2.71
         (8.10)   (16.66)   (13.37)   (1.90)   (2.95) (-3.34)

(2) PC = 1.17 GDEF + 0.52 PCL + 1.55 ΔM1 + 1.52 EXPTNA - 15.47 r^2 = 0.995; F = 1314.8; DW = 2.77
         (8.75)   (4.51)   (1.96)   (4.62)   (-3.69)

(3) PC = 1.97 GDEF + 1.06 PCL + 3.41 ΔM1 + 0.13 PCN + 0.35 ΔPENAN - 10.00 r^2 = 0.995; F = 1157.5; DW = 2.52
         (7.96)   (19.81)   (6.05)   (3.32)   (2.71)   (-2.72)

(4) PC = 4.73 GDEF + 0.63 PCL + 2.59 GENAN - 8.93 r^2 = 0.983; F = 463.03; DW = 2.99
         (5.64)   (6.44)   (2.97)   (-2.45)

Real Private Credit (PCP)

(5) PCP = 1.19 EXPTNA + 0.08 PCNP + 0.78 GDEF - 16.12 r^2 = 0.983; F = 531.66; DW = 1.90
          (11.11)   (7.16)   (5.99)   (-4.07)

(6) PCP = 0.90 PCPL + 2.70 ΔM1 + 0.67 GDEF + 6.27 r^2 = 0.971; F = 269.57; DW = 1.83
          (6.52)   (6.15)   (3.53)   (2.32)

(continued)

101

Table 3.16 (continued)

(7) PCP = 0.90 PCPL + 3.29 ΔM1 + 1.01 GDEF + 0.34 MANP - 6.13
      (8.02)   (8.42)   (5.60)   (3.66)   (-1.52)
   $r^2 = 0.979$; F = 310.25; DW = 2.52

(8) PCP = 0.86 PCPL + 3.17 ΔM1 + 0.90 GDEF + 0.43 PCNP - 5.99
      (7.56)   (8.25)   (5.32)   (3.54)   (-1.45)
   $r^2 = 0.981$; F = 302.73; DW = 2.37

(9) PCP = 1.00 PCPL + 0.46 ΔM2 + 0.26 GDEF + 0.69 ΔPENANP + 2.29
      (12.88)   (13.99)   (4.14)   (1.99)   (1.49)
   $r^2 = 0.987$; F = 312.98; DW = 2.26

(10) PCP = 0.90 PCPL + 2.70 ΔM1 + 0.67 GDEF + 6.27
       (6.52)   (6.15)   (3.53)   (2.32)
   $r^2 = 0.992$; F = 751.64; DW = 1.89

(11) PCP = 0.72 PCPL + 2.91 ΔM1 + 0.78 GDEF + 0.37 MANP - 243.7 DUMDV - 5.12
       (6.42)   (8.16)   (4.61)   (4.57)   (-3.08)   (-1.18)
   $r^2 = 0.987$; F = 341.6; DW = 1.78

(12) PCP = 1.01 PCPL + 0.47 ΔM2 + 0.31 GDEF + 0.02 PCNP - 2.38
       (4.46)   (15.60)   (5.40)   (3.02)   (-1.02)
   $r^2 = 0.990$; F = 419.7; DW = 1.63

Note: See Appendix for definition of symbols. Ordinary least squares estimates; TSP estimation program.
Source: Compiled by the author.

TABLE 3.17

Mexico: Estimated Structural Equations—Interest Rate Block (1951-79)

Real Rate of Interest (MRI)

(1) $MRI = -0.75 \, INFD + 1.55 \, MI - 0.082 \, GDEFPL - 0.44 \, GM2 - 0.25$
$\quad\quad\quad (-6.00) \quad\quad (3.01) \quad\quad (2.62) \quad\quad\quad (-4.32) \quad\quad (-0.69)$
$\quad r^2 = 0.917; \; F = 57.38; \; DW = 2.26$

(2) $MRI = -0.76 \, INFD + 1.28 \, MI - 0.071 \, GDEFPL - 0.35 \, GM2 + 0.92$
$\quad\quad\quad (-5.87) \quad\quad (2.64) \quad\quad (2.28) \quad\quad\quad (-3.52) \quad\quad (0.25)$
$\quad r^2 = 0.910; \; F = 53.03; \; DW = 2.37$

(3) $MRI = -1.47 \, \Delta EX - 0.97 \, MI + 1.11 \, MI - 0.82 \, \Delta USTB$
$\quad\quad\quad (-4.72) \quad\quad (-10.92) \quad\quad (12.02) \quad\quad (-1.85)$
$\quad DW = 2.56$

(4) $MRI = -0.15 \, MRIL - 1.85 \, MI + 1.45 \, MIL - 0.98 \, INFD - 0.84 \, \Delta EX + 11.09$
$\quad\quad\quad (-1.27) \quad\quad (-2.16) \quad\quad (1.53) \quad\quad (-6.75) \quad\quad (-2.15) \quad\quad (2.70)$
$\quad r^2 = 0.881; \; F = 31.13; \; DW = 1.93$

(5) $MRI = -0.60 \, INFD + 0.48 \, INFC + 8.11$
$\quad\quad\quad (-2.03) \quad\quad (-2.10) \quad\quad (7.27)$
$\quad r^2 = 0.806; \; F = 53.23; \; DW = 2.14$

(6) $MRI = -1.13 \, INFD - 0.70 \, USTB + 9.61$
$\quad\quad\quad (-9.81) \quad\quad (-2.16) \quad\quad (5.88)$
$\quad r^2 = 0.824; \; F = 53.81; \; DW = 2.07$

(7) $MRI = -0.81 \, INFD - 0.75 \, \Delta EX - 0.55 \, INF + 0.91 \, MI$
$\quad\quad\quad (-6.47) \quad\quad (-2.22) \quad\quad (-4.63) \quad\quad (10.14)$
$\quad DW = 2.28$

(8) $MRI = -1.41 \, \Delta EX - 0.94 \, INFC + 0.90 \, MI - 0.73 \, \Delta USTB + 1.87$
$\quad\quad\quad (-4.25) \quad\quad (-8.49) \quad\quad (2.41) \quad\quad (-1.51) \quad\quad (0.61)$
$\quad r^2 = 0.893; \; F = 43.63; \; DW = 2.54$

(9) $MRI = -0.43 \, INFD - 1.04 \, \Delta EX - 0.49 \, INFC + 8.26$
$\quad\quad\quad (-1.66) \quad\quad (-3.06) \quad\quad (-2.47) \quad\quad (8.64)$
$\quad r^2 = 0.858; \; F = 51.53; \; DW = 2.32$

(10) $MRI = -0.69 \, INFD - 0.69 \, INF - 0.75 \, \Delta EX - 0.26 \, GGDPNP + 0.89 \, MI + 2.53$
$\quad\quad\quad (-4.17) \quad\quad (-2.93) \quad\quad (-2.20) \quad\quad (-1.20) \quad\quad (1.79) \quad\quad (0.60)$
$\quad r^2 = 0.90; \; F = 34.31; \; DW = 2.32$

(continued)

Table 3.17 (continued)

(11) MRI = -1.41 ∆EX - 0.94 INFC + 0.89 MI - 0.73 ∆USTB + 1.84
$\quad$ (-4.35) $\quad$ (-8.82) $\quad$ (2.45) $\quad$ (-1.54)
$\qquad r^2 = 0.878; F = 47.83; DW = 2.55$

(12) MRI = -1.26 INFD + 0.085 GDEFPL + 0.70 GM1
$\quad$ (-6.56) $\quad$ (2.10) $\quad$ (4.27)
$\qquad DW = 1.80$

(13) MRI = -1.19 ∆EX - 0.014 INF - 1.05 INFD + 0.68 MI
$\quad$ (-2.70) $\quad$ (-0.79) $\quad$ (06.77) $\quad$ (6.75)
$\qquad DW = 1.64$

Nominal Rate of Interest (MI)

(14) MI = -0.24 MIL + 0.083 CPI - 0.05 GREV + 50.61 EXCESSA + 5.00
$\quad$ (-1.20) $\quad$ (5.12) $\quad$ (-3.30) $\quad$ (2.81) $\quad$ (3.10)
$\qquad r^2 = 0.973; F = 199.96; DW = 1.94$

(15) MI = -0.34 MIL - 0.023 GENAN - 0.11 GDEFL + 6.09 EXCESSB + 10.55
$\quad$ (-1.22) $\quad$ (-2.14) $\quad$ (-3.64) $\quad$ (1.73) $\quad$ (4.82)
$\qquad r^2 = 0.957; F = 122.10; DW = 2.27$

(16) MI = 0.68 MIL + 5.11 EXCESSB + 2.58
$\quad$ (3.06) $\quad$ (1.96) $\quad$ (1.75)
$\qquad r^2 = 0.916; F = 130.55; DW = 2.04$

(17) MI = 0.56 MIL + 0.13 ∆CPI + 3.67
$\quad$ (4.27) $\quad$ (4.52) $\quad$ (3.39)
$\qquad r^2 = 0.947; F = 215.30; DW = 2.76$

(18) MI = 0.93 MIL + 0.071 INFW + 0.50
$\quad$ (10.79) $\quad$ (2.86) $\quad$ (0.68)
$\qquad r^2 = 0.927; F = 152.83; DW = 3.27$

(19) MI = 0.08 WPI - 0.053 GREV + 38.05 EXCESSA + 3.51
$\quad$ (4.07) $\quad$ (-2.90) $\quad$ (1.84) $\quad$ (3.41)
$\qquad r^2 = 0.965; F = 210.39; DW = 2.18$

(20) MI = 0.02 GCN + 0.075 ∆CPI + 8.21
$\quad$ (5.27) $\quad$ (2.33) $\quad$ (67.13)
$\qquad r^2 = 0.957; F = 266.56; DW = 1.86$

(21) MI = 0.04 GCN - 0.007 BMRM + 8.19
$\quad$ (16.54) $\quad$ (-4.33) $\quad$ (80.53)
$\qquad r^2 = 0.970; F = 392.87; DW = 2.41$

(22) $MI = 0.04\ GCN - 0.006\ BMRM - 0.0043\ BMRML + 8.20$
$\quad\quad\quad (17.25) \quad\quad (-4.47) \quad\quad\quad (-2.55) \quad\quad\quad (89.33)$
$\quad\quad r^2 = 0.978;\ F = 324.19;\ DW = 2.28$

(23) $MI = -0.01\ BMRM - 0.009\ BMRML - 0.056\ GDEF + 8.12$
$\quad\quad\quad (-8.61) \quad\quad (-6.21) \quad\quad\quad (-23.03) \quad\quad (115.50)$
$\quad\quad r^2 = 0.987;\ F = 565.33;\ DW = 2.44$

(24) $MI = -0.004\ BMRM - 0.003\ BMRML - 0.22\ MIL + 0.077\ CPI + 7.25$
$\quad\quad\quad (-3.01) \quad\quad\quad (-1.51) \quad\quad\quad (-1.02) \quad\quad (7.17) \quad\quad (4.97)$
$\quad\quad r^2 = 0.977;\ F = 238.79;\ DW = 1.89$

(25) $MI = -0.03\ GENAN + 0.13\ USTB - 0.024\ GENANL + 11.46\ DFGDP + 3.32$
$\quad\quad\quad (1.93) \quad\quad\quad (1.79) \quad\quad\quad (-2.66) \quad\quad\quad (4.28) \quad\quad\quad (2.95)$
$\quad\quad r^2 = 0.996;\ F = 141.51;\ DW = 2.19$

(26) $MI = 32.01\ EXCESSA + 0.077\ CPI - 0.022\ GENAN + 4.07$
$\quad\quad\quad (2.03) \quad\quad\quad\quad (4.73) \quad\quad\quad (-2.72) \quad\quad (4.82)$
$\quad\quad r^2 = 0.968;\ F = 233.97;\ DW = 2.36$

(27) $MI = 0.68\ MIL + 5.11\ EXCESSB + 2.58$
$\quad\quad\quad (3.06) \quad\quad (1.96) \quad\quad\quad\quad (1.47)$
$\quad\quad r^2 = 0.908;\ F = 130.58;\ DW = 2.04$

(28) $MI = -0.011\ BMRM - 0.010\ BMRML - 0.017\ GCN - 0.078\ GDEF + 8.13$
$\quad\quad\quad (-7.13) \quad\quad\quad (-5.46) \quad\quad\quad (-1.23) \quad\quad (-4.31) \quad\quad (114.38)$
$\quad\quad r^2 = 0.987;\ F = 433.94;\ DW = 2.28$

(29) $MI = 0.036\ GGENAN + 0.25\ USTB - 0.049\ GENAN + 18.98\ GDPDF$
$\quad\quad\quad (2.25) \quad\quad\quad\quad (3.32) \quad\quad\quad (-18.98) \quad\quad (20.06)$
$\quad\quad DW = 2.35$

(30) $MI = -0.047\ GENAN + 185.44\ EXCESSAL$
$\quad\quad\quad (-13.06) \quad\quad\quad\quad (26.14)$
$\quad\quad DW = 1.23$

(31) $MI = 0.186\ GENAN + 0.94\ USTB + 0.025\ WP1$
$\quad\quad\quad (3.27) \quad\quad\quad\quad (3.56) \quad\quad\quad (1.72)$
$\quad\quad DW = 0.97$

(32) $MI = -0.097\ GDEF + 0.21\ \Delta GDEF - 0.54\ \Delta EX + 7.77$
$\quad\quad\quad (-7.59) \quad\quad\quad (4.76) \quad\quad\quad (-5.66) \quad\quad (29.97)$
$\quad\quad r^2 = 0.865;\ F = 60.78;\ DW = 1.66$

Note: See Appendix for definition of symbols. Ordinary least squares estimates; TSP estimation program.
Source: Compiled by the author.

105

The Bank of Mexico reserve money (BMRM) was also included, yielding good results (equations 21, 22, 23, 24, and 28, Table 3.17). In all cases it and its lagged value BMRML had negative signs. One possible explanation is that this term simply is reflective of increasing reserve requirements during periods of monetary tightness and is thus not a causal factor but only reflective of the monetary environment.

In any case, it appears that the links to the U.S. interest rates are important, as are the government deficit, excess monetary conditions and changes in price (or inflation). The results for the real rate of interest (nominal deflated by the wholesale price index) are in general not as satisfactory as were the nominal estimations. One would expect inflation to affect adversely the real rate, as well as changes in the exchange rate (ΔEX); the difference between the Mexican and U.S. rate of consumer price inflation (INFD) also has an adverse affect on the real rate.

The growth in money GM2 and GM1 also tended to reduce the rate, as theory would predict. Partially because credit is rationed in Mexico and because the financial markets are not developed, one should not place a great deal of confidence in these estimates. They are suggestive, however, of several of the more important quantifiable factors at work.

Conclusions

From these empirical tests and those in the main body of the chapter, it is apparent that two major requirements for the effectiveness of monetary policy—namely the existence of a well-defined money demand function and a significant relationship between money and prices—are in Mexico's case firmly established.

Notes

1. Thomas Mayer, "The Structure of Monetarism (I)," in The Structure of Monetarism, ed. Thomas Mayer (New York: Norton, 1978), p. 2.

2. See the general framework developed in Thomas Sargent and Neil Wallace, "Rational Expectations and the Theory of Economic Policy," Journal of Monetary Economics, April 1976, pp. 169-85.

3. Following the formulation developed by Chorng-huey Wong, "Demand for Money in Developing Countries," Journal of Monetary Economics, January 1977, pp. 59-86.

4. For an excellent elaboration of this formulation, see David Morgan, "Fiscal Policy in Oil Exporting Countries, 1972-1978," International Monetary Fund Staff Papers, March 1979, pp. 55-86; and Andrew Crockett and Owen Evans, "Demand for Money in Middle Eastern Countries," International Monetary Fund Staff Papers, September 1980, pp. 543-77.

4

MECHANISMS OF
OIL-INDUCED GROWTH

INTRODUCTION

From the events of the last decade—in particular the escalation in oil revenues following the oil discoveries in 1974, the increased levels of production in the latter 1970s, the publication of the National Plan for Urban Development in May 1978 and the National Industrial Development Plan in 1979, and finally the country's experience during the latter 1970s to early 1980s in utilizing its greatly augmented revenues for domestic development—it is now apparent that much of the direction of the Mexican economy in the 1980s and 1990s will depend on the ability of the government to implement the above plans while getting inflation under control.

This is particularly the case given that the Mexican government is at present (1982) at something of a watershed, having just devalued the peso under pressure of slackening oil revenues, internal inflation, and increasing government deficits and levels of foreign debt.

Several economic forecasting models for optimization of the country's long-range objectives are developed in the following chapters. These are used to make a number of projections of the economy's major macroeconomic variables. Ultimately, the purpose of these exercises is the identification of a feasible set of production opportunities open to the economy during the 1980s and 1990s while at the same time being consistent with the country's overall economic and social objectives.

STEPS IN FORECASTING THE ECONOMY

With these points in mind, the steps in the analysis comprising the remainder of the study consist of—

1. determining, through an examination of the discussion
in previous chapters, the growth options open to the country
2. selecting, given the general preferences of the Mexican
authorities, the growth strategy that will likely characterize
the country's pattern of economic development over the next
two decades
3. identifying the manner in which oil revenues empirically
impact on the economy as a necessary first step in constructing
a realistic econometric model capable of assessing the feasibility
of the economy staying on the forecast growth path. This step
entails quantifying the mechanisms largely responsible for the
economy's past growth performance.
4. estimating the structural relationships hypothesized
by the model
5. projecting on a preliminary basis the major macroeconomic
variables for the 1980-90 period with an eye to extending these
into the year 2000
6. drawing on the analysis in previous chapters to identify
any possible side effects associated with this growth path
7. assigning priority to the macroeconomic constraints
(identified in 6 above) given the country's social, philosophical,
and institutional system
8. analyzing, in light of the National Industrial Development Plan's targets, an optimal growth path for the 1980s together
with its concomitant policy requirements
9. examining the implications of the above analysis for an
oil production strategy that is compatible with Mexico's long-run
interests, given the country's economic and social constraints.

PROBABLE DEVELOPMENT STRATEGY

The cornerstone of Mexico's strategy of development has
been fairly well established under Lopez Portillo and is unlikely
to change fundamentally under his successor, Miguel de la Madrid
Iturtado.

In essence the strategy consists of the timed channeling
of resources earned by the petroleum sector into expanding the
nonoil production base. This in turn involves anticipating several
likely eventualities.

Firstly, an expanding economy requires an increasing flow of resources to maintain its momentum. Given (1) estimates of known oil reserves, (2) the likely expansion of needs for domestic energy sources, and (3) the plans to supply the petrochemical industry and refineries with enough crude oil and gas to meet domestic and export requirements.

Secondly, because oil reserves are not infinite, the country will have to prepare for the day when its hydrocarbons have been economically depleted. Mexico still has one of the largest reserves of crude petroleum in the world. The huge Chiapas-Borasco "Reforma" discovery in 1974 combined with the 1977 Bay of Campeche discovery boosted Mexico's proved reserves from a meager 5.2 billion barrels in 1972 to 16.8 billion barrels by 1978. Additional finds and refined figures on the depths of existing fields allowed PEMEX to announce proved reserves of 40 billion barrels by the end of 1978, more than double the figure given earlier that year. Mexico's probable reserves lie at around 200 billion barrels.[1]

While production levels have not been clearly defined into the future, one condition has been emphasized by President Lopez Portillo: Mexican oil development will now proceed at a pace consistent with sound economic management. So far development of the new fields has been so rapid that production targets established for 1982 were reached in 1980. However, Mexico is obviously uneasy about the possibility that rapid increases in production will result in PEMEX incurring heavy debts, dislocating the economy and increasing the rate of inflation.[2]

Considerable new investment is required to develop new fields if production is to expand significantly. PEMEX is spending around $19 billion in 1977-82 to develop Mexico's petroleum industry both vertically and horizontally. Continued exploration, expanding refinery capacity to facilitate greater exports, and expansion of the country's petrochemical industry are prime concerns.[3]

Thirdly, the longer-term problem of economic diversification is intimately tied with the country's strategy of economic development and the possibilities for developing an international comparative advantage in the production of certain commodities.

In the manufacturing area, Mexico's comparative advantage appears to lie in two broad areas. First, some manufactured exports can be and are based on local primary raw materials; progress in these industries will depend heavily on the associated primary producing sectors. Second, there is an especially promising feature in exporting products to the U.S. that combine substantial inputs of manual labor and moderate transport costs (and/or need for fast delivery). In products for which transport costs are too high, Mexico cannot compete with U.S. producers; where transport costs are very low, Mexico cannot, at least at present, compete on even terms with many Asian countries as a source of cheap labor.

Oil revenues and expenditures out of them will not of course be sufficient for the development of a wide number of new areas in which the country has a comparative advantage. Mexico's potential can be realized rapidly by adopting a more outward oriented development strategy. The essence of this strategy is to create a stable policy environment with a strong government commitment to expand exports and keep them profitable. This in turn requires giving producers access to the inputs and other help they need to be competitive, and having an exchange rate relative to domestic wages and other costs at a level where local prices appear low and the country becomes a really attractive place to invest and expand output. In this strategy the exchange rate would become a main source of protection against imports as well as assuring export competitiveness. By compressing the foreign currency value of incomes, nonessential imports could be kept in check while increased nonoil export earnings would enable the country to increase its imports of capital equipment and intermediate goods. [4]

In essence the role of the government during the forecast period will likely continue to be constrained along the lines established in the National Industrial Development Plan:

1. designing a domestic infrastructure network capable of supporting a modern industrial apparatus

2. implementing health, welfare, and education policies necessary for maintaining the human element in the development process while at the same time contributing to improvements in labor and managerial quality

3. investing in selected heavy industries into which the private sector is reluctant to venture

4. guiding the future spatial configuration of population and economic activity through locational investment decisions.

The continued increasing role of government in the economy is simply a logical consequence of the development strategy already adopted by the government and the constraints facing Mexican planners. Government activity will continue to be directed toward economic activities that the private sector will be reluctant to enter because of the risk involved or size of the investment required.

In essence the government will continue to face the basic problem of utilizing its petroleum revenues to support consumption while ensuring that eventual self-sustained growth is achieved. This perception of the growth process will be incorporated in the forecasting model through the separation of the petroleum sector from the remainder of the economy. As noted, linkages (forward and backward) between the petroleum industry and other sectors of the economy are minimal, and consequently the influence of the economy on the petroleum sector is negligible, as is the direct influence of that sector on the rest of the economy.

Finally, the model is structured to anticipate high levels for both government investment and government consumption reflecting the government's desire to: (1) diversify the economy in preparation for the ultimate depletion of their oil reserves, (2) employ the revenues immediately to improve standards of living, and (3) minimize the risk and uncertainty surrounding the level of petroleum revenues in the short run and the number of periods during which the revenues will be available in the long run.

ECONOMETRIC MODELS

Econometric models, despite their limitations,[5] are increasingly being used by planners in developing countries for two basic purposes: simulation and policy analysis. Simulation can be easily performed by simply forecasting values of the exogenous variables over the desired horizons, introducing them into the model, and obtaining the values for the key macrovariables.[6] Yet simple forecasts are not the only uses of the models. Indeed, forecasts under alternative conditions with respect to the exogenous variables and policy instruments are invaluable. This is where the structural analysis of the economy, which an econometric model involves, makes it superior to other forecasting techniques. Aside from the alternative results, one can check other sensitivity of the key macrovariables to particular exogenous variables and/or policy instruments.

The institutional characteristics and the historical background of Mexico presented in the earlier chapters provide the foundation for the econometric model developed below.

With the model's ultimate objectives and structure in mind and following the work of Theil[7] and Timbergen,[8] the following model is developed to aid in overcoming that deficiency. In its entirety the model consists of—

1. a characterization of the policy problem, specification of a preference function, the quantitative model, and the constraints or boundary problem facing Mexican planners
2. the selection problem, i.e., classification of variables by their properties (such as randomness, direct or indirect controllability, and time dependence)
3. the steering problem, i.e., derivation of optimum decisio rules in static and dynamic senses

As formulated here the model consists of the following basic ingredients:

1. a welfare function (W), representing the objectives of policy, which is a function of the policy variables (z_j) and the target variables (y_i)
2. an empirical model (M) (in this case an econometric model), which expresses the empirical relationships between the target variables and the policy variables under specified boundary conditions
3. the structural relations of the model, which come in three groups: behavioristic, technical, and definitional. The most important are the behavioristic equations as they express quantitative hypotheses about economic and social behavior.
4. boundary conditions on all the variables.

The key element in this framework is the model (M). The first task, therefore, in any attempt at rationalizing economic policy making in Mexico is to estimate the structural relationships that make up the model.[9]
The remainder of this chapter presents the estimated structural equations for the major macroeconomic variables, discusses several insights provided by these equations to the structure and operation of the economy, and draws several implications for policy suggested by the equations.

PRODUCTION FUNCTION

Conceptually, output may be determined primarily by input (or productive capacity constraints) on the one hand or demand factors on the other. On the basis of the discussion in previous chapters, it is reasonable to assume that Mexico's GDP is constrained by a broad range of input factors. Supporting evidence for this may be found in the structure of the country's imports, which indicates that a significant part of domestic demand for

capital goods and intermediate industrial products is still being
met by imports.

Gross domestic product is assumed to be a simple linear
function of the capital stock and employment. The employment
variable is, of course, important from the point of view of the
government's strategy designed to eliminate unemployment eventually by the end of the century. In equation form:

$$GDPNP = f(KP, EMPT, T), \text{ where } KP = \sum_{t=1}^{3} TINP$$

Capital stock is in gross terms and is a three-year summation of
total (private + government) investment (TINP).

In the absence of any consistent time series data on man/
hours or unemployment, the total population (POP) was used
as a measure of labor input. The time trend (T) was initially
included to capture any technological change not embodied in
capital or labor.

Best results were obtained with capital and time (equation
1, Table 4.1). Of note is the positive effect of nominal U.S.
gross domestic product (USGDP).

$$GDPNP = 0.33 \text{ USGDP} + 23.00 \text{ TIME} + 0.38 \text{ RHO} - 33.71$$
(1951-80)   (13.48)   (11.33)   (2.21)   (-2.12)
$$r^2 = 0.994; F = 2020.72; DW = 1.53$$

and the lack of technological change

$$GDPNP = 0.67 \text{ KP} + 19.99 \text{ POP} - 4.80 \text{ TIME} - 420.81$$
          (3.26)   (2.14)   (-0.50)   (-1.93)
$$r^2 = 0.994; F = 1234.35; DW = 1.63$$

Formulations with population and government expenditures
(equation 7, Table 4.1) were also quite satisfactory.

Private Consumption

Several patterns have tended to characterize the movement
of private consumption over time, with the most interesting being
its increase at a significantly slower rate than GDP. Both the
average and marginal propensity to consume were quite high in
the early 1950s. Since then, the average private propensity
to consume GDP has declined from 84.9 percent in 1951 to 71.8
percent in 1970 and finally to 62.0 percent in 1980 (Table 4.2).

TABLE 4.1

Mexico: Estimated Structural Equations—National Income Accounts Block (1951-79)

Real Gross Domestic Product (GDPNP)

(1) GDPNP = 0.71 KP + 20.25 TIME + 55.85
$\quad$ (10.69) $\quad$ (11.18) $\quad$ (6.14)
$r^2 = 0.998$; F = 6485.23; DW = 0.946

(2) GDPNP = 0.44 KP + 23.53 TIME + 0.06 USGDP + 36.46
$\quad$ (3.00) $\quad$ (10.11) $\quad$ (2.06) $\quad$ (2.87)
$r^2 = 0.998$; F = 4912.48; DW = 0.93

(3) GDPNP = 0.71 KP + 18.26 TIME - 33.32 DUMDV + 0.05 USYP + 26.63
$\quad$ (8.78) $\quad$ (8.03) $\quad$ (-2.31) $\quad$ (0.72) $\quad$ (0.60)
$r^2 = 0.998$; F = 4006.3; DW = 1.22

(4) GDPNP = 0.32 KP + 30.33 TIME + 0.038 USYP - 960.32 ZB - 138.68
$\quad$ (2.97) $\quad$ (7.68) $\quad$ (0.63) $\quad$ (-3.66) $\quad$ (-2.69)
$r^2 = 0.999$; F = 5194.77; DW = 1.03

(5) GDPNP = 0.75 KP + 19.37 TIME - 36.58 DUMDV + 57.79
$\quad$ (12.29) $\quad$ (11.78) $\quad$ (-2.70) $\quad$ (7.10)
$r^2 = 0.999$; F = 5455.77; DW = 1.34

Nominal Gross Domestic Product (GDPN)

(6) GDPN = 1.64 K + 1.51 POP + 12.58 EX - 163.37
$\quad$ (30.61) $\quad$ (1.89) $\quad$ (4.39) $\quad$ (-3.45)
$r^2 = 0.999$; F = 5830.03; DW = 2.15

(7) GDPN = 0.74 K + 1.86 POP + 2.48 GENAN
$\quad$ (2.29) $\quad$ (5.34) $\quad$ (3.42)
DW = 1.75

(8) GDPN = 1.84 K + 0.83 POP
$\quad$ (83.82) $\quad$ (4.01)
DW = 1.69

Real Public Consumption (PCNP)

(9) PCNP = 0.80 GDPNP - 29.79 DFGDP - 1.18 GCNP
$\quad$ (25.08) $\quad$ (-3.88) $\quad$ (-5.98)
$r^2 = 0.998$; F = 3982.06; DW = 2.07

(10) PCNP = 0.84 GDPNP - 22.68 DFGDP - 0.49 GIP - 1.09 GCNP + 22.70
$\quad$ (21.27) $\quad$ (-2.55) $\quad$ (-1.48) $\quad$ (-3.66) $\quad$ (2.37)
$r^2 = 0.998$; F = 5501.11; DW = 2.19

(11) $PCNP = 0.91\ GDPNP - 0.96\ GIP - 1.48\ GCNP + 2.83$
  $(33.39)\quad\quad (-3.06)\quad\quad (-5.31)\quad\quad (0.46)$

Nominal Private Consumption (PCN)

(12) $PCN = 0.32\ GDPN + 0.21\ GDPNL + 2.20\ CPI - 42.15$
  $(4.13)\quad\quad (2.37)\quad\quad (3.61)\quad\quad (-2.28)$

(13) $PCN = 0.90\ GDPN - 1.34\ IG - 1.06\ GCN + 4.17$
  $(22.37)\quad\quad (7.34)\quad (-3.56)\quad (1.01)$

(14) $PCN = 0.84\ GDPN - 1.10\ IG - 1.44\ GCN + 10.15\ MI + 0.23\ SNL - 76.25$
  $(21.56)\quad\quad (-4.87)\quad (-5.42)\quad\quad (3.51)\quad\quad (1.32)\quad\quad (-3.29)$

(15) $PCN = 0.44\ GDPN + 0.39\ GDPNL + 11.65\ MI - 0.85\ SNL - 80.01$
  $(7.89)\quad\quad (5.45)\quad\quad (3.82)\quad\quad (-4.02)\quad\quad (-3.33)$

(16) $PCN = 0.53\ GDPN + 0.39\ GDPNL - 1.11\ SNL + 10.54$
  $(8.28)\quad\quad (4.36)\quad\quad (-4.41)\quad\quad (2.32)$

(17) $PCN = 0.81\ GDPN + 0.86\ GDPNL - 0.98\ SN + 8.67$
  $(20.73)\quad\quad (2.21)\quad\quad (-13.29)\quad\quad (4.39)$

Real Government Consumption (GCNP)

(18) $GCNP = 0.72\ GREVP + 0.60\ GCNPL - 0.02\ GDPNP + 17.48\ DUMDV - 20.3\ DUMEX - 1.08$
  $(6.97)\quad\quad (6.13)\quad\quad (-2.29)\quad\quad (6.67)\quad\quad (-5.76)\quad\quad (-0.76)$

(19) $GCNP = 0.58\ GREVP + 0.61\ GCNPL - 2.47\ MI + 15.98$
  $(3.46)\quad\quad (3.90)\quad\quad (-2.81)\quad\quad (2.71)$

(20) $GCNP = 0.31\ GREVP + 0.59\ GCNPL + -0.018\ GDPNP - 4.65$
  $(2.05)\quad\quad (3.24)\quad\quad (1.96)\quad\quad (-1.70)$

Nominal Government Consumption (GCN)

(21) $GCN = 0.34\ GREV + 0.81\ GCNL - 0.33\ MRI + 0.95$
  $(2.35)\quad\quad (4.01)\quad\quad (-2.77)\quad\quad (0.82)$

$r^2 = 0.997;\ F = 3797.95;\ DW = 2.25$

$r^2 = 0.999;\ F = 11643.7;\ DW = 1.06$

$r^2 = 0.999;\ F = 24784.9;\ DW = 2.68$

$r^2 = 0.999;\ F = 22543.4;\ DW = 1.46$

$r^2 = 0.999;\ F = 16022.4;\ DW = 1.99$

$r^2 = 0.999;\ F = 13647.0;\ DW = 2.72$

$r^2 = 0.999;\ F = 63067.6;\ DW = 1.22$

$r^2 = 0.996;\ F = 1110.04;\ DW = 1.25$

$r^2 = 0.994;\ F = 1258.03;\ DW = 1.22$

$r^2 = 0.993;\ F = 1090.89;\ DW = 1.13$

$r^2 = 0.998;\ F = 3824.71;\ DW = 1.28$

(continued)

117

Table 4.1 (continued)

(22) GCN = 0.39 GREV + 0.64 GCNL + 3.50 MI - 29.26
       (2.34)   (2.42)   (2.19)   (-2.25) $r^2 = 0.998$; F = 3466.40; DW = 1.49

(23) GCN = 0.48 GREV + 0.05 GDPN + 4.25 MI - 39.01
       (4.04)   (2.75)   (3.18)   (-3.74) $r^2 = 0.998$; F = 3680.02; DW = 1.55

(24) GCN = 0.31 GREV + 0.39 GCNL + 3.18 MI + 0.03 GDPN - 29.50
       (1.92)   (1.36)   (2.07)   (1.87)   (-2.38) $r^2 = 0.998$; F = 2862.37; DW = 1.63

(25) GCN = 20.83 GREV + 6.05 MI - 49.24
       (20.83)   (4.58)   (-4.48) $r^2 = 0.997$; F = 4324.11; DW = 1.73

Real Private Investment (IPP)

(26) IPP = 0.09 KPL + 0.85 GIPL + 0.25 MR1 - 2.61 M1 + 26.09
       (3.21)   (4.45)   (1.46)   (-2.56)   (3.40) $r^2 = 0.987$; F = 331.04; DW = 1.25

(27) IPP = 0.20 PCPL + 0.14 PENANPL + 0.10 ΔGDPNP - 8.01
       (3.70)   (16.27)   (2.01)   (-2.40) $r^2 = 0.976$; F = 324.30; DW = 1.12

(28) IPP = 0.58 IPPL + 0.51 GIPL + 0.11 PCPL - 1.20 MIL + 0.17 ΔGDPNP + 10.74
       (5.49)   (3.44)   (2.22)   (-1.37)   (3.40)   (2.05) $r^2 = 0.988$; F = 395.51; DW = 1.82

(29) IPP = 0.10 KPL + 0.61 GIPL + 1.11 MI + 0.10 ΔGDPNP - 2.06 ΔEX + 8.89
       (2.95)   (2.83)   (3.45)   (2.25)   (-2.83)   (1.47) $r^2 = 0.986$; F = 368.52; DW = 1.45

(30) IPP = 0.13 PCPL + 1.15 GIPL + 4.46 MI - 2.02 EX + 10.04
       (1.51)   (11.57)   (3.71)   (-2.34)   (3.78) $r^2 = 0.978$; F = 304.61; DW = 1.35

(31) IPP = 0.50 IPPL + 0.74 GIPL + 0.12 PCPL + 0.10 ΔGDPNP - 2.83 MI - 0.87 ΔEX + 25.25
       (6.29)   (6.20)   (2.99)   (4.13)   (-3.72)   (-1.89)   (4.37) $r^2 = 0.994$; F = 631.27; DW = 1.88

(32) IPP = -1.80 ΔEX + 1.42 GIPL - 0.36 ΔWPI + 11.73
       (-2.29)   (22.73)   (-2.04)   (5.20) $r^2 = 0.979$; F = 366.20; DW = 1.01

(33) IPP = -2.01 ΔEX + 0.10 ΔGDPNP + 1.28 GIPL + 11.24
       (-2.75)   (2.29)   (27.97)   (4.96) $r^2 = 0.979$; F = 380.18; DW = 0.98

118

(34) $\text{IPP} = 0.76\,\text{GIPL} + 0.08\,\text{PCNP} + 0.16\,\text{PCPL} - 0.73\,\text{EX} + 8.70$
    $\qquad\quad (5.62)\qquad\quad (4.37)\qquad\quad\;\; (2.90)\qquad\quad (-1.78)\quad (1.51)$

$r^2 = 0.986;\ F = 419.23;\ \text{DW} = 1.09$

Nominal Private Investment (IP)

(35) $\text{IP} = 0.30\,\Delta\text{GDPN} - 7.99\,\text{MI} + 0.18\,\text{PENANL} - 1.30\,\Delta\text{CP1} + 59.07$
    $\qquad\;\; (5.39)\qquad\qquad (-3.39)\qquad\; (9.35)\qquad\qquad (-2.12)\qquad (3.26)$

$r^2 = 0.996;\ F = 1461.73;\ \text{DW} = 1.61$

(36) $\text{IP} = 0.34\,\Delta\text{GDPN} - 5.66\,\text{MI} + 0.15\,\text{PENANL} - 1.18\,\Delta\text{WP1} + 42.02$
    $\qquad\;\; (6.92)\qquad\qquad (-2.45)\qquad\; (7.59)\qquad\qquad (-3.41)\qquad (2.39)$

$r^2 = 0.997;\ F = 1842.27;\ \text{DW} = 1.90$

(37) $\text{IP} = 0.37\,\Delta\text{GDPN} - 5.07\,\text{MI} + 0.14\,\text{PENANL} - 1.55\,\Delta\text{WP1} + 1.04\,\Delta\text{EX} + 38.39$
    $\qquad\;\; (6.74)\qquad\qquad (-2.21)\qquad\; (6.52)\qquad\qquad (-3.61)\qquad\quad (1.41)\qquad\;\; (2.21)$

$r^2 = 0.997;\ F = 1536.93;\ \text{DW} = 2.00$

(38) $\text{IP} = 0.18\,\Delta\text{GDPN} + 0.30\,\text{KL} - 1.46\,\Delta\text{EX} + 74.32$
    $\qquad\;\; (4.12)\qquad\qquad (10.61)\qquad\; (-1.82)\qquad (3.64)$

$r^2 = 0.994;\ F = 987.89;\ \text{DW} = 1.62$

(39) $\text{IP} = 0.22\,\Delta\text{GDPN} + 9.02\,\text{MI} + 0.31\,\text{KL} - 2.07\,\text{EX} + 94.13$
    $\qquad\;\; (5.00)\qquad\qquad (-3.73)\qquad (11.41)\qquad (-2.40)\qquad (4.86)$

$r^2 = 0.995;\ F = 1080.45;\ \text{DW} = 1.60$

(40) $\text{IP} = 0.04\,\Delta\text{GDPN} - 1.35\,\text{MI} + 1.60\,\text{IGL} - 1.39\,\Delta\text{EX} + 14.55$
    $\qquad\;\; (1.86)\qquad\qquad (-1.30)\qquad (24.84)\qquad (-3.75)\qquad (1.68)$

$r^2 = 0.999;\ F = 4682.59;\ \text{DW} = 1.26$

(41) $\text{IP} = 0.08\,\Delta\text{GDPN} - 5.11\,\text{MI} + 0.57\,\text{IG} + 0.18\,\text{KL} - 0.94\,\text{EX} + 0.76\,\Delta\text{DFGDP} + 53.35$
    $\qquad\;\; (1.85)\qquad\qquad (-2.81)\qquad (5.27)\qquad (5.84)\qquad (-1.48)\qquad\quad (0.20)\qquad\qquad (3.46)$

$r^2 = 0.998;\ F = 1531.23;\ \text{DW} = 1.54$

(42) $\text{IP} = 0.22\,\Delta\text{GDPN} + 9.02\,\text{MI} + 0.31\,\text{KL} - 2.08\,\text{EX} + 94.13$
    $\qquad\;\; (3.73)\qquad\qquad (3.73)\qquad\;\; (11.41)\qquad (-2.39)\qquad (4.86)$

$r^2 = 0.995;\ F = 680.45;\ \text{DW} = 1.59$

Real Imports (ZP)

(43) $\text{ZP} = -108.88\,\text{EW} + 106.89\,\text{DUMEX} - 83.55\,\text{DUMDV} - 10.84\,\text{DUMTDV} + 6.60$
    $\qquad\quad (-12.26)\qquad\qquad (7.30)\qquad\qquad (-5.91)\qquad\qquad (-1.55)\qquad\qquad (1.04)$

$r^2 = 0.956;\ F = 123.96;\ \text{DW} = 1.42$

(44) $\text{ZP} = -0.49\,\text{EP} - 0.26\,\text{TINP} - 0.90\,\text{EXL} - 14.49\,\text{TTA} + 19.03$
    $\qquad\quad (-2.98)\qquad (-6.24)\qquad\; (-1.76)\qquad (-1.50)\qquad (1.45)$

$r^2 = 0.991;\ F = 625.06;\ \text{DW} = 1.09$

(45) $\text{ZP} = -0.40\,\text{TINP} - 0.70\,\text{EX} - 3.29\,\text{EXL} + 15.81\,\text{DFGDP} - 34.12\,\text{TTA} + 57.74$
    $\qquad\quad (-22.05)\qquad\; (-1.55)\qquad (-5.88)\qquad\quad (3.76)\qquad\qquad (-2.90)\qquad\; (3.23)$

$r^2 = 0.992;\ F = 569.20;\ \text{DW} = 1.96$

(continued)

119

Table 4.1 (continued)

(46) ZP = 0.41 ZPL - 0.10 WPI + 1.34 EX - 0.92 EP - 19.87 TTA + 20.14
     (5.77)   (-1.26)   (2.16)   (-7.95)   (-2.04)   (1.33)
     r^2 = 0.992; F = 543.84; DW = 2.04

(47) ZP = -0.40 TINP - 0.70 EX - 3.29 EXL + 15.80 DFGDP - 34.12 TTA + 57.74
     (-22.05)   (-1.55)   (-5.88)   (3.76)   (-2.89)   (3.23)
     r^2 = 0.992; F = 569.20; DW = 1.96

Nominal Imports (ZNAN)

(48) ZNAN = -0.49 EXPTNA - 0.25 TIN - 0.22 ΔTIN + 5.98 DUMEX - 2.37
     (-10.02)   (-12.26)   (-3.83)   (1.92)   (-2.77)
     r^2 = 0.999; F = 11091.8; DW = 1.66

(49) ZNAN = -0.44 EXPTNA - 0.24 TIN - 0.29 ΔTIN - 3.45
     (-10.19)   (-11.47)   (-5.98)   (-5.05)
     r^2 = 0.999; F = 13281.7; DW = 2.09

(50) ZNAN = -0.55 EXPTNA - 0.29 TIN - 12.30 TTA + 2.34
     (-10.06)   (-9.17)   (-2.23)   (2.06)
     r^2 = 0.999; F = 6429.0; DW = 1.27

(51) ZNAN = -0.52 EXPTNA - 0.29 TIN - 0.88
     (-8.27)   (-9.41)   (-1.07)
     r^2 = 0.998; F = 8323.6; DW = 1.27

(52) ZNAN = -0.94 EXPTNA - 0.95 GDPN + 0.97 WPI - 29.28
     (-11.22)   (-5.86)   (4.43)   (-4.12)
     r^2 = 0.997; F = 2871.5; DW = 1.03

Real Exports (EW)—deflated by industrial countries export index

(53) EW = 1.16 + 0.01 INFD - 0.00003 GDNP + 0.21 ΔUSYP - 0.14
     (14.67)   (4.03)   (-0.27)   (3.31)   (-3.31)
     r^2 = 0.976; F = 229.00; DW = 2.06

(54) EW = 1.00 EWL + 0.0026 CPP + 0.0019 ΔUSYP - 0.16
     (6.19)   (1.32)   (2.41)   (-3.05)
     r^2 = 0.961; F = 196.62; DW = 1.61

(55) EW = 0.70 EWL - 0.16 DUMTDV + 0.057 EX + 0.00091 ΔUSYP - 0.44
     (9.90)   (-2.36)   (6.54)   (1.95)   (-9.14)
     r^2 = 0.986; F = 484.53; DW = 2.78

(56) EW = 0.60 EWL - 0.19 DUMTDV + 0.063 EX + 0.00011 ΔUSYP - 0.54
     (6.62)   (-2.59)   (7.09)   (1.44)   (-6.67)
     r^2 = 0.985; F = 453.21; DW = 2.24

(57) EW = 1.14 EWL + 0.013 INFD + 0.0021 ΔUSYP - 0.14
     (25.10)   (4.12)   (3.38)   (-4.11)
     r^2 = 0.975; F = 317.56; DW = 2.01

Real Exports (EP)—deflated by Mexican gross domestic product deflator

(58) $EP = 0.58\ EPL + 0.24\ CPP + 0.069\ \Delta USYP + 1.21\ EX - 7.80$
       (3.14)   (1.38)   (1.69)   (2.47)   (-1.81)
       $r^2 = 0.973$; $F = 209.47$; $DW = 2.03$

(59) $EP = 0.82\ EPL + 0.46\ INFD + 0.23\ \Delta USYP - 15.16$
       (5.09)   (1.78)   (1.73)   (-1.87)
       $r^2 = 0.949$; $F = 148.0$; $DW = 1.58$

Nominal Exports (EXPTNA)

(60) $EXPTNA = 0.11\ GDPNL - 48.00\ DUMDV + 3.95\ EX - 50.26$
          (8.15)   (-3.85)   (3.06)   (-3.73)
       $r^2 = 0.981$; $F = 415.59$; $DW = 1.05$

(61) $EXPTNA = 1.19\ EXPTNAL + 35.89\ DUMEX + 0.21\ \Delta USGDP - 2.93$
          (13.83)   (5.01)   (0.30)   (-0.89)
       $r^2 = 0.986$; $F = 577.54$; $DW = 3.04$

(62) $EXPTNA = 0.74\ EXPTNAL + 60.57\ DUMEX - 49.12\ DUMDV + 0.39\ GDPNPL - 0.67$
          (4.28)   (5.94)   (-4.45)   (2.02)   (-0.30)
       $r^2 = 0.993$; $F = 779.47$; $DW = 2.64$

(63) $EXPTNA = 1.41\ EXPTNAL - 5.76$
          (33.91)   (-1.99)
       $r^2 = 0.978$; $F = 1150.14$; $DW = 2.42$

(64) $EXPTNA = 1.08\ EXPTNAL + 3.47\ EX - 42.66$
          (12.72)   (4.19)   (-4.68)
       $r^2 = 0.98$; $F = 949.22$; $DW = 2.66$

Note: See Appendix for definition of symbols. Ordinary least squares estimates; TSP estimation program.
Source: Compiled by the author.

TABLE 4.2

Mexico: Patterns of Consumption, 1951-80
(current prices, billions of pesos)

	Private Consumption	Government Consumption	Gross Domestic Product	Private Consumption GDP	Government Consumption GDP
1951	45.0	2.2	53.0	84.9	4.2
1955	70.7	3.8	88.2	80.2	4.3
1960	123.9	8.0	155.9	79.5	5.1
1965	190.7	17.7	252.0	75.7	7.0
1970	300.8	32.6	418.7	71.8	7.8
1971	331.9	36.7	452.4	73.4	8.1
1972	375.3	43.7	512.3	73.3	8.5
1973	446.1	56.1	619.6	72.0	9.1
1974	628.3	82.3	899.7	69.8	9.1
1975	755.9	113.5	1100.7	68.7	10.3
1976	933.4	150.9	1371.0	68.1	11.0
1977	1226.1	199.0	1849.3	66.3	10.8
1978	1543.8	255.2	2337.4	66.0	10.9
1979	1975.9	334.3	3067.5	64.4	10.9
1980	2651.5	462.8	4276.5	62.0	10.8

Source: Bank of Mexico, Annual Report, various issues.

The reasons for this decline may be the crowding out effect of government expenditure, as evidenced by the negative relationship between both government consumption and private consumption (equations 9, 10 and 14, Table 4.1), and government investment and private consumption (equations 10, 11 and 14, Table 4.1).

It has become common practice to assume that effects on demand due to changes in prices or income are distributed over time,[10] rather than being felt instantaneously. In the case of the permanent income hypothesis,[11] for example, permanent income is approximated by a weighted average of all past observed incomes. The distribution is assumed known, the weights declining geometrically.

In a stock adjustment model, the distributed lag is only incidentally implied and pertains to a dynamic model of consumer behavior.[12] If several assumptions are made, the so-called Nerlove model can be derived and estimated as a special case of the stock adjustment model.[13]

Since there was no a priori basis for assigning weights to reflect the importance of past incomes in affecting the consumption decision, one of the equations tested utilized a modified version of the simple Keynesian function in which previous levels of consumption (in addition to nonoil income) were included as an explanatory variable:

$$PCNP = a + GDPNP + cPCNPL$$

This is sometimes referred to as the Brown-Klein consumption function.[14] Its main hypothesis is that consumers react to changes in income in a gradual manner, trying to maintain the levels of consumption they are used to. This relationship has been well established by both budget surveys and cross-country analyses in numerous countries, and there is no reason to believe that Mexico is an exception to this pattern.

The result,

$$PCNP = 0.42 \, GDPNP + 0.30 \, PCNPL + 71.41$$
$$(1.71) \qquad (2.37) \qquad (2.91)$$
$$r^2 = 0.986; \quad F = 334.6$$

indicates that the short-run marginal propensity to consume of 0.42 and a long-run marginal propensity to consume equals 0.60.

Inflation may have inhibited that adjustment.[15] While the ratio of consumption to both GDP and nonoil GDP declined over the 1951-80 period, the fall seems a bit sharper in the 1970s.

This period was characterized by money creation at an accelerating rate with a corresponding rise in the rate of consumer price increases. Thus a situation may have been created whereby inflation acted as an effective tax, causing real disposable incomes to slow down or even decline.

This hypothesis is borne out by the following two regressions, both with a negative sign for the change in the consumer price index (ΔCPI).

$$PCNP = 0.53 \text{ GDPNP} - 0.44 \Delta WPI + 0.94 \text{ RHO} + 231.19$$
$$(17.21) \qquad (-2.36) \qquad (14.81) \qquad (4.41)$$
$$r^2 = 0.928; \ F = 102.98; \ DW = 1.5?$$

$$PCNP = 0.57 \text{ GDPNP} - 1.29 \Delta WPI - 0.92 \text{ MRI} + 0.93 \text{ RHO} + 163.72$$
$$(19.76) \qquad (-4.18) \qquad (-2.77) \qquad (13.60) \qquad (4.17)$$
$$r^2 = 0.948; \ F = 146.68; \ DW = 1.7?$$

where GDPNP = real gross domestic product; PCNP = real private consumption; ΔWPI = the change in wholesale price index; and MRI = the real interest rate.

The negative inflation-consumption pattern suggests some sort of forced savings mechanism was present in the 1970s.

Using the gross national product identity,

(1) $Y = C + I + X - M$

where C = (private and public) consumption; I = gross domestic capital formation; X = exports (including factor income from abroad); and M = imports (including factor payments to foreigners), it is possible to depict the IS (investment, savings) identity as

(2) $I = S + F$

where F is foreign capital outflow (defined as $F = M - X = I - S$).

Equations (1) and (2) should hold not only as ex post identities, but also as equilibrium conditions. This assumes that commodity markets are cleared at equilibrium prices. If ex ante or desired levels of investment exceed ex ante savings at prices that prevailed in the preceding period,[16] however, the nature of this adjustment will depend on F or net capital outflow, which was, of course, negative during this period. If, for example, the capital inflow were perfectly elastic, the initial adjustment problem would be mitigated since any excess of I over S would simply be filled by a positive F, thus relieving the excess domestic demand.

It is quite likely, however, that in the short run, especially because large amounts of foreign funds are exogenously determined, F cannot be relied upon as an equilibrating variable.

Also during the 1970s, output was not capable of expanding rapidly enough in the short run (firms at full capacity, infrastructure bottlenecks) to aid fully in the equilibration process.

In other words, if output were flexible enough and responded to demand stimulus in the short run (within the given period), then I and S could adjust to establish an equilibrium Y (given the exogenously determined level of F). For this Keynesian type of adjustment process to be effective, it is also necessary for the savings and investment functions to be responsive to changes in GNP (with movements that are in the right direction and magnitude). As noted in the private investment functions above, however, changes in price had a negative impact on private investment (Table 4.1).

The same negative relationship holds between changes in price or inflation and total real investment (TINP).

$$TINP = 0.31 \text{ GDPNP} - 0.54 \text{ INFW} + 0.90 \text{ RHO} - 90.13$$
$$(12.27) \qquad (-1.90) \qquad (10.70) \qquad (-2.91)$$
$$r^2 = 0.858; \ F = 72.34; \ DW = 2.06$$

$$TINP = 1.03 \text{ TINPL} + 0.41 \ \Delta\text{GDPNP} - 0.68 \text{ INFW} - 0.14 \text{ RHO} - 6.86$$
$$(34.24) \qquad (5.80) \qquad (-2.23) \qquad (-0.78) \qquad (-2.60)$$
$$r^2 = 0.995; \ F = 1494.87; \ DW = 2.06$$

$$TINP = 0.36 \text{ GDPNP} - 0.63 \ \Delta\text{CPI} + 0.93 \text{ RHO} - 161.83$$
$$(9.77) \qquad (-2.09) \qquad (3.82) \qquad (-3.81)$$
$$r^2 = 0.820; \ F = 54.81; \ DW = 1.84$$

Because the public sector's fiscal actions are more or less independent of movements in GDP, all the pressure for macroeconomic adjustment was placed on private savings; i.e., increases in private savings at the expense of consumption may, along with the government's crowding out effect, have accounted for the sharp decline in private consumption

Several formulations of total national savings do in fact show a positive relationship between measures of inflation and real savings (SNP).

$$SNP = 0.30 \text{ GDPNP} + 1.14 \ \Delta\text{CPI} + 0.94 \text{ RHO} - 112.91$$
$$(9.72) \qquad (4.66) \qquad (14.41) \qquad (-2.55)$$
$$r^2 = 0.909; \ F = 119.37; \ DW = 1.55$$

$$SNP = 0.36 \text{ GDPNP} + 0.55 \text{ INFC} + 0.94 \text{ RHO} - 176.62$$
$$(11.35) \qquad (1.99) \qquad (14.07) \qquad (-3.49)$$
$$r^2 = 0.855; \ F = 70.70; \ DW = 1.44$$

Government Consumption

Government consumption expenditures (GCNP) consist of the government's purchases of goods and services to provide social, administrative, and military services and therefore are not subject to the same type of behavioral constraints as private consumption. Even less is known about the behavior of public consumption in Mexico than about private consumption. A logical case could be made for treating them as autonomous, disaggregated according to the type of factors purchased, or as a function of revenues.

In the absence of disaggregated time series data, government consumption was regressed on revenues (GREVP), gross domestic product, and lagged government consumption, together with a number of dummy variables reflecting devaluations of the peso. Several formulations give good results (equations 18 through 25, Table 4.1).

INVESTMENT

Investment is defined as the sum of imported and domestically produced machinery and equipment together with expenditures for new structures and repair outlays. Imported capital is a significant part of total capital formation and also represents a channel through which new technology from abroad may enter the system.

Since 1951 private investment has increased at a slightly faster rate than gross domestic product, and as a result its share in GDP has increased from 9.1 percent in 1951 to 12.2 percent in 1979.

The government's investment has increased somewhat faster, especially in the 1970s, and as a result its share in GDP has increased from 5.4 percent in 1951 to 7.3 percent in 1970, and to 10.5 percent in 1979 (Table 4.3).

As with consumption, the empirical estimates below have divided capital formation in Mexico into that controlled by the government and that influenced (private investment) by market developments. A number of observers have noted that government investment has helped to break down some of the discontinu-

TABLE 4.3

Mexico: Patterns of Investment, 1951-79
(billions of pesos, current prices)

	Private Investment	Government Investment	Gross Domestic Product	Private Investment/GDP	Government Investment/GDP
1951	4.82	2.84	53.0	9.1	5.4
1955	9.51	4.41	88.2	10.8	5.0
1960	17.13	8.38	155.9	11.0	5.4
1965	27.99	16.30	252.0	11.1	6.5
1970	51.72	30.58	418.7	12.4	7.3
1971	53.46	28.54	452.4	11.8	6.3
1972	55.94	42.06	512.3	10.9	8.2
1973	69.49	57.61	619.6	11.2	9.3
1974	104.19	69.05	899.7	11.6	7.7
1975	124.15	99.05	1100.7	11.3	9.0
1976	155.10	111.79	1371.0	11.3	8.2
1977	185.10	154.0	1849.3	10.0	8.3
1978	254.4	221.7	2337.4	10.9	9.5
1979	375.0	323.1	3067.5	12.2	10.5

Source: Bank of Mexico, Annual Report, various issues.

ities inherent in economic development. Most importantly in this regard, it has helped create an environment in which economies of scale could be obtained for the first time in many areas by private entrepreneurs. Government investment has thus performed a dual role. The first has been to create an institutional, financial, and infrastructural environment that has been conducive to private enterprise and initiative. In this role it has complemented private investment by filling gaps in areas where the private sector was clearly unable to participate. The second and much less important role to date has been to serve as a signal to the private sector by inducing a flow of private resources into activities and regions that the planners perceive as having high social, but not necessarily private, profitability.

PRIVATE INVESTMENT

Accepted theory on private investment tells us that its main determinants should be the stock of capital and output.[17] The model specification with this information usually revolves around the manner in which private investors close the gap between their actual and their perceived optimal or most profitable stock of capital. The absence of capital stock figures for Mexico, however, rules out formulations along these lines. Instead, private real investment was regressed on various factors that are likely to have affected to one degree or another the profitability of investment.

Profitability in turn (particularly that of investment in machinery and construction) is generally considered to be reflected in certain lagged variables.[18] Decisions concerning investment not only take time to make but also are based on past experiences. The existence of a very definite lag structure for investment behavior in most countries confirms this general formulation. Specification of the probable length of the lags for Mexico, however, is more difficult to make.

The evidence for the United States suggests two separate lag sequences in investment decision. The first is the so-called administrative lag, representing the time necessary to have plans approved by management committees and designs completed. This lag is usually relatively short, anywhere from three to six months. The second lag, the appropriations lag, is nearly always longer.[19]

Tom Mayer suggests, on the basis of his exhaustive study of United States data, a 15-month interval between the start and completion of construction;[20] in an earlier study, it was suggested that during World War II and the Korean War this lag was about ten months.[21] Also for the United States, Almond concluded that three to four quarters was a realistic estimate for the appropriations lag.[22] This, combined with the usual three- to six-month administrative lag, would yield a total lag of eighteen months or six quarters.

There are several reasons, however, for believing that a six quarter lag, while perhaps relevant for the U.S. type of environment, should be reduced to around a year in the case of Mexico. First, Mexican entrepreneurs, while undertaking more and more investments in heavy industry, are still predominantly involved in lighter manufacturing. Given that it is quite likely large, complex investments in heavy industry that yield larger than average appropriations lag, there is likely an upward bias in the United States figure. Second, because entrepreneurial ability to carry out detailed, in-depth cost-benefit analysis is limited in Mexico and because of the general high profitability of investment in that country, the administrative lag in the Mexican case should be much lower than in the United States.

In addition, many investments in Mexico take place in areas protected from foreign competition and, while not guaranteed by the government, often receive aid if survival becomes a problem. Therefore, they are not subject to the risks and resulting committee and board meetings characteristic of U.S. business practice. Thus, for a number of reasons all pointing in the same direction, we would expect the investment lag in Mexico to be shorter than in the United States. On the average, four quarters would seem to be a realistic figure.

The one-year lags examined in the investment equations consisted of: (1) lagged total private expenditure (PENANPL), (2) private consumption (PCNPL), (3) money (M1PL), (4) private credit (PCPL), (5) government investment (GIPL), (6) nominal interest rate (M1L), and (7) the capital stock (KPL).

The inclusion of government expenditure is based on the underlying theory that this type of outlay is undertaken in part to unbalance the economy, thus raising the profitability of private investment. Changes in gross domestic product (GDPNP) should stimulate investment through an accelerator type mechanism. As for private consumption, a good case could be made for either a positive effect, through creating a direct demand for goods and services, or a negative impact through increasing the competition for financial resources. Capital rationing, therefore, may be a problem as private consumers compete with businesses for funds.

There are several special characteristics of the Mexican
financial markets worth mentioning.

1. The demarcation between money and capital markets is
not clear because many short-term loans are automatically renew
able and long-term bonds can be redeemed on demand.
2. While the government financial institutions influence
capital formation and the securities market, private institutions
affect liquidity.
3. Since many large enterprises are owned by the government, government bonds or bonds issued by its agencies have
priority over private issues.
4. Most small- and medium-size corporations prefer interna
financing to short-term bank loans since security issues involve
high cost and control problems.
5. The middle income group in Mexico has not been developed as in many industrialized nations. Most savings are trans-
ferred to financial institutions, which become dominant forces
in the financial markets. Wealthy individuals may be interested
more in the real estate and commodities markets than the securities markets since they still remember the problems associated
with inflation in the 1950s.
6. The stock exchanges are dominated by fixed income
securities. Variable income securities are not actively traded.
Furthermore, brokerage firms and specialists are not important
in Mexico since they do not perform the same sophisticated functions as in the United States.

In short, most of Mexico's financial development has taken
place through the growth of the banking system, consisting of
public, private, and mixed enterprises in both commercial and
development banking. Direct financing of firms through the
public issue of stocks and bonds is much less important. During
the 1960s and into the 1970s, resources available to the banking
system grew substantially faster than GDP, allowing credit to
the private sector to grow about twice as fast as GDP.
In general nonmonetary deposits made up more than half
of the financial system's liabilities and amounted to around 30
percent of GDP in the early 1970s. Economic stability, a positive
interest rate differential (with respect to foreign interest rates)
with spreads of 2 to 5 percentage points during the last ten
years, full convertibility of the peso, and, until 1972, a positive
real interest rate in the domestic market were all responsible
for the development of the financial system. On the negative
side, however, a large portion of those nonmonetary deposits

were held in very short-term instruments, the longest being a one-year promissory note; about one-third of the value of the deposits were completely liquid.

Historically, the liquidity of the liabilities of the banking system has made the system highly vulnerable. For example, in 1973 and 1974, nonmonetary deposits fell in real terms, as real interest rates turned negative and the interest rate differential between foreign and domestic rates was reversed. Rising inflation relative to the country's trading partners induced devaluationary expectations, thereby further reducing the incentive to invest in peso denominated financial assets. This trend was reversed in 1975 because of the decline of inflationary and devaluationary expectations and the fall in interest rates prevailing in international markets. However, resumption of speculation against the peso early in 1976 combined with the effects of the subsequent devaluations was undoubtedly responsible for the drop by almost 30 percent in nonmonetary deposits in real terms by the end of the year. The result was that total credit fell by about 10 percent for the year 1976.

Availability of domestic credit to the private sector has in recent years been reduced because the public sector has often preempted funds from the financial system. For example, during the stabilization crisis in the mid-1970s, public sector credit increased from around 4.5 percent of GDP in 1972 to 9 percent by 1976. These trends resulted in the real stock of domestically financed credit to the private sector falling by 23 percent between 1972 and 1976.

The regression results (Table 4.1) were quite satisfactory for a number of alternative formulations. These are discussed in more detail below in conjunction with the alternative development strategy open to the country. Suffice it to say that the accelerator (ΔGDPNP) lagged government expenditures (GIPL), lagged private investment (IPPL), and lagged interest (MIL). Equation 28 gives one of the better statistical results and is consistent with our speculation as to entrepreneurial behavior outlined above.

The statistical significance of lagged government expenditure indicates the important role that the government performs in order to create all infrastructural and institutional environment conducive to the growth of private investment. The lag undoubtedly reflects the gestation period between government initiation and the private response.

Contrary to the theories stressing credit rationing rather than the interest rate in influencing private investment, the nominal rate of interest (MI) was significant (with a negative sign) in all regressions in which it was included.

The negative sign on the change in exchange rate (ΔEX) undoubtedly reflects the effect of uncertainty during periods of exchange crisis.

IMPORTS

Imports play a crucial role in the Mexican economy. They provide a multitude of goods without which growth and expansion are not possible. They include heavy machinery and equipment as well as a wide range of intermediate goods and an increasing amount of food.

Imports tend to mirror domestic aggregate economic activity rising with booms and falling with recessions. There are at least two components to this mechanism. The first takes place during a boom, whereby increases in domestic demand elicit increases in spending on intermediate goods, many of which must in turn be imported. The second and more important component is the increased demand for productive capacity during a boom. Expanded aggregate demand leads to increased domestic investment and, concomitantly, increased imports of capital goods and raw materials.

In the actual formulation of the import equations, the role of relative prices was assumed likely to be significant from two points of view. The first is that high import prices relative to domestic prices should induce import substitution if the factors (including managerial talent) are domestically available. The plausibility of this expectation is increased by the government's active campaign to diversify the economy.

The second is the terms of trade effect; i.e., high import prices relative to domestic prices could imply a reduced ability to import unless export prices have increased commensurately. The terms of trade were measured as the ratio of the price index for domestic goods to that of imported goods. The index used was the ratio of the domestic wholesale price index to the U.S. wholesale price index (TTA).

The results (Table 4.1) are consistent with the above formulation. It should be noted that since the original data for imports used negative signs based on national income accounting, the signs of the coefficients may seem the opposite of what was expected.

In general, real imports (imports deflated by the U.S. export price index) are positively related to exports, apparently reflecting foreign exchange availability, the terms of trade (TTA) investment (TINP), and the gross national product. The investment term was consistently significant while that for private consumption was not, thus reflecting the nature and effectiveness of the country's import licensing system.

EXPORTS

As might be expected, exports are positively related to the U.S. economy through real U.S. GDP (USYP) and changes in the U.S. real GDP (ΔUSYP). Dummies reflecting devaluation together with the exchange rate (EX) have helped exports expand during the 1951-79 period (Table 4.1, equations 55, 56, 60, 61, 62).

MECHANISMS OF GROWTH

The manner in which exports act as a leading sector and the determinants of the overall impact of changes in exports on national economies has been discussed in the literature for some time.[23] The consensus among economists seems to be that exports can contribute to economic growth through their direct contribution to gross domestic product since they are included as part of GDP, and indirectly through linkages created with nonoil sectors in a sequence of multiplier accelerator mechanisms. Theoretically, these indirect contributions to the economy may continue to operate long after a particular change in exports has occurred.[24]

Thus, while the petroleum sector may not participate directly in the buying and selling of goods in the domestic market, as was historically the case of the leading export growth sectors, it may still act as they did in providing an engine of growth for the economy, rather than a direct effect through large backward and forward linkages. The mechanism may be one of a series of demand responses that result once the sector's revenues begin to interact with the rest of the economy.

In sum, the overall impact of a change in exports will depend on: (1) changes in technology that result, (2) the propensity to import, (3) the extent to which investment opportunities are generated, (4) the ability to attract foreign factors, and (5) other, nonquantitative effects. Obviously, neither the exhibited nor relative sizes of exports' direct and indirect contributions to the growth of the economy need to be fixed, and they could conceivably vary over time and between different time periods. Clearly, if the opportunities generated by the

growth of the export sector are exploited, then a pattern of
economic growth will evolve and be characterized as a process
of diversification about an export base. 25

While the relationship between the growth of oil exports
and the growth of GDP over time is central to an export base
model of growth, the literature has never been specific as to
the operational nature of this relationship, i.e., exactly what
effect the time period or time pattern changes in exports should
have on income. The problem of conceptualizing the time lag
between oil export growth and economic growth in Mexico must
therefore be central to any investigation that attempts to forecast the economy's likely growth path. 26

More precisely, to have any credibility at all a forecasting
model of the Mexican economy must identify the extent to which
demand increasing effects of petroleum revenues have induced
movements in the country's indigenous (nonoil) income. As a
first step in constructing an econometric model of the economy,
therefore, an attempt was made to determine the likely manner
in which the oil sector will interact with the rest of the economy
during the 1980s and into the 1990s.

Several schools of thought seem to have developed concerning the country's development strategy in general and the use
of the oil revenues in particular. Two strikingly different pro-
posals as to the government's best investment strategy have
emerged. 27

The first, or planner, view (i.e., that of the Secretariat
of Planning) appears to be that the resources should be channeled
through direct public expenditure on welfare, infrastructure
(such as schools and hospitals), and productive public enterprises (particularly in heavy industry and capital goods).
Simultaneously, national income would be distributed away from
profit and toward wages. The idea seems to be to extend the
import substituting industrialization process into full maturity
on the basis of large mass markets, state enterprises, restrictions on multinationals, technological independence, and continued tariff protection for the private sector. In other words,
it is proposed to reinstigate the strategy initiated during the
Echeverria administration, but this time without the shortage
of foreign exchange or fiscal resources that frustrated that
effort.

The second position or the treasury view (i.e., that of
the Secretary of Finance and the Bank of Mexico) contends that
the revenues should be transformed through indirect public
expenditure so as to stimulate consumption and investment by
the private sector. Presumably, various tax incentives and

development credits from state banks would play an important
role in this strategy. This approach also calls for wage restraint,
a reduction in tariffs, increased foreign investment, and a stable
peso (supported by the oil revenues).

If this strategy is successful, the likely outcome would be
a shift towards more higher-investment and capital goods imports
for the private (rather than the public) sector, while the pattern
of consumption would probably be shifted more toward those
products consumed by the upper income groups rather than the
basic items of the lower income groups. In general this strategy
would like to return the country's development path to one re-
sembling that experienced in the 1960s, one of steady noninflationary growth with fiscal and exchange balance.[28]

To date, of the two approaches, the treasury view has
characterized the country's postdevaluation development strategy.
Still, there is evidence of greater direct government involvement
in the economy than the 1960s. Also there does not appear to
be any firm commitment on the part of the government to increased
integration into the world economy.

Any discussion of the relative merits of the two strategies
ultimately comes down to the behavior of private investment.
Clearly, given the likely level of oil revenues during the foreseeable future, the government would be in a position to undertake the volume of investment required for the socially necessary
rate of job creation. The treasury position does not deny this,
but rather argues that the private sector is also capable of
investing at this rate while at the same time utilizing the country's resources more efficiently.

Clearly, ultimate success of a strategy along the lines ad-
vocated by the treasury would depend critically on the manner
in which the private sector responded to the investment incentives
generated by government expenditures.

The orthodox interpretation of private investment behavior
in Mexico begins with the assumption that the rate of return to
investors is greater than the rate charged by banks.[29] If this
is true, the factor largely determining the rate of investment
is the availability of funds and not their cost.

Considerations along these lines formed the theoretical
rationale for many of the government's policies in the 1960s,
the argument being that a low level of government funding from
the domestic money market (usually achieved through central
bank reserve requirements on financial intermediaries) was
necessary to assure adequate funds for private investors.

In contrast, the planning view is that finance is not a
constraint on private investment in Mexico—at least for medium

and large corporations, which account for the greater part of productive capital formation.[30] According to this line of argument—

1. high profit levels and the absence of an active equity market mean that Mexican firms finance most of their fixed asset formation from retained earnings and use bank loans for working capital—particularly for credit to their customers
2. most large national firms are closely connected to major banking groups—often through interlocking shareholders—and receive preference in financing over government or individuals (as well as providing the bulk of bank deposits)
3. multinational corporations—which may account for half of manufacturing output—have direct access to foreign capital markets and are thus not affected by domestic credit conditions.

This is essentially a Keynesian position whereby private investment is assumed determined largely by profit expectations, with market size and consumer credit also important factors. It would follow that bank credit (and thus variations in the budget deficit or development bank outlays) would, in the short run at least, affect consumption rather than investment.

One implication of this line of reasoning is that government attempts at stimulating private investment through channeling the oil revenues through development banks will not be successful, at least in the short run; i.e., that whatever effect these funds would have on private investment would result from increased consumption, with the expansion in markets stimulating new productive capacity only after a lag of some time. Furthermore, it might be argued, the pattern of capacity expansion would not in any case necessarily correspond to the development goals of the government. Instead investors might find it more profitable to concentrate on luxury consumer goods, services, and real estate speculation; i.e., credits would have little effect on a corporate sector already possessing adequate funds.

Put differently, there is a suspicion in Mexican planning circles that a sector with low profitability, such as capital equipment and wage goods (which have had a high priority for the government), would be automatically chosen by private investors strictly on their perceived profitability. More likely, given the continued overvaluation of the peso (made possible only by increased oil revenues), high manufacturing wage levels, and low tariff protection, would be a shift away from industry toward investment in tertiary activities. In other words, economic development aims would become difficult if not impossible to achieve if policy were designed along the lines of the 1960s.

The strategy finally adopted will depend not only on its relative economic merits but also on the pressures the government feels from the country's labor organizations. Currently organized labor is pressing for still greater state participation in the economy, wider welfare benefits, and continued industrial protection, clearly a position more compatible with the Keynesian planning approach to development than the actual strategy followed in the 1960s.

In order to determine the major factors that underlay the decision of the private sector to invest, additional regressions were estimated and corrected for serial correlation in both constant (1975) and current prices. The main independent variables found significant (for the current price case) were: (1) government investment lagged one year (IGL), (2) the nominal interest rate (MI), (3) the change in gross domestic product from the previous year (ΔGDPN), (4) changes in government investment (ΔIG), (5) last year's total capital stock (KL), (6) change from last year's wholesale price index (ΔWPI), (7) change from last year's exchange rate (ΔEX), (8) the exchange rate (EX), and (9) the level of real (1975 constant prices) private sector credit from the banking system during the previous year (PCPL).

The results (Table 4.4) indicate a strong positive response to previous year's government investment (IGL), presumably reflecting the hypothesized model of the government intentionally creating profitable investment opportunities through its capital plan, i.e., a Hirschman type unbalanced growth mechanism whereby the creation of public projects lowers the cost of production, thus eliciting a positive response from the private sector. Next in order of importance was the negative response of private sector investment to the nominal interest rate, clearly indicating that the cost of capital and not just its availability (as implied in a number of studies) is a major factor influencing the investment decision in Mexico. The positive effect of changes in gross domestic product (ΔGDPN) depicts an accelerator type response whereby the private sector attempts to expand its plant and equipment to maintain a capital stock in line with expanded sales volume.

The positive response to changes in government investment is of interest because it implies that added government investments have not crowded out private investors from the financial markets (as perhaps in the United States and other countries).

The negative response of investment to changes in the wholesale price index seems to indicate a disinclination on the part of private investors to engage in speculative inventory accumulation (although a tightening of credit during inflationary periods may be a better explanation for the observed association).

TABLE 4.4

Mexico: Determinants of Private Investment, 1951-79 (current prices)

Private Investment	IGL	MI	ΔGDPN	ΔIG	KL	ΔWPI	ΔEX	EX	PCPL	RHO	Intercept	r^2	F	DW
IP =	1.42 (25.12)	-3.07 (-3.04)	0.05 (2.59)	0.45 (5.17)						0.65 (4.44)	31.76 (3.44)	0.996	1299.02	1.73
IP =	1.01 (6.17)	-1.83 (-1.42)	0.21 (5.42)		0.06 (1.56)	-0.96 (-4.59)				0.41 (2.36)	19.18 (1.91)	0.997	1974.28	1.79
IP =	1.26 (11.83)	-1.83 (-1.48)	0.16 (2.39)	0.23 (1.44)		-0.62 (-1.70)				0.67 (4.73)	22.07 (2.03)	0.996	1114.30	1.70
IP =	1.37 (7.91)	-4.22 (-2.67)	0.06 (2.00)		0.06 (1.62)					-0.05 (-0.24)	36.39 (2.90)	0.998	3017.26	2.01
IP =	1.17 (13.93)		0.23 (6.10)			-1.06 (-5.37)				0.58 (3.71)	6.31 (3.46)	0.997	2213.36	1.74
IP =	1.50 (32.08)	2.98 (-2.55)		0.51 (5.32)		-0.21 (-1.77)				0.57 (3.65)	30.21 (2.94)	0.996	1406.27	1.83
IP =	1.32 (8.61)	-2.74 (-2.11)		0.40 (4.21)	0.06 (1.53)					0.31 (1.67)	25.26 (2.52)	0.998	2397.63	1.88
IP =	1.68 (104.57)						-1.61 (-4.63)			0.31 (1.67)	3.14 (2.81)	0.998	5670.11	2.16
IP =	1.50 (24.57)	-2.37 (-2.50)	0.05 (2.68)	0.25 (2.15)			-0.98 (-2.38)			0.62 (4.11)	25.13 (2.93)	0.998	1423.29	1.87
IP =	1.53 (29.97)	-1.48 (-1.55)		0.42 (4.37)						0.41 (2.31)	16.93 (2.06)	0.997	2540.06	2.03
IP =	0.62 (3.46)	-10.38 (-1.84)	0.56 (8.21)							-0.22 (-1.16)	83.28 (1.88)	0.978	364.95	2.09
IP =	1.40 (15.03)		0.10 (5.52)					-1.83 (-4.89)	0.08 (2.52)	0.58 (3.68)	26.06 (5.66)	0.997	1860.50	2.06
IP =			0.52 (24.82)							0.06 (0.31)	13.58 (3.36)	0.959	616.24	1.89
IP =		-9.21 (-4.04)	0.08 (1.79)		0.37 (12.12)					0.57 (3.61)	66.91 (3.45)	0.984	418.28	1.40

Note: See text for definition of symbols. Ordinary least squares estimation with Cochrane-Orcutt procedure; TSP estimation program.
Source: Compiled by the author.

The negative relationship between private investment and changes in the exchange rate may also reflect tightening credit—uncertainty associated with periods of deteriorating economic conditions.

Surprisingly, private sector credit (a number of alternative formulations were used in the estimates) does not appear very important in explaining the observed fluctuations in private investment.

More or less the same results were obtained (Table 4.5) when the variables were estimated in constant prices. Again, real government investment lagged one year (IGPL) appears to have the strongest association with real private investment, followed by the positive impact of last year's real capital stock (KPL) and the negative relationship to the nominal interest rate.

In general the results suggest a stable environment whereby output is flexible and private investment is responsive (positive relationship with changes in GDP) and in the right direction (negative relationship with changes in price and negative with interest rates) to restore macroeconomic equilibrium.

Because of the complexity of sorting out all the impacts government policy has on private investment, these results should be viewed as only suggestive.

It should be noted, however, that the regressions on private investment are quite consistent with those obtained in the analysis of the impact of government expenditure contained in Chapter 2.

CONCLUSIONS

The equations estimated above have numerous implications, many of which are better discussed in the context of the forecasts made in the following chapter. Several general observations can be made, however.

1. The importance of the government in early all the key macroeconomic relationships is perhaps the most significant yet hardly surprising result established in the regressions.

2. The fact that the oil industry is under the control of the government makes it possible to delineate clearly the role of the public sector in the economy. Equations for consumption and investment indicate the strong impact of government expenditure on the activity of the private sector and upon key macroeconomic aggregates such as the capital stock.

3. In general, econometric model building in Mexico appears to be a very feasible and desirable endeavor. The results pre-

TABLE 4.5

Mexico: Determinants of Private Investment, 1951-79
(constant 1975 prices)

Private Investment	IGPL	KPL	MI	ΔIGP	ΔGDPNP	ΔWPI	ΔEX	PCP	GIP	RHO	Intercept	r^2	F	DW
IPP =	1.13 (5.97)	0.05 (1.67)	-3.86 (-3.08)	0.48 (3.44)						0.36 (2.03)	41.45 (4.72)	0.973	182.41	1.62
IPP =	1.11 (6.86)	0.06 (2.11)	-3.40 (-3.01)	0.30 (2.06)			-1.43 (-2.61)			0.36 (2.03)	37.82 (4.77)	0.980	194.69	1.61
IPP =	0.94 (6.08)	0.08 (3.09)	-2.69 (-2.60)		0.65 (1.79)		-1.73 (-3.41)			0.36 (2.00)	29.91 (4.22)	0.979	189.82	1.85
IPP =	1.10 (6.44)	0.06 (2.11)		0.29 (2.00)						0.35 (1.96)	43.99 (3.71)	0.981	154.82	1.64
IPP =	0.89 (4.73)	0.08 (2.51)				-0.41 (-2.72)				0.31 (1.68)	12.28 (4.19)	0.971	231.71	1.62
IPP =	1.34 (13.50)		-3.64 (-1.74)	0.41 (2.40)		-0.25 (-1.15)		0.11 (1.56)		0.45 (2.63)	42.32 (2.71)	0.966	114.96	1.78
IPP =	1.20 (19.49)									0.42 (2.43)	18.74 (5.20)	0.938	379.96	1.86
IPP =	0.95 (5.80)	0.08 (2.94)	-2.19 (-2.29)				-2.02 (-3.96)			0.23 (1.25)	28.99 (4.28)	0.983	290.47	1.67
IPP =	0.82 (4.45)	0.09 (2.92)	-2.64 (-2.14)		0.10 (2.35)					0.33 (1.81)	28.35 (3.36)	0.970	163.78	1.56
IPP =	0.98 (6.16)	0.06 (2.52)				-0.33 (-2.53)	-1.67 (3.32)			0.53 (1.82)	12.59 (4.98)	0.979	236.84	1.67
IPP =	1.20 (14.59)					-0.61 (-3.41)		0.14 (2.65)		0.45 (2.64)	16.46 (4.96)	0.957	154.50	1.99
IPP =	1.35 (14.58)		-4.74 (-2.44)							0.16 (0.85)	50.96 (3.58)	0.972	241.85	2.00
IPP =	1.39 (14.46)		-3.46 (-3.69)	0.56 (4.15)				0.14 (1.98)		0.43 (2.54)	40.96 (4.32)	0.963	183.66	1.76
IPP =		0.13 (4.88)	-3.83 (-2.88)						0.64 (3.93)	0.16 (0.82)	39.53 (4.20)	0.975	269.93	1.82

Note: See text for definition of symbols. Ordinary least squares estimation with Cochrane-Orcutt procedure; TSP estimation program.

Source: Compiled by the author.

sented above would tend to support such an assertion. The importance of this type of activity seems self-evident. It is hard to see how the pursuit of national policy goals could take place efficiently without a framework capable of examining in a quantitative fashion the economic forces at work in the country.

NOTES

1. These findings together with their margins of error are discussed at length in Richard Mancke, Mexican Oil and Natural Gas (New York: Praeger, 1979). For background on the petroleum industry, cf. Edward Williams, The Rebirth of the Mexican Petroleum Industry (Lexington, Mass.: Lexington Books, 1979).

2. David Ronfeldt, Richard Nehring, and Arturo Gandara, Mexico's Petroleum and U.S. Policy: Implications for the 1980s (Santa Monica, Calif.: Rand Corporation, 1980), pp. 5-6.

3. Frank E. Niering, Jr., "Mexico: A New Force in World Oil," Petroleum Economist, March 1979, p. 113. See also "Mexico's Reluctant Oil Boom: A Tight Rein on Development to Promote Balanced Growth," Business Week, January 15, 1979, p. 74.

4. A. Nowick, et al., Mexico: Manufacturing Sector, Situation, Prospects and Policies (Washington, D.C.: International Bank for Reconstruction and Development [World Bank], 1979), p. 15.

5. Excellent critiques are given in Raymond Vernon, "Comprehensive Model Building in the Planning Process: The Case of Less Developed Economies," Economic Journal, March 1966, pp. 57-69; and Aron Shourie, "The Use of Macroeconomic Regression Models of Developing Countries for Forecasts and Policy Prescription," Oxford Economic Papers, March 1972, pp. 1-35.

6. Jere Behrman and L. Klein, "Econometric Growth Models for the Developing Economy," in Induction, Growth and Trade, Essays in Honour of Sir Roy Harrod, ed. W. A. Eltis (London: Oxford University Press, 1970), p. 169.

7. H. Theil, "On the Theory of Economic Policy," American Economic Review, May 1956.

8. J. Timbergen, On the Theory of Economic Policy (Amsterdam: North Holland, 1952).

9. In terms of estimation procedures, ordinary least squares were used as a first screening of the numerous variables considered for each equation. When the model was essentially

complete, the equations were estimated using two-stage least squares procedures. Since there was little difference in the coefficients, only the ordinary least square results are presented here. The two-stage model is available from the author on request. All estimations were made with the program developed by Bronwyn Hall and Robert E. Hall, Time Series Processor, Version 3.5, Stanford, Calif., April 6, 1980.

10. C. Beeker, "A Theory of the Allocation of Time," Economic Journal, September 1965, pp. 493-517.

11. See M. Friedman, A Theory of the Consumption Function (Princeton, N.J.: National Bureau of Economic Research, 1957) for an explanation of the methods used.

12. Michael Evans, Macroeconomic Activity: Theory, Forecasting and Control (New York: Harper & Row, 1969), pp. 23-24.

13. S. Almon, "The Distributed Lag Between Capital Appropriations and Expenditures," Econometrica, January 1965, p. 188.

14. See Robert Ferber, "Consumer Economics: A Survey," Journal of Economic Literature, September 1973, pp. 1303-42.

15. A hypothesis originally proposed by Arthur Smithies, The Economic Potential of the Arab Countries (Santa Monica, Calif.: Rand Corporation, 1978), p. 41.

16. See N. Leff and K. Sato, "Macroeconomic Adjustment in Developing Countries: Instability, Short-run Growth and External Dependency," The Review of Economics and Statistics, May 1980, pp. 170-79, for a detailed elaboration of this approach.

17. Thomas Mayer, "Plant and Equipment Lead Times," Journal of Business, April 1960, pp. 127-32; and Edwin Kuhand and Richard Schmalensee, An Introduction to Applied Macroeconomics (Amsterdam: North Holland, 1973), p. 59.

18. E. Greenberg, "Fixed Investment," in David Heathfield Topics in Applied Macroeconomics (New York: Academic Press, 1976), p. 97.

19. Evans, Macroeconomic Activity, pp. 100-01.

20. Mayer, "Plant and Equipment Lead Times," p. 128.

21. Thomas Mayer and S. Sonenblum, "Lead Times for Fixed Investment," Review of Economics and Statistics, August 1955, pp. 300-304.

22. Almon, "The Distributed Lag," p. 188.

23. See for example G. W. Bertram, "The Relevance of the Canadian Wheat Boom in Canadian Economic Growth," Canadian Journal of Economics, August 1973; and R. E. Caves, "Export Lead Growth and the New Economic History," in Trade, Balance of Payments and Growth, Essays in Honor of Charles Kindleberger, ed. J. Bhagwati (Amsterdam: North Holland, 1972), pp. 403-42.

24. Raymond Mikesell, "The Contribution of Petroleum and Mineral Resources to Economic Development," in Foreign Investment in the Petroleum and Mineral Industries, ed. Raymond Mikesell (Baltimore, Md.: Johns Hopkins University Press, 1972), pp. 3-28.

25. An exhaustive analysis is given in G. Nankani, Development Problems of Mineral-Exporting Countries, World Bank Staff Working Paper no. 354 (New York: International Bank for Reconstruction and Development [World Bank], August 1979).

26. Cf. M. M. Metwally and H. V. Tamaschke, "Oil Exports and Economic Growth in the Middle East," Kyklos, 1980, pp. 499-521.

27. Summarized in E. V. K. Fitzgerald, "Mexico: A New Direction in Economic Policy?" Bank of London & South America Review, October 1978, p. 533.

28. Ibid.

29. As developed in John Koehler, Economic Policy Making with Limited Information: The Process of Macro Control in Mexico (Santa Monica, Calif.: Rand Corporation, 1968).

30. Cf. Ernesto Marcos, "Design of a Development Policy for Mexico: Industry and Oil," in Public and Private Enterprise in a Mixed Economy, ed. William Baumol (New York: St. Martin's Press, 1980), pp. 57-68.

5

OPTIMAL GROWTH PATHS TO 1995:
THEORETICAL CONSIDERATIONS

INTRODUCTION

By early 1982 the National Industrial Development Plan
had been overtaken by events, including sharp rises in the
price of crude oil in 1979-80, depressed market conditions in
the United States, continuing high inflation in Mexico, and a
glut in world oil markets.[1]

The 1981 oil glut forced Petroleos Mexicanos to lower its
export price by $2 a barrel in June 1981, but its director general
was promptly dismissed for doing so, and his successor reversed
the decision. Mexico's clients began canceling contracts and
within weeks exports had dropped by 50 percent.

Since then, Mexico has slowly recovered its markets, selling
its oil at prevailing, and still sinking (as of April 1982), world
rates. For all of 1981 Mexico earned $6 billion less than it antici-
pated; its current account balance of payments deficit rose to
a record $10.8 billion, and the public foreign debt grew by
$14.9 billion to $48.7 billion. That figure, combined with the
private sector's estimated $15 billion exposure abroad, made
Mexico one of the world's most indebted developing countries.

On February 18, 1982, the peso was abruptly devalued by
about 30 percent after the government announced it would no
longer intervene in exchange markets to support the currency.
Devaluation had been in the offing since the oil price reductions.

In addition to the direct revenue loss, the price cut had
caused a loss of confidence in the government's ability to maintain a stable peso, and capital outflows began to increase. But
the government continued to live beyond its means and increased

its external debt by $14 billion during 1981 to $48.7 billion at
the end of the year. Most of this debt was contracted after
the oil price reductions.

President Lopez Portillo repeatedly said all through 1981
that he would "defend the peso like a dog." He appealed to
Mexicans to have faith in their country and not transfer their
money into dollars. Mexicans, therefore, realized that devaluation was a possibility. Capital outflows are estimated at between
$2 billion and $3 billion alone from December 1981 to January
1982. The government was therefore forced into propping up
its reserves and sustaining an artificially high exchange rate
with expensive short-term borrowings.

Whether the devaluation averts or brings on a major economic crisis depends on the government's success in enforcing
the additional austerity measures that it introduced in the latter
part of February 1982. These ruled out an across-the-board
emergency wage increase and proposed a 3 percent cut in the
budget.

The 1982 gross domestic product is expected to grow by
about 4.5 percent, some three points less than in 1981. This
means that the 800,000 new jobs needed because of the rapid
increase in population will not be created.

DEFECTS OF THE PLAN

In retrospect it is fairly easy to point out the plan's technical defects, together with errors in judgment made by the
government in its general conduct of macroeconomic policy over
the last several years.

For one thing, the National Industrial Development Plan
appears to have greatly understated the amount of fixed investment required to generate the rates of GDP growth of over 10
percent that it envisaged for the mid-1980s.

Probably the greatest defect in the plan, however, is its
treatment of inflation. The plan refers to a "framework of
growth that had been increasingly conditioning all economic
sectors to depend financially on the outside world." It describes
what happened in the post-1972 inflation in terms of the progres-
sive subjection of monetary policy to international financial
discipline associated with the inflexible management of the rate
of exchange, whose maintenance was at times converted into an
end in itself. "The government responded to the pressures
on the external sector by supporting the parity. Thus, the
debt generated by the whole economy necessary to cover the

deficit on current account in the balance of payments and the speculative outflow of capital was gradually converted into public debt."

The empirical work in the previous chapters suggests otherwise. These results point to excessive government spending, financed by the Bank of Mexico and reflected in an increase in the money supply, as one of the prime sources of inflationary pressures. Further, a careful reading of government statements during the early to mid-1970s reveals that the government, even when confronted with an excessive rate of increase in imports and a declining rate of increase in exports of goods and services, refused to admit that the peso was overvalued.

The plan actually has very little to say about the problem of inflation other than asserting that the goal of 8 to 10 percent annual growth in real GDP, although higher than any in Mexican history, "is compatible with reducing inflation." No estimate of the rate of inflation that will occur in implementing the government's programs is given in the plan. What analysis of the problem there is simply dismisses the notion that diminishing public spending or restricting credit to overcome an inflationary crisis is incorrect since such policies "attack only the symptoms and not the causes."

This analysis is clearly faulty, and yet it is possible to show that there was great merit to the government's overall approach toward policy, and that, under certain circumstances, the plan's goals could have been met within tolerable inflationary limits. The best way to illustrate this argument is through the construction of a macroeconomic forecasting model.

The quantification and discussion of a number of key macroeconomic relationships involved in the government's 1978-90 development strategy, as outlined in the plan documents, has been undertaken in the last three chapters. The sections below combine a number of the most important variables into an overall model of the economy. The model is constructed so that it is capable of identifying the simultaneous interaction of these variables over time. Thus it should be able to determine, among other things, whether or not the economy will be close to the government's long-run growth objectives. In addition, the model is of the optimum control type, and thus capable of indicating the best path for the economy given likely constraints and the overall objectives of the government.

The model is also capable of depicting what might have been if the government had timed its expenditures more wisely and thus gained control over the inflationary buildup that eventually undermined most of the plan's major objectives.

In this regard the model draws upon the alternatives provided within the National Industrial Development Plan and its
excellent insights into the directions of structural change considered desirable by the Mexican policy makers (together with
the measures that might have been taken in order to attain them)

BASIC FEATURES OF THE FORECASTING MODEL

The model consists of a system of stochastic equations and
identities containing the key economic variables. The latter
fall into two main categories:

1. endogenous variables—those that are jointly determined
in the system and are influenced by other economic variables
2. exogenous variables—those that are not influenced by
the system and whose values are assumed to be given. These
consist of the following types:

   a. variables external to the system, such as international prices, United States growth, and so on
   b. lagged variables, including predetermined lagged
   endogenous variables (whose values before the current
   time period are given)
   c. policy variables, whose values are determined by
   the government, such as the foreign exchange rate, government expenditures, and the like.

The policy variables are not entirely exogenous, since the
economic behavior of the system often requires their modification
by the government, but we refer to them as endogenous because
the government can determine the size and timing of changes in
them in accordance with its policy objectives.

The substitution of values for the exogenous variables
enables one to arrive at a solution of the model, i.e., a calcula-
tion of values for all the endogenous variables. The model can
then be used for forecasting. Treating the policy variables as
exogenous makes it possible to compare the results of alternative
policy measures. The model both for describing and explaining
past developments and for prediction was employed. The analysis
was made in connection with the National Industrial Development
Plan, and many of the implications of the plan were examined
with the help of the model. One of the chief advantages of a
formal model of this type is that it makes it possible to investi-
gate various alternatives to the original plan and thus to analyze
the sensitivity of the economic variables to changes in recom-

mended policy measures (e.g., the effect of increased rates of oil production on various macroeconomic variables).

In many respects the model is similar to several other Keynesian type forecasting models built in the last several years; i.e., it expands the basic Keynesian structure of aggregate demand and supply relationships through an econometric estimation of the economy's major structural relationships. The model differs from most other efforts, however, in that it extends the analysis to a higher level through incorporating optimal control methods for forecasting purposes.[2]

The construction of such a model may be of substantial interest in its own right. The parameters of the individual equations do have a number of policy implications and also yield insights that a nonquantitative examination of the economy would not be capable of deducing. The standard reasons for constructing the model of this general type are that it can be used for multiplier analysis, policy simulation, and prediction. More importantly, however, exploration of these properties, together with the optimal control methods of forecasting, presents numerous insights into various aspects of the economy.

Many of these insights are not intuitively obvious and are unlikely to have been arrived at even by the best analysts using more traditional methods.

In summary, the model is based on the following assumptions:

1. that only a limited number of exogenous variables determine all the country's basic macro variables;

2. that government expenditures follow a pattern similar to that anticipated by the National Industrial Development Plan;

3. that there are no major alterations in world economic conditions during this period.

THE FORECASTING MODEL

The institutional characteristics and the historical background of Mexico presented in the previous chapters provide a foundation for the econometric-optimal control projections presented below. From these exercises we will try to determine why the National Industrial Development Plan's development strategy was not a feasible one, and what constraints are likely to be met in pursuing strategies of this type in the future, particularly during the forecast period for the plan (1978-90).

Model Characteristics

The model examines the economy from the point of view of the resources and requirements of implications associated with alternative growth scenarios. The forecasts determine the inflation rate, government deficits, and balance of payments position associated with alternative levels of government investment.

Structural Equations

While a detailed description of the equations used in the forecasting model can be found in the previous three chapters, it should be noted that the model itself incorporates a number of interesting features that are particularly relevant for a country like Mexico. These include special equations to reflect: (1) the increasing dependence of government revenues and expenditures on oil production, (2) consideration of the special links with the United States economy in terms of export demand for Mexican products and the effect of U.S. inflation rates on the Mexican price level, and (3) the basic Keynesian nature of many of the major economic forces present; i.e., the importance of real factors and to a certain degree the endogenous nature of the money supply functions.

The model's equations (Table 5.1) were estimated with annual data for the 1951-79 period. As with the National Industrial Development Plan, real variables were measured in 1975 constant prices.

All the equations are estimated by ordinary least squares techniques. The rationale underlying selection of independent variables has been discussed in some detail in the previous three chapters, and since the econometric statistics associated with each equation were presented earlier, they are not repeated here

For convenience and manageability, the model was broken down into a set of four main blocks consisting of—

1. oil-government expenditure (Keynesian national income forecasting model) in constant prices
2. oil-government expenditure (Keynesian national income model) in nominal prices
3. monetary supply
4. inflation equations

Since the major assumptions implicit in the model equations have been discussed at length in the previous three chapters,

TABLE 5.1

Mexico: Optimum Control Model—Endogenous Variables
(1951-79)

---

(1) Real Private Consumption (PCNP)
   PCNP = 0.88 GDPNPL - 1.94 GCNPL + 26.36

(2) Real Private Investment (IPP)
   IPP = 0.76 IGPL + 0.08 PCNP - 0.73 EX + 8.70

(3) Real Private Expenditures (PENANP)
   PENANP = PCNP + IPP

(4) Real Government Consumption (GCNP)
   GCNP = 0.72 GREVP + 0.60 GCNPL - 0.02 GDPNP + 0.17
   DUMDV - 20.3 DUMEX - 1.08

(5) Real Government Investment (GIP)
   GIP = Exogenous

(6) Real Government Expenditure (GENANP)
   GENANP = GCNPP + GIP

(7) Real Imports (ZP)
   ZP = 0.40 TINP - 0.70 EX - 3.29 EXL + 15.81 GDPDF - 34.12
   TTA + 57.74

(8) Real Exports - Deflated by Gross Domestic Product Deflator (EP)
   EP = 0.58 EPL + 0.24 CPP + 0.069 ΔUSYP + 1.21 EX

(9) Real Exports - Deflated by Industrial Country Export Index (EW)
   EW = 0.60 EWL - 0.19 DOMTDU + 0.063 EX + 0.00011 USYP -
   0.54

(10) Real Total Investment (TINP)
   TINP = IPP + GIP

(11) Nominal Exports (E)
   E = 1.08 EL + 3.47 EX - 42.66

(12) Real Capital Stock (KP)
   KP = TINP + TINPL + TINPL2

(13) Real Gross Domestic Product (GDPNP)
   GDPNP = 0.44 KP + 23.53 T1ME + 0.06 USGDP + 36.46

(14) Real Government Revenue (GREVP)
   GREVP = 0.024 GDPNP + 0.81 GREVPL + 0.045 E - 2.65

(15) Nominal Government Revenue (GREV)
   GREV = 0.036 GDPN + 1.07 GREVL - 4.76

(16) Real Government Deficit (GDEFP)
   GREVP - GENANP

(continued)

Table 5.1 (continued)

(17) Nominal Government Deficit (GDEF)
    GDEF = GREV - GENAN

(18) Nominal Government Consumption (GCN)
    GCN = 0.57 GREV + 0.64 GCNL + 3.50 MI - 29.26

(19) Nominal Government Investment (GI)
    GI = Exogenous

(20) Nominal Government Expenditure (GENAN)
    GENAN = GCN + GIN

(21) Nominal Private Consumption (PCN)
    PCN = 0.90 GDPN - 1.34 GIN - 1.06 GCN + 4.17

(22) Nominal Total Investment (TIN)
    TIN = TINP - GDPDF

(23) Gross Domestic Product Deflator (GDPDF)
    GDPDF = 0.0065 USWP + 0.0009 M2 + 0.38 GDPDFL - 0.11

(24) Time (TIME)
    TIME = Exogenous, 1, 2, 3 - -

(25) Nominal Gross Domestic Product (GDPN)
    GDPN = GDPNP - GDPDF

(26) Consumer Price Index (CPI)
    CPI = 0.82 CPIL + 36.88 EXCESSB + 0.37 USEUVL - 11.49

(27) Broad Money - Income Balance (EXCESSB)
    EXCESSB = M2/GDPNP

(28) Narrow Money - Income Balance (EXCESSA)
    EXCESSA = M1/GDPNP

(29) Narrow Money (M1)
    M1 = 0.98 M1L + 0.16 BMRM + 14.14 DUMEX + 0.74

(30) Broad Money (M2)
    M2 = 1.16 BMRM + 0.39 M2L + 54.15 DUMEX + 0.019

(31) Bank of Mexico Reserve Money (BMRM)
    BMRM = -2.07 GDEFL - 149.9 DUMDV + 64.31 DUMEX - 8.09

(32) Bank of Mexico Net Foreign Assets (BMFA)
    BMFA = 0.16 E - 11.11 DUMEX + 1.60 EX + 5.15 DUMDV - 3.75 DUMTDV - 12.41

(33) Nominal Imports (Z)
    Z = -0.49 E - 0.25 TIN - 0.22 ΔTIN + 5.98 DUMEX - 2.37

(continued)

152

(34) Commercial Bank Reserves (CBR)
$$CBR = 0.20\ CBRL + 1.80\ BMFA + 1.85\ GENAN - 60.43\ DUMDV + 3.41\ GDEF - 18.58$$

(35) Measure of Openness (ZB)
$$ZB = Z/GDPN$$

(36) Nominal Interest Rate (MI)
$$MI = -0.24\ MIL + 0.083\ CPI - 0.053\ GREV + 50.61\ EXCESSA + 5.00$$

(37) Real Interest Rate (MRI)
$$MRI = -0.15\ MRIL - 1.85\ MI + 1.45\ MIL - 0.98\ INFD - 0.84\ \Delta EX + 11.09$$

(38) US-Mexico Inflation Rate Differential (INFD)
$$INFD = INFC - INFUS$$

(39) Private Credit (PC)
$$PC = 1.17\ GDEF + 0.52\ PCL + 1.55\ \Delta M1 + 1.52\ E - 15.47$$

(40) Terms of Trade (TTA)
$$TTA = USEUV/WPI$$

(41) Wholesale Price Index (WPI)
$$WPI = 1.68\ EX + 2.84\ EXL + 68.46\ EXCESSB + 0.68\ USEUV - 45.57$$

(42) Inflation - Consumer Price Index (INFC)
$$INFC = 0.81 + 0.45\ GM2 + 0.50\ GGDPNP + 0.16\ INFCL - 6.46$$

(43) Inflation Gross Domestic Product Deflator (INF)
$$INF = 1.29\ INFUS + 0.35\ GM2 - 0.16\ GDPNP - 3.30$$

(44) Inflation - Wholesale Price Deflator (INFW)
$$INFW = 0.69\ INFUS + 0.56\ GM2 + 0.44\ GGDPNP - 7.73$$

Note: See Appendix for full listing of the variables.
Source: Compiled by the author.

suffice it to note that in large part the model reflects the overall picture of an economy characterized by a number of rigidities
in the pattern of resource use. As the economy continues to
grow and expand, immobility should gradually give way to a
greater degree of adaptability in both the utilization of factor
inputs and the composition of goods produced during any given
time period.

Because factor substitution at the present time is somewhat
limited, imports of both labor and capital have special significanc
in determining the country's growth path; i.e., as domestic
factors cannot readily be adjusted to produce substitutes for
imported producer goods, some minimum proportion of imports
(both labor and capital) is required to utilize the country's
domestic resources in an efficient manner. [3]

As in the two gap analyses discussed earlier, it is assumed
that, because the economy has some structurally determined and
rigid relationships between factor inputs, it is impossible for it
to achieve its full growth potential without a certain amount of
imported goods and services. The country's factor proportions
problem has, of course, been relieved over the last several
years with exports expanding sufficiently to assure an increased
supply of the required imports. In addition, the beginnings
of the development of a domestic capital goods industry should
help to reduce the country's external dependence. Still, as
with most developing countries, the problem of underdevelopment faced by Mexico is essentially that of short-run rigidities
in resource use. [4]

The forecasts from this type of export based model can be
used to derive a number of policy implications. There are, for
example, several implications pertinent to the country's economic
planning and the efficiency of the National Industrial Development Plan. More generally, the model is used to make a broad
assessment in quantitative terms of the rates of economic growth
implied by alternative crude petroleum production rates. As
constructed, the model should provide reasonably reliable orders
of magnitude on the basis of specified assumptions about the
magnitudes of the various parameters to allow for probable
future changes in the country's economic structure. The gap
between government revenues and expenditures can, for example
be used to determine the need for possible policy changes.

The model also makes several critical assumptions about
the economy's absorptive capacity. The analysis focuses on
the role of capital in expanding the productive capacity of the
economy. While capital availability is recognized as a prerequisit
for the country's economic growth, emphasis is mainly on the

relationship between capital assimilation and capital formation. Specifically, the notion that Mexico's economic growth is principally constrained by capital is qualified. It is assumed that the country faces little difficulty in absorbing, as it has done so successfully in the past, moderate volumes of capital over time. On the other hand, the country is likely to encounter serious impediments, due to the implied government deficit and the associated higher rate of economic growth, in maintaining a noninflationary environment at substantially higher rates of investment.

Indeed, if the absorptive capacity of the country is broadly conceived as that magnitude of oil revenues necessary to sustain a feasible level of public expenditures consistent with the government's borrowing capacity, preferences, and objectives (without strictly differentiating between investment and consumption outlays), then there is a wide range of values that can be realistically forecast as within the range of the authorities' implementation capability. If a problem of absorptive capacity is likely to develop in the future, it would most likely be because of the direct inflationary impact of the government deficits and the indirect effect higher rates of growth would have on available supplies rather than an allocation constraint. (Cf. especially the equations in Table 5.1 linking the monetary base to the government deficit, the money supply to the monetary base, and the rate of inflation to the money supply and growth in real GDP).

In sum, the forecasting model described above is suitable in selecting optimum planned growth rates and the associated levels of investment requirements. It is especially useful in assessing the realism and consistency of such documents as the National Industrial Development Plan; i.e., it is designed to examine the implications of planned changes in the economy's structural parameters, especially the ability of the private sector to participate in the country's anticipated expansion and the ability of the government to transform its financial resources into productive activities.

OPTIMAL CONTROL FUNCTIONS

The optimal control aspect of the model consists of—

1. the set of estimated equations (Table 5.1) that represent those aspects of the economy that are to be controlled
2. a set of constraints on the variables of the system

3. a set of boundary conditions on the variables
4. a cost functional or performance index, which is to be minimized.

The essential idea of optimal control is precisely to derive the optimal policy in order to steer the economy to a specified set of targets.[5] A necessary step in this regard is to specify an objective function or a welfare loss function by which the outcome associated with the optimal policy or its alternatives can be evaluated.[6] Given this welfare loss function and the econometric model outlined above, a policy sequence can be found minimizing the expectation of the welfare loss[7] for either the entire 1974-95 time period or selected segments.

In very general terms, the solution to the optimal control problem with unknown parameters using a quadratic loss function can be written as

(1) $y(t) = A(t)y(t+1) + C(t)x(t) + b(t) + u(t)$

where $y(t)$ is a vector of endogenous variables at time t; $x(t)$ is a vector of policy variables at time t; $b(t)$ is a vector combining the effects of all exogenous variables not subject to control; the matrices $A(t)$ $C(t)$ and $b(t)$ consist of unknown parameters whose probability distribution is assumed to be given; and $u(t)$ is a vector of random disturbances having mean 0, co-variance matrixes V, and being serially uncorrelated. Endogenous variables and policy variables with higher order lags can be eliminated by defining new endogenous variables so as to retain the form (1) of a system of first order linear stochastic difference equations in which only the current control variables $x(t)$ appear. We can include the policy variables in the vector $y(t)$ so that $x(t)$ need not be an argument of the loss function.[8]

The loss function mentioned above can be depicted as

(2) $W = \sum_{t-1}^{T} (yt - at)^1 K_t (yt - at)$

where $a(t)$ is a vector of targets for the variables $y(t)$, and $K(t)$ is a diagonal matrix giving the relative penalties for the squared deviations of the various variables from their targets. The problem becomes essentially one of minimizing the expected value of the loss function for T periods by choosing a strategy for $x(1)$, $x(2)$, . . . $x(T)$. The control variables will be selected

sequentially, the vector x(t) for each period being determined
only after the up-to-date information is available. This information consists mainly of y(t-1), which includes the observations
of all past endogenous variables and policy variables affecting
the current endogenous variables at time (t).

The specific optimal control exercise developed for Mexico
is designed for analyzing the problems that tend to develop in
oil based economies—that is, economies for which petroleum acts
as a major source of revenue. For Mexico increasing dependence
on an easy income does involve a long-term risk. Such a risk
would be seldom encountered in other less developed countries
that are not so fortunate as to have a bounty of income and
thus have to resort to the more traditional means of finance.
The obvious danger of this reliance has recently been thrust
upon the country by declining oil revenues, increasing government deficits, and the February 1982 devaluation of the peso.
Even in times where there was an overriding need for tax reform,
the government was reluctant to move ahead. It is little wonder
that the stepped-up oil revenues in the late 1970s removed any
sense of urgency to develop alternative sources of revenues.
The result is now an incongruity that has emerged in the long
run between the mounting requirements of the economy for such
income and the country's inability to generate sufficient alternative revenues. For sure, whether oil will act as a stimulant or
a barrier to Mexico's economic development is a question that
in the long run will depend to a large extent on the government's
expenditure policies and related economic and tax measures.

It may be argued that decisions of the planners and policy
makers in Mexico, particularly after the 1974 discoveries, were
not made in a context of marginal optimization. However, the
manner in which the planning authorities approached their
responsibilities can be approximated by the optimization of a
well-defined objective function.[9] After all, the responsible
officials in the government, the Secretariat of the President of
the Bank of Mexico, the Ministry of National Property and Industrial Development, and the Ministry of Programming and Budget,
were all reasonably knowledgable men and concerned with national
income, the price level, the balance of payments, and so on.
Clearly, a deviation between actual developments and the desired
ones on any of these aspects can be regarded as having caused
disutility to this group.

The question posed by the model in its simplest form is,
therefore, Given the fact that the country's oil revenues are
finite, can this wealth be transformed so that, as it is depleted,
it is replaced by an alternative source of revenue? More specif-

ically, the objective function is formally stated as, What is the maximum stock of domestic capital that can be accumulated before the depletion of oil, if one takes into account the identifiable macroeconomic and political constraints on the conversion of oil wealth into other forms of wealth? This objective function is initially chosen mainly because it portrays the interests and long-term objectives of the Mexican government, and because it is consistent with the country's priorities as outlined in the National Industrial Development Plan.

In this context it is important to note that global profit maximization is probably not the real objective of the Mexican government (as is mistakenly assumed by some economists when trying to explain the behavior and the economic goals of the country's decision makers). Indeed, the government's foremost concern appears to be in designing an investment strategy that will have the ability to generate real economic development in the domestic nonoil sectors as the nation's stock of oil is exhausted.

While there is no particular problem conceptualizing the optimization function, there remain some ambiguities in putting into operation a meaningful function.[10]

Several approaches can be used to gain insights as to what Mexico's optimal oil production rate should be. In fact, the economic literature on the subject of optimal depletion of exhaustible resources has burgeoned in recent years. What is fascinating about this field is the intellectual heterogeneity of the problems that the subject raises. A wide range of alternative objectives in the choice of an optimal depletion rate have been considered by those working in the field. G. Heal, for instance, has been concerned with the problem of exhaustion of natural resources in general. In one of his earlier papers, he considered the question, Is there any sense in which the stock of exhaustible resources are being depleted too fast?[11] His work with P. Dasgupta emphasizes the role of uncertainty due to the length of the time horizon involved.[12] By adopting a utilitarian approach, it is possible to extend this analysis to the specification of the characteristics of an optimal depletion policy. Given a production function of the economy, the elasticity of substitution between reproducible capital and exhaustible resources becomes the element in the determination of an optimal plan.

In contrast, it is possible to approach the problem of optimal consumption of exhaustible resources incorporating market behavior aspects. Here the analysis usually attempts to determine whether market depletion rates are acceptable. One school of thought argues that in a perfectly competitive commodity and capital market, the optimal price of the resources rises with the rate of interest. If true, it would follow that free market behavior under certain conditions would allocate a fixed supply strictly depletable resource in an intertemporally efficient manner.[13]

The approaches above have one common feature: they all analyze the problem from the consumer's point of view, thus focusing largely on the demand for nonreplenishable resources. Perhaps a more productive approach for gaining insights into Mexico's optimal strategy with regard to rates of crude oil production would be one that gave prominence to the problem of achieving an equitable balance between present and future generations. Solow,[14] for example, has considered a reformulation of the objective more in the spirit of certain ideas of fairness advanced primarily by J. Rawls.[15] The basic idea underlying this approach is that consumption per head should be the same for all generations. In operational terms, a straightforward application of the Max-Min principle to the intergenerational problems of capital accumulation indicates that, if there is a finite pool of exhaustible resources involved, "earlier generations are entitled to draw down the pool so long as they add to the stock of reproducible capital."[16]

Solow's work comes closest to the problems dealt with in the forecasts undertaken here, at least as far as equity between generations and optimal planning are concerned. However, there is a key point on which we diverge. This involves the treatment of the rate of extraction of the resources. Solow regards it as endogenous, but it would seem to be more accurate to treat it as exogenous in the Mexican context. Endogeneity of the rate of depletion would imply that production rates were determined within the system. In other words, while the form and size of the optimal plan are determined by the rate of extraction, the latter in turn is determined according to the needs of the optimal plan and the level of investment. The interaction of the two would simultaneously determine both variables: the rate of extraction and the level of investment.

As Williams has observed:

In both policy making and politics, the new oil has catalyzed drawn out and intense disputes characterized by ongoing agony, much backing and filling, frequent explosions of vituperative recrimination and even occasional examples of the decisionmakers acknowledging and responding to the charges of their opponents.

At the level of policymaking, the decision-makers' stance on production illustrates the agony of the process. From the outset it has been clouded by a vacillation and indecision, shifting from posture to posture. Official policy has reflected the vicissitudes of the moment, the novelty of the situation and the interplay of forces on both the international and domestic scene. Early on, the conservationists appeared to dominate official rhetoric; in midstream the expansionist forces gained the upper hand and by 1978 the government's policy had once again assumed a more cautious tone with the promulgation of a "production platform"; and in 1980 the expansionists won a minor victory when the platform was raised from 2.25 million barrels per day to 2.7 million b/d.[17]

Still, the matter was far from settled in 1980. The official definition of the original production platform by no means implied an unalterable decision to shut off further increases in hydrocarbon production and exportation. Rather, it conferred a reflective policy review, which might preclude further growth in the industry, but might also result in a decision to push ahead with increasing production and exportation. The Director General of Petroleos Mexicanos (PEMEX) set out the policy in his 1978 annual report:

After the production platform of 1980 is attained Mexico can decide if the same pace of production is to continue or if it is convenient to increase or reduce it with the tremendous advantage of having by then enough income and ease to project the execution of a master development plan.[18]

It is certainly reasonable to expect ongoing controversy as the influence of the two sides waxes and wanes. The policy will undoubtedly continue to reverberate with the clash of roles pro and con as they press their respective positions.

An examination of the Mexican budgetary and planning process reveals that in all likelihood there is no way one could make a convincing argument that the decision to produce oil for export at any given time was determined by internal economic planning. Rather, production rates are very much if not exclusively determined by political considerations.

Moreover, endogeneity of the depletion rate is meaningful only when the country has the ability to determine its oil receipts

over a certain length of time and can vary them at will to suit
its requirements. Determination of the time path of its oil revenue
in turn calls for the country's ability to decide on its price of
oil in each time period over the planning horizon. This is not
the case as far as Mexico is concerned. The price of Mexican
oil is for all practical purposes kept in line with OPEC prices,
while bargaining with the United States has set the natural gas
price.

Even if OPEC were to break up, Mexico would not gain
true autonomy over oil pricing, but would instead have to price
with due regard to whatever the competitive world market price
was at the time.

In light of the above arguments, it seems best to view both
oil revenue and production rates as exogenous, recognizing
that significant deviations of anticipated government expenditures
from anticipated revenues would create pressures over time for
an adjustment in the depletion rate.

CONCLUSIONS

From a policy perspective, the most meaningful forecasts
of the Mexican economy are those that are able to address the
issue of the optimal expenditure of revenue from oil (or out of
total revenue, for that matter).

The literature cited above on the question of optimal rate
of depletion gives upon a second reading surprisingly few insights
into this most important issue. While a variety of models have
been developed concerning the price sequence that such paths
generate, the question of optimal choice of investment of oil
revenues has been rather neglected. With such vast amounts
of funds accruing to the Mexican government and the pressing
development needs of the country, the problem merits serious
investigation.

With this objective in mind, an intertemporal planning model
is formulated and forecasts made in the next chapter using optimal control theory. The advantage of this particular method
lies in the fact that it is capable of guiding the economy toward
a given target. After analytical solutions have been reached,
the model is subsequently tested by means of computing algorithm
known as the method of feasible directions.

This is a technique first developed in the control engineering field. It is used in the Mexican context to arrive at numerical solutions identifying the country's optimal growth path over
time; i.e., the routine is used to estimate the optimal trajectory

of investment if oil resources are to be transformed into an
alternative source of wealth over a specified time horizon.
Operationally, this involves maximizing the country's terminal
stock of capital at the end of each forecasting period, subject
to certain constraints with regard to inflation and private consumption. Although this choice is very aggregated, it highlights
the special nature of the current economic state of Mexican
economic affairs—underdeveloped yet financially rich, faced
with the problem of absorption capacity while compelled to create
large numbers of new viable jobs for a rapidly expanding population.

NOTES

1. Cf. Alan Riding, "Oil Glut Threatens Mexico's Economy,
New York Times, July 6, 1981; William Chislett, "Mexico Faces
Crucial Economic Decisions," Financial Times, December 10,
1981, "Lopez Portillo Plays for High Economic Stakes," Financial
Times, February 23, 1982, and "U.S.-Mexico Friendship Dogged
by Growing Policy Differences," Financial Times, February 12,
1982; Alan Riding, "Mexico's Mood is Pessimistic," San Francisco
Chronicle, February 15, 1982, and "Mexico's Road to Trouble
Is Coated with Oil," New York Times, February 21, 1982.
2. Cf. A. Ando and C. Polash, "Some Stabilization Prob-
lems of 1971-1975 with an Application of Optimum Control Algo-
rithms," American Economic Review, May 1976; A. H. Gelb,
"Optimal Control and Stabilization Policy: An Application to the
Coffee Economy," Review of Economic Studies no. 1, 1977;
J. E. Stiglitz, "Growth with Exhaustible Natural Resources:
Efficient and Optimal Growth Paths," Review of Economic Studies,
October 1974; and F. Vakil, Estimating Iran's Financial Surplus
1352-1371 (Tehran: Economic Research Institute, 1975).
3. These assumptions are summarized in H. Kitamura,
"Trade and Capital Needs of Developing Countries and Foreign
Assistance," Weltwirtschaftliches Archiv, 1966, pp. 303-24.
4. J. Vanek, Estimating Foreign Resource Needs for
Economic Development (New York: McGraw-Hill, 1967), Chap. 3.
5. Gregory C. Chow, "Control Methods for Macroeconomic
Policy Analysis," American Economic Review, May 1976, p. 341.
6. H. A. Simon, "Dynamic Programming Under Uncertainty
with a Quadratic Criterion," Econometrica, January 1956, pp.
74-81.
7. H. Theil, "A Note on Certainty Equivalence in Dynamic
Planning," Econometrica, April 1957, pp. 346-49.

8. A complete description is given in Gregory C. Chow, Analysis and Control of Dynamic Economic Systems (New York: McGraw Hill, 1975).

9. Cf. C. H. Wong and O. Pettersen, "Financial Programming in the Framework of Optimal Control," Weltwirtschaftliches Archiv no. 1, 1979, pp. 20-37.

10. A discussion of this problem for the U.S. is given in L. R. Klein, "Political Aspects of Economic Control," in Theory of Economic Efficiency: Essays in Honor of Abba Lerner, ed. H. Greenfield, et al. (Cambridge, Mass.: MIT Press, 1979), pp. 76-91.

11. G. M. Heal, "The Depletion of Exhaustible Resources: Some Theoretical Issues," in Issues in Contemporary Economics, ed. M. Parkin and R. Nobay (Manchester: Manchester University Press, 1974), p. 211.

12. P. Dasgupta and G. M. Heal, "The Optimal Depletion of Exhaustible Resources," Review of Economic Studies, October 1974, pp. 1-29.

13. M. C. Weinstein and R. J. Zeckhauser, "The Optimum Consumption of Depletable Natural Resources," Quarterly Journal of Economics, August 1975, pp. 371-92.

14. R. M. Solow, "Intergenerational Equity and Exhaustible Resources," Review of Economic Studies, October 1974, pp. 29-47.

15. J. Rawls, A Theory of Social Justice (Cambridge, Mass.: Harvard University Press, 1971).

16. Solow, "Intergenerational Equity," p. 41.

17. Edward Williams, "Petroleum and Political Change," in Mexico's Political Economy, ed. Jorge Dominquez (Beverly Hills, Calif.: Sage Publications, 1982), p. 33.

18. Petroleos Mexicanos, Report Delivered by the Director General, 1978 (Mexico, D.F., 1978), p. 5.

6

OPTIMAL GROWTH PATHS TO 1995: ANALYSIS OF THE NATIONAL INDUSTRIAL DEVELOPMENT PLAN TARGETS

INTRODUCTION

President Lopez Portillo has described Mexico's oil based industrialization strategy as representing the country's first genuine opportunity to establish an independent model of economic development. The publication of the National Industrial Development Plan in March 1979 clarified the nature of this model; the debate around the plan since then has thrown light on the fundamental policy choices that have been made by the government and that the authorities feel will determine the socioeconomic course of Mexico until the end of the century.[1]

Previous chapters have shown how the plan represents the determination of the Mexican government to overcome the structural problems of the economy by applying its oil resources to public and private investment in heavy industry and manufacturing exports. Incentives are geared to reducing regional imbalances, providing employment (through the decentralization of plants and the support of small business), and expanding capacity. The participation of foreign firms is encouraged in branches involved in technology transfers and exports.

The initial reaction to the industrial plan was generally good in business circles because it helped to reduce uncertainty about the future, but the industrial strategy has been questioned by different groups because of the overall ideological orientation and role of the government in the economy espoused by each. A more fundamental criticism of the plan can be raised, however, from a purely technical point of view. As the following sections demonstrate, the plan is weak in its identification of several key

economic relationships, makes unrealistic assumptions about
certain exogenous factors, and could be considerably improved
upon at little cost or loss of goal attainment simply through a
rescheduling of several of its key expenditure streams.[2]

This argument has been borne out by the recent (February
1982) devaluation, mounting government deficits, and the austerity program introduced by the government. The origins of these
problems are identified in the sections that follow, together with
a revised forecast to 1995, which indicates that despite the
economy's current plight many of the plan's goals are still potentially achievable.

The application of optimal control to the problem of planning
a development strategy through the 1980s to 1995 is presented
below. The approach is straightforward. On the basis of the
analysis in previous chapters, the economic system is represented
by an econometric model—consisting of a set of difference equations. There are constraints; for example, inflation is not
allowed to deviate significantly from the anticipated United
States rate of price increase. The boundary conditions are
the initial values of the variables, while the real capital stock
is maximized for 1995 in the objective function.

Since the model is intended to be the basis for comparison
with the forecasts in the National Industrial Development Plan,
a critique of that plan is given in the sections below.

ANALYSIS OF THE NATIONAL INDUSTRIAL
DEVELOPMENT PLAN'S MACRO FORECASTS

Previous chapters have examined the National Industrial
Development Plan in general terms. In terms of specific forecasts, the average annual rate of growth (Table 6.1) in GDP
for the first years of the Lopez Portillo administration (1977-79)
was forecast by the plan to be 7.5 percent, and, having reached
10.6 percent in 1982, it was expected to stay at about that level
until 1990 and into the 1990s. The plan implies, therefore, a
gradual acceleration and then leveling off in the country's
growth profile. The higher rate of growth from the mid-1980s
on is possible notwithstanding the precipitous decline forecast
by the plan in the growth of the petroleum and the petrochemical
group in 1982, after which real income growth will remain relatively constant until 1990, with the production of crude oil
remaining at a platform of 2.25 million bpd (or possibly slightly
higher).

TABLE 6.1

Growth of Real[a] GDP: Plan and Base Projections 1970-90

				Annual Rates of Growth Percent				
	1975/1970[b]	1978	1979	1980	1981	1982	1985/1982[b]	1990/1985[b]
GDP Total								
Plan	5.4	6.5	7.1	8.2	9.5	10.5	10.2	6.4
Base	5.4	6.5	7.1	6.8	6.4	6.9	6.4	6.4
Sectors								
Primary								
Plan	1.1	0.8	2.5	2.7	2.9	3.5	3.5	2.9
Base	1.1	0.8	2.5	1.7	1.5	1.9	1.8	1.5
Mining								
Plan	3.3	-2.4	6.1	9.1	8.6	10.5	8.3	7.7
Base	3.3	-2.4	6.1	9.1	8.6	8.7	6.5	5.6
Petroleum and petrochemicals								
Plan	6.3	36.5	38.3[c]	24.6	22.0	8.9	6.7	8.3
Base	6.3	36.5	38.4	22.6	19.2	5.8	3.3	3.9
Manufactures								
Plan	5.1	6.4	6.6	8.2	9.7	12.4	12.1	10.8
Base	5.1	6.4	6.6	6.4	5.6	7.4	7.0	6.5

(continued)

167

Table 6.1 (continued)

	1975/1970[b]	1978	1979	1980	1981	1982	1985/1982[b]	1990/1985[b]
				Annual Rates of Growth Percent				
Construction								
Plan	9.4	14.4	6.6[c]	10.4	11.4	13.4	13.2	14.8
Base	9.4	14.4	6.5	8.6	6.8	9.7	10.4	9.5
Electricity								
Plan	5.9	9.0	9.0[c]	11.1	12.5	14.7	14.5	14.0
Base	5.9	9.0	10.0	9.7	9.1	10.6	10.5	10.3
Commerce and services								
Plan	5.9	4.6	5.4	6.8	8.4	10.6	10.1	10.5
Base	5.9	4.6	5.4	5.7	5.6	6.9	6.4	6.6

[a]Expressed in 1975 prices.
[b]Annual average.
[c]The difference between Plan and Base probably reflects an error in one of the tables.
Source: National Industrial Development Plan.

168

INVESTMENT REQUIREMENTS

High rates of investment are clearly the link to increases in real GDP counted on by the plan. Total investment in 1975 pesos comes to 243 billion in 1978, 291 billion in 1980, 357 billion in 1982, 510 billion in 1985, and finally 634 billion in 1990, for a total increase of 161 percent. The average annual increase in 1978-80 is 9.9 percent, and in 1980-82 it is 11.3 percent. In the next three years (1982-85) it is 14.3 percent, while in 1985-90 it averages 4.5 percent. From 1978 to 1990, therefore, the average annual rate of real investment is 8.3 percent. How growth in GDP is to be sustained while the rate of increase in real investment falls is not spelled out by the plan. Nor is it clear how the overall rates of GDP can be achieved with the rates of investment listed above.

It should be noted that during the 1971-79 period, Mexican GDP increased at 5.4 percent per annum on average in real terms while fixed investment expanded at 7.0 percent per annum. During the 1960s, growth was higher but the rate of expansion of fixed investment moved ahead proportionately more rapidly. In the peak growth years of 1963, 1964, 1972, 1978, and 1979, the GDP growth exceeded 7 percent. The rate of growth in fixed investment however expanded more rapidly at between 15 and 20 percent during these years.

The same reservations apply to the initial period; i.e., the growth rates averaging 10.3 percent per annum anticipated by the mid-1980s were expected to be produced as a result of average real increases in fixed capital formation of as little as 12.2 percent.

To judge from historical experiences in Mexico and in other countries, however, it would appear that an acceleration in the annual rate of increase of fixed investment to 12.2 percent would merely raise growth onto a plateau of 6.5 to 7.5 percent. By contrast, moving GDP growth ahead to a steady rate of 10 percent per annum or more would appear to require a sustained rate of increase in fixed investment volume in excess of 20 percent per annum.

The most rapid increase in federal government investment is from 1980 to 1982 (Table 6.2), increasing by 10, 15, and 20 percent per annum. While private investment increases more moderately at 9, 10.4, and 14.0 percent, expansion at this pace is still high by past trends. During this period, private investment forecast by the plan is proportionately further above the base forecast than is the case with federal government investment. Beginning in 1982 and through 1990 the government's

TABLE 6.2

Real Gross Fixed Capital Investment: Plan and Base, 1978-82

	Percentage Annual Rates of Increase—1975 Prices						
	1978	1979	1980	1981	1982	1985/80[a]	1990/85[a]
(1) Federal Government							
Plan	8.0	9.1	10.0	15.0	20.0	20.4	25.6
Base	8.0	9.1	9.5	14.0	17.0	14.6	15.5
(2) Public Enterprises							
Plan	36.8	10.5	15.3	1.6	6.2	4.8	4.8
Base	36.8	10.5	15.3	1.6	6.2	4.8	4.8
(3) Private Enterprises							
Plan	11.9	6.5	9.0	10.4	14.0	12.6	8.9
Base	11.9	6.5	7.7	6.6	9.6	9.3	7.4

Percentage Average Annual Rates of Increase 1970-90

	1975/70	1980/75	1982/77	1985/80	1990/85	1990/75
(1) Federal Government						
Plan	14.2	3.8	12.3	20.4	25.6	16.2
Base	14.2	3.7	11.5	14.6	15.5	11.1
(2) Public Enterprises						
Plan	19.6	8.4	13.5	4.8	4.8	6.0
Base	19.6	8.4	13.5	4.8	4.8	6.0
(3) Private Enterprises						
Plan	7.2	4.0	10.3	12.6	8.9	8.4
Base	7.2	3.8	8.4	9.3	7.4	6.5

[a]Annual average.
Source: National Industrial Development Plan.

deviation from the base path is greater, with the differential over the base rising in the federal government investment from 17.6 percent to 65.2 percent, while falling in the private sector from 45.8 percent to 20.3 percent.

It can be seen from the five-year averages that investment by the federal government increases continually to 1990, while in the private sector it declines from the annual peak of 14.0 percent in 1982 and from the quinquennial average peak of 12.6 percent in 1980-85 to an annual average of 8.9 percent over the last five years of the plan.

The rate of increase in investment by the public enterprises reaches a peak of 15.3 percent in 1980 when production of PEMEX reaches its "platform" of 2.25 million barrels a day. This decline is very steep indeed in 1981 (to 1.6 percent from 15.3 percent in 1980), and thereafter the next two five-year periods show an average rate of growth less than one-fourth that by the federal government and about one-half that by the private sector.

As a result of these trends, public sector investment increases from 37.0 percent of total investment in 1975 to 46.6 percent in 1990 (Table 6.3), while private sector investment declines from 63.0 percent of total investment in 1975 to 45.6 percent in 1990.

FINANCING THE PLAN

In terms of the financing of investment, the plan forecasts that the proportion contributed by domestic savings grows steadily until 1981 when it is 101 percent, because foreign savings make a negative contribution indicating that foreign debt is being repaid. Thereafter domestic savings decline and foreign savings increase until they reach 5.0 percent of the total in 1990 (Table 6.3). These projections indicate that policy makers never really take seriously the popularly expressed view that increased petroleum resources will make Mexico a capital exporting country in the foreseeable future.

Unfortunately, fiscal reform in Mexico has been postponed, if not abandoned, in favor of selected improvements in the tax rate structure and in the administration, budgeting, and tax collecting procedures, including the coordination of federal, state, and local systems.[3] In large part petroleum revenues have stifled any sense of urgency in developing a modern, efficient tax system. One reform has recently been introduced, however.

TABLE 6.3

Public and Private Shares in Fixed Capital Investment 1975-90

	1975	1978	1979	1980	1981	1982	1985	1990
Total Fixed Investment (billions of 1975 pesos)	227	243	263	291	316	357	510	634
Percentage Shares in Total								
Public investment	37.0	38.3	39.1	40.4	39.2	37.8	38.0	46.6
Social investment	12.7	11.8	12.0	11.6	12.8	13.6	17.7	31.8
Productive activities	24.2	26.5	27.1	28.8	26.4	24.2	20.3	14.8
PEMEX and CFE	14.9	20.1	19.7	22.7	20.6	19.0	15.8	11.6
Other	9.3	6.4	7.4	6.1	5.9	5.2	4.5	3.3
Private investment	63.0	61.7	60.9	58.2	56.5	54.9	48.4	45.6
Housing	25.3	30.8	30.6	28.7	27.0	24.2	20.0	15.3
Productive activities	37.7	30.8	30.3	29.5	29.5	30.6	31.7	30.3
Additional required by Plan	0.0	0.0	0.0	1.3	4.3	7.4	8.4	7.8
Shares in Productive Investment	100	100	100	100	100	100	100	100
Public sector	39.1	46.2	47.2	48.3	43.9	38.9	32.5	27.9
Private sector	60.9	53.8	52.8	49.5	48.9	49.3	53.9	57.4
Additional required by Plan	0.0	0.0	0.0	2.2	7.2	11.8	13.6	14.7
Total Savings	100	100	100	100	100	100	100	100
Domestic	79.3	86.2	92.7	97.4	101.1	100.0	96.0	95.0
Foreign	20.7	13.8	7.3	2.6	-1.1	0.0	4.0	5.0

Source: National Industrial Development Plan.

As of January 1, 1980, Mexico substituted a value-added tax (VAT) for its old tax on gross business receipts (impuesto sobre ingressos mercantiles) and for seventeen other indirect taxes on specific commodities and services.

The VAT is an improvement of sorts since it avoids the cascade effect of multiple taxing that is characteristic of the gross receipts tax, and the VAT may be rebated to exporters even under the rules of GATT. But the value-added tax has created considerable confusion among consumers and small businessmen in Mexico, since computation of taxable value added requires considerably more sophisticated bookkeeping than did the simpler flat rate tax on gross sales receipts. Moreover, VAT hurts in the same way that the gross receipts tax hurts: it must be paid by every business firm whether it sustains profit or loss. Small businesses everywhere have opposed the VAT because it is not based on the ability to pay; they much prefer a tax on business profits. The VAT hurts most—as did the gross receipts tax—those very sectors of the economy that the Mexican government says it wants to help: small, labor intensive firms in industry, construction, and the service trades. The VAT, whatever its name, is still a sales tax with a regressive impact. Large oligopoly firms can shift it forward to consumers in the form of higher prices; all firms will try to shift it backward to labor in lower wages; small competitive firms may not be able to shift it at all. The VAT in Mexico states a uniform rate of 10 percent (except for the border areas and free zones where a preferential 6 percent will prevail), and it is estimated not to collect any larger share of the GDP than the taxes it replaces. But neither does it ameliorate any of the adverse effects of those indirect taxes on Mexicans of low incomes.[4]

In short, despite the Mexican government's commitment to capital formation as the major source of national income growth no significant improvements were or have been made in the methods of financing public expenditure (other than of course indirectly through investment in the oil sector). Given that current expenditures have historically outrun revenues, there is little reason to believe this pattern will be broken by the plan. Furthermore, given its emphasis on development and employment, the government has little choice but to maintain aggregate demand with the sharp increases in the deficits likely at times resulting in rapid expansion in the money supply and inflationary pressures. The social costs of slower growth or of recession would include an increase in political unrest, more violence, increased illegal migration to the United States, and more land invasions by campesinos without employment alternatives.

Monetary policy measures in Mexico have largely reflected the needs for financing the federal deficit. The Mexican authorities have allowed rapid growth in the money supply in all but a few of the recent years—perhaps by as much as 37 percent in 1979. Mexican money markets have grown more integrated with world money markets; the authorities have recently created a treasury certificate that can be used in open market operations, and they will move slowly toward the use of general quantitative credit controls, gradually giving up the elaborate quantitative system of direct credit and managed interest rates that characterize Mexico's monetary policy. Growing exports of petroleum could create future inflationary pressures as foreign exchange is sold for pesos to commercial banks and to the central bank of Mexico.[5]

EXTERNAL BALANCE

The external accounts over the plan period should reflect the changes anticipated in the domestic economy. In this regard it is interesting to note that, in spite of the fact that the petroleum industry and the surplus that it is yielding are the key elements of the plan, the production and exportation of petroleum and petrochemicals are identical in the base and the plan projections. Enormous differences do exist, however, between the plan and base in the various items that make up the balance of payments.

The greatest difference between plan and base (the plan differential) exists in the current account balance, which shows a deficit in 1990 of -$26.4 billion in the plan and a surplus of $4.6 billion in the base. The plan differential is also large in 1982, when both the plan and the base show a surplus, although under the plan it is about to turn into a deficit[6] (Table 6.4).

The differential in factor payments is zero or small through 1982, but by 1990 it is very large. Total receipts from capital and labor are identical in the base and in the plan. The chief items in receipts are interest and remittances, and in the 12 years to 1990 the former increases more than five times while the latter quadruples. The plan differential of 230 percent must obviously be entirely due to payments abroad. And within payments abroad, the differential is caused entirely by payments of interest on public debt. In fact these interest payments are ten times the amount forecast for the base while, for the same period, foreign direct investment is forecast as identical in the plan and the base.

The large plan differential in the importation of goods reflects the intention to borrow more abroad. Presumably, the

TABLE 6.4

External Accounts: Deficits (-) and Surpluses (+) 1978-90
(billions of dollars, current prices)

		1978	1979	1980	1981	1982	1985	1990
1. Current Account[a]	Plan	-2.54	-1.65	-0.80	0.48	0.03	-5.31	-26.39
	Base	-2.54	-1.66	-0.48	1.92	3.42	3.24	4.62
2. Factor Payments (8-11)	Plan	-2.14	-2.43	-2.48	-2.33	-2.20	-2.60	-8.08
	Base	-2.14	-2.43	-2.47	-2.25	-1.97	-1.35	-0.44
3. Goods & Services	Plan	-0.40	0.78	1.68	2.81	2.23	-2.71	-18.3
	Base	-0.40	0.77	1.99	4.17	5.38	4.59	6.34
4. Trade balance (5-6)	Plan	2.02	-1.38	-1.23	-1.14	-3.08	-12.75	-22.45
	Base	2.02	-1.39	-0.87	0.38	0.42	-0.88	6.02
5. Exports of Goods	Plan	5.21	7.43	9.68	12.32	14.21	19.43	37.60
	Base	5.21	7.43	9.56	12.04	13.63	17.15	26.94
6. Imports of Goods	Plan	7.23	8.81	10.91	13.46	17.29	32.18	60.05
	Base	7.23	8.82	10.43	11.66	13.2	18.03	20.92
7. Exports of Processing Services[b]	Plan	0.63	0.69	0.76	0.81	0.88	1.03	1.38
	Base	0.63	0.69	0.76	0.81	0.88	1.07	1.53

Factor Payments

8. Total Receipts[c]		0.66	0.74	0.85	0.95	1.08	1.54	2.88
i) Emigrant remittances		0.08	0.09	0.10	0.11	0.13	0.18	0.36
ii) Interest		0.25	0.29	0.33	0.38	0.44	0.67	1.35
9. Total Payments Abroad	Plan	2.80	3.17	3.33	3.28	4.14	7.57	10.95
	Base	2.80	3.17	3.31	3.21	3.04	2.90	3.32
i) Interest on Public Debt	Plan	2.07	2.37	2.44	2.30	2.18	2.66	8.49
	Base	2.07	2.37	2.42	2.22	1.94	1.41	0.86
ii) Foreign Direct Investment	(d)	0.57	0.62	0.69	0.77	0.86	1.16	1.91

aDefined as balance of exports and imports of goods and services plus balance on payments to factors of production (capital and labor).

bThe maquiladoras. The values are given in the Plan Nacional in 1975 pesos, so the exchange rate of 12.50 to the dollar was used in converting.

cNo difference between the plan and the base projections.

Source: National Industrial Development Plan.

foreign borrowing base increased identically in the two projections, insofar as it depends on the oil surplus. It makes little sense, therefore, to forecast such different volumes of borrowing in the base and plan forecasts. The plausibility of these forecasts is all the less because past policy, on which the base projection is founded, is accused of having borrowed abroad too much. It is, therefore, somewhat inconsistent to project that it will borrow too little in the plan period.

In terms of exports of hydrocarbons (Table 6.5), the production and export of crude petroleum and derived products is projected identically for the base and the plan. This is another apparent inconsistency, i.e., that the exports of petrochemicals will be identical in view of the large plan differentials in other important respects. For example, the plan differential for total goods exported is 38.7 percent in 1990. It is negligible until 1982, and then it becomes only 2.6 percent. In the plan, petroleum and petrochemicals exports will have risen to 61.0 percent of total exports of goods by 1982 (from 34.4 percent in 1978), after which they will fall to nearly 40 percent in 1990. In contrast, they will fall to only 51.2 percent of the total in the base forecast. This difference between the base and the plan is, of course, entirely the result of the much greater increase of non-petroleum exports under the plan. It would seem, however, that exports of this magnitude will ultimately depend on American policy toward Mexican imports, and it is by no means clear, given the growing sentiment of protectionism in the United States, that accommodations anywhere near these levels will be made.

ROLE OF THE GOVERNMENT

As noted earlier, the government is to play a more active part in directing the economy.[7] This is readily apparent by comparison of the levels of public sector expenditures in the plan and base forecasts. Available resources consist of gross domestic product plus imports. Resources are used by intermediate demand, which consists of industrial inputs, private consumption of final products, government consumption, fixed capital investment, allocations to inventories, and exports.

Clearly, an effort is being made at least up to 1982 to increase investment rather than consumption (Table 6.6). The share of intermediate demand (industrial inputs) diminished, but it was accompanied by the biggest proportional change (66.7 percent) in the share of addition to inventories. Presumably, the plan anticipates industry will be stocking up in view

TABLE 6.5

Exports of Petroleum and Petrochemicals and of Total Goods 1978-90 (billions of 1975 dollars)[a]

		1978	1979	1980	1981	1982	1985	1990
1. Petroleum and petro-chemicals[b]		1.54	2.83	3.95	5.13	5.56	5.56	5.56
2. Total Exports of Goods	Plan	4.48	5.90	7.11	8.43	9.12	10.38	15.06
	Base	4.48	5.90	7.07	8.33	8.89	9.40	10.86
3. Percentage (1)/(2)	Plan	34.4	48.0	55.6	62.9	61.0	53.6	36.9
	Base	34.4	48.0	55.9	61.6	62.5	59.1	51.2

[a]In the Plan Nacional the values were expressed in 1975 pesos, when the exchange rate was 12.50 pesos to the dollar, and this rate is used here in converting to dollars.
[b]Exports are identical in the base and the plan projections.
Source: National Industrial Development Plan.

179

TABLE 6.6

Changing Shares in the Use of National Resources 1975-90

	Percentages			Percentage Change in Shares	
	1975	1982	1990	1982/75	1990/82
Intermediate demand	34.1	33.4	35.6	-2.1	6.6
Private consumption	44.1	40.0	39.1	-9.3	-2.2
Government consumption	1.1	1.1	1.3	0.0	18.2
Gross fixed capital investment	14.7	16.4	19.1	11.6	16.5
Addition to inventories	0.9	1.5	1.6	66.7	6.7
Exports	4.8	7.6	5.2	58.3	-31.6

Source: Compiled by the author, based on National Industrial Development Plan.

of the high rate of fixed investment to be achieved during the 1982-90 period (increasing its share to 16.5 percent as compared with 11.6 percent in 1978-82). This is the only category that declines continuously (from 44.1 percent of resources in 1975 to 39.1 percent in 1990). The share of government consumption is to be constant until 1982, but then is forecast to increase by a larger percentage than any other category over the 1982-90 period. Then the share of exports is forecast to decline heavily after 1982 because exports of petroleum products and petrochemicals are held at their platform rates.

OIL PRODUCTION—EXPORTS

Mexico's oil industry had begun to show signs of slowing down in the 1960s (Table 6.7). In mid-1973 a group of international petroleum experts estimated that Mexican imports of petroleum products would have to rise from 100,000 bpd to 4.5 million bpd by the end of the century. Assuming that the price of crude would triple to $9 a barrel (a pre-1973 estimate), the cost of imports would be about $15 billion a year. The dramatic nature of the improvement resulting from the new finds is indi-

TABLE 6.7

Growth of the Petroleum Industry by Decades 1938-78

	Total Percentage Increase in the Period				Annual Amounts	
	1938 to 1948	1948 to 1958	1958 to 1968	1968 to 1978	1938	1978
Total exploration wells (number)	78	742	1,224	1,218	5	83
Productive (percent of total)	25.3	31.4	24.3	25.5	3	30
Total development wells	312	2,444	4,665	3,459	12	223
Productive (percent of total)	67.9	74.8	79.6	79.6	8	173
Total proven reserves	10.2	197.7	35.9	626.7	1.2[a]	40.2[a]
Crude oil and condensates	59.6	156.3	26.1	797.0	0.8	28.4
Natural gas	-9.2	302.6	51.7	398.6	0.4	11.8
Production volume						
Crude oil	54.0	68.4	59.5	202.4	38.8[b]	485.3[b]
Natural gas	47.8	637.9	119.9	61.9	0.7[c]	934.9[c]
Refining						
Volume processed	43.7	88.7	69.0	103.0	35.1[b]	326.6[b]
Employment						
Number	65.3	56.6	48.7	n.a.	17.6	n.a.
Payments	282.1	343.4	208.2	305.8	67.0	14,194[d]
Exports of petroleum & products	45.8	-11.2	38.8	728.9	9.0[b]	133.9[b]
Imports of petroleum & products	178.8	165.5	-8.4	-5.8	1.7[b]	10.6[b]

(continued)

Table 6.7 (continued)

	Total Percentage Increase in the Period				Annual Amounts	
	1938 to 1948	1948 to 1958	1958 to 1968	1968 to 1978	1938	1978
Gross Income	347.9	315.9	121.8	809.0	0.3d	100.3d
From exports (percent of total)	32.3	17.1	5.9	21.7	0.1	41.8
Gross fixed investment	2,052.5	831.8	221.5	1,341.6	0.008d	69.5d
Taxes paid	471.4	132.9	154.6	1,912.4	0.042d	27.2d

aReserves of oil and natural gas (oil equivalent) are expressed in billion barrels.
bProduction, refining, exports and imports of oil are expressed in million barrels.
cProduction of natural gas is expressed in billion cubic meters.
dPayments to employees, gross income, gross fixed investment, and taxes are expressed in billion pesos.

eThe peso-dollar exchange rate was 4.52 pesos from March 18, 1938 to the end of the year, 5.19 in 1939, 5.40 in 1940 through September, 4.85 from October 1940 to June 1948, and then 8.65 until April 1954 when it stayed at 12.50 until September 1976. It has been at about 22.80 since mid-1977.

Note: n.a. = not available.

Source: Nacional Financiera, Statistics on the Mexican Economy, for data to 1975 and PEMEX, Memoria de Labores (annual report) thereafter.

cated by the fact that the National Plan for Industrial Development estimated that exports of petroleum products would be earning $15 billion in foreign exchange by the year 2000.

While the outlook was made even more favorable by the rise in international oil prices after the plan was published, the country's export prospects have been dimmed somewhat by the 1981-82 worldwide oil glut.

The effects of the Reforma discoveries in 1972 were not felt immediately as the production of crude increased in 1973 by only 1.9 percent. But in 1974 crude production increased by nearly 25 percent and, except for a drop in 1976 to 11.2 percent, it increased by over 20 percent in each of the following years through 1978.

The percentage increase in the gross income of PEMEX (Table 6.8) has been greater than that of production because of the international price increases together with a very considerable rise in prices to domestic consumers.

The production of crude in 1979 was expected to increase by nearly 28.0 percent and of gas by 29 percent. Refining, however, was to increase by less than 5 percent over 1978. Exports of crude petroleum alone in 1979 were expected to increase by 83 percent over the 1978 combined total of crude and refined products. The total number of wells planned to be drilled was 409 in 1979, of which 359 were to be onshore and 50 offshore.

As a result, the petroleum sector's contribution to GDP increased 17.5 percent from 1979 to 1980, the second highest annual growth registered by this sector since 1950. Crude oil, gas liquids, and condensate production averaged 2.1 million bpd, an increase of 32 percent over 1979.

In November 1980 Mexico announced a National Energy Plan with goals for 1990 and projections for the year 2000. The goals and priorities established in the plan are: (1) to export petroleum only insofar as the country can productively absorb resources from abroad, (2) to attempt to increase the value-added content of petroleum exports, (3) to use the export of petroleum to diversify Mexico's foreign trading partners, (4) to take advantage of petroleum sales to absorb modern technology, develop more rapidly the production of capital goods, obtain access to new markets abroad for manufactured goods, and obtain better terms of financing, and (5) to cooperate with other countries in the development and supply of petroleum and in the exploitation of local sources of energy.[8] For the decade of the 1980s, the plan proposed an export limit of 1.5 million bpd of petroleum and 300 million cubic feet of gas. In

TABLE 6.8

Annual Growth of PEMEX, 1973-79

	1973	1974	1975	1976	1977	1978	1979[a]
Exploration wells	103	100	87	79	79	83	n.a.
Percentage productive	23.3	20.0	14.9	31.6	38.0	33.7	n.a.
Development wells	319	309	226	257	228	223	n.a.
Percentage productive	78.1	26.6	76.1	77.8	77.2	77.6	n.a.
Petroleum reserves (billion barrels)	5.4	5.8	6.3	11.2	16.0	40.2	n.a.
Oil	3.3	3.5	4.0	n.a.	10.4	28.4	n.a.
Natural gas	2.2	2.2	2.4	n.a.	5.6	11.8	n.a.
Production							
Crude oil (million barrels)	191.5	238.3	294.8	327.3	396.2	485.3	620.0
Natural gas (billion m³)	19.2	21.1	22.3	21.9	21.1	26.5	34.3
Refining							
Volume processed (million barrels)	210.8	240.5	247.6	273.8	308.7	326.6	337.3

184

Employment							
Number (000's)	77.3	81.0	86.8	125.0	137.5[b]	151.3[b]	167.0
Payments (billion pesos)	5.0	6.4	8.3	8.8	11.5	14.2	n.a.
Petroleum and products (million barrels)							
Exports	8.7	6.5	37.0	35.7	75.4	133.9	245.3[c]
Imports	25.4	21.6	18.2	9.3	3.5	10.6	n.a.
Gross income (billion pesos)	18.4	32.4	38.4	45.3	76.3	100.3	162.0
From exports (percent of total)	0.4	1.6	5.3	7.0	23.4	41.8	88.0
Exports (percent of total)	2.4	4.9	13.8	15.4	30.7	41.7	54.9
Gross fixed investment (billion pesos)	7.2	9.7	14.0	23.9	34.9	69.5	73.0
Taxes paid (billion pesos)	2.7	4.3	8.6	7.6	18.9	27.2	48.0

[a]Estimated.
[b]Estimated on the basis of the fact that the increase in number employed from 1976 to 1979 was 34 percent.
[c]Crude only.
Note: n.a. = not available.
Source: Annual Reports of Petróleos Mexicanos (Memoria de Labores); and for estimates 1979, speech of Mr. Jorge Díaz Serrano, March 18, 1979.

185

keeping with a more general goal to diversify foreign trade,
Mexico will try to avoid concentrating more than 50 percent of
hydrocarbon exports to any one country. [9]

FUTURE SUPPLIES OF PETROLEUM PRODUCTS

In October 1977, PEMEX presented its official forecast to
1982 of production of oil and gas, domestic consumption on
availabilities for export of gas, and the total investment that
would be necessary to achieve the predicted production. At
the time it was assumed that the August 1977 agreement with
the private U.S. gas distributors would be soon consummated. [10]
The original estimates (Table 6.9) of gas available for
export have been affected by the decision to convert Mexican
industry to gas. It will take a considerable amount of time,
however, before the conversion will affect domestic consumption
of natural gas (and therefore how big the surplus available for
export will be). Similar uncertainties affect the estimates of
future U.S. demand for foreign gas. The proposed two billion
cubic feet a day of gas through Reynosa would represent only
about 4 percent of current U.S. consumption. Some experts
believe, however, that the existing Mexican reserves of natural
gas would justify the production of as much as 14 billion cubic
feet a day, and that quantity would leave much more for export.
It should be noted that past efforts to forecast hydrocarbor
production have encountered a wide margin of error. For example, estimates of 954,000 bpd for crude production in 1977 (Tabl
6.9) was in fact exceeded by about 137,000 bpd, while that for
1978 was deficient by about 110,000 bpd. The estimate for 1979
was also about 131,500 bpd above the latter estimate of 620 millio
barrels for that year (or 1,700,000 bpd). The 1977 forecast
envisaged that in 1982 production would be 2.7 million bpd
instead of the production platform of 2.25 million bpd, which
was subsequently reached in 1980, two years earlier.
The Industrial Development Plan published its estimates
of the value in constant 1975 pesos during 1978-90 of production
and exports of petroleum products and petrochemicals (Table
6.10). These estimates were based on the assumption that the
price of crude oil would increase by 6.6 percent annually until
1982, and by 5 percent annually thereafter. The annual rates
of increase are greater for the combined item than for crude
above, except in 1978 when the increase for crude alone is 50.4
percent as against 26.3 percent for the combined item. The
actual figure for crude in 1978 was an increase of 22.5 percent—

TABLE 6.9

Estimated Supplies of Crude Oil and Gas 1977-82

	1977	1978	1979	1980	1981	1982
Crude oil (million barrels per day)	0.954	1.435	1.831	2.169	2.466	2.678
Annual increase percent	—	50.4	27.6	18.5	13.7	8.6
Gas (billion cubic feet per day)						
Gross production[a]	2.2	3.4	4.1	4.5	4.8	4.9
Available for consumption[b]	1.74	3.04	3.59	3.95	4.21	4.33
Annual increase percent	—	74.7	20.6	9.8	6.7	2.1
Domestic demand	1.55	1.70	1.85	2.03	2.05	2.14
Annual increase percent	—	9.7	8.8	9.7	1.0	4.4
Available for export	0.19	1.34	1.74	1.92	2.16	2.18
Value (US $ billion)[c]	—	—	1.65	1.82	2.05	2.07

(continued)

187

Table 6.9 (continued)

	1977	1978	1979	1980	1981	1982
Total Investment (billion pesos)		87.1	59.0	49.6	47.0	50.8
Exploration (including estimates)		2.6	2.8	3.6	4.6	5.6
Development		28.0	24.8	25.1	26.2	28.4
Refining		14.7	6.8	6.0	4.8	6.0
Petrochemicals		15.2	12.3	5.9	3.4	3.2
Transport		24.9	11.3	8.0	7.0	6.4
Social & Administration		1.6	0.87	0.94	0.99	1.05

aThe more conservative of two estimates.

bAfter deducting for gas flared, contraction (removal of liquids) and injection in fields.

cAt $2.60 per 1,000 c.f. Since mid-1978 the exchange rate has been at or near 22.80 pesos to 1 dollar. No value was put on the exports of gas by Mr. Díaz Serrano.

Source: Statement to the Mexican Congress by Jorge Díaz Serrano, Director General of PEMEX, October 1977 (constructed from tables at pages 2-23 for total investment figures, and at pages 3-34 and 35).

TABLE 6.10

Predicted Gross Production and Exports of Petroleum and Derivatives and Petrochemicals 1978-90 (billions of constant pesos—1975 prices)

	1978	1979	1980	1981	1982	1985	1990
Production	67.8	88.0	10.6	127.5	139.3	174.5	271.7
Annual increase %	26.3	29.8	21.1	19.6	9.3	10.4[a]	9.3[b]
Exports	19.6	35.4	49.4	64.1	69.5	69.5	69.5[b]
Annual increase %	102.9	80.8	39.6	29.9	8.3	7.1[a]	0.0
Exports/production (ratio T)	28.9	40.2	46.3	50.3	49.9	39.8	25.6

[a]Annual average 1980 to 1985.
[b]Annual average 1985 to 1990.
Source: National Industrial Development Plan.

189

a considerable difference. In 1978 the increase in exports of
the combined items were anticipated to be at a maximum, declining
very rapidly in 1980, when the production and the export of
crude are to reach their platform. The increase in exports was
forecast to be zero in 1990. At that time the ratio of exports to
production was expected to be at its minimum.

THE PETROLEUM SURPLUS

The exports of crude, refined products, and petrochemicals
constitute the "financial surplus from petroleum." This is defined in the plan "in the broad sense, as the additional spending
power that hydrocarbon exports give the economy." The concept
is said not to be limited to the extra tax revenue the oil surplus
brings to the public treasury, nor the additional receipts that
it brings to the balance of payments. Having larger external
resources at its disposal, the economy can generate more internal
resources. The sum of both is the correct measure to the surplus
This is only partially correct, since both the magnitude and time
profile of the surplus are critically dependent on the manner in
which the surplus is utilized in the government's budget.[12]
In measuring the financial oil surplus, account must be
taken not only of the additional exports and the savings on
imports of petroleum products, but also of the increase in foreign
borrowing power that is associated with the expanded level of
petroleum production. The report does not give specific recog-
nition to this fact. Yet this increase in foreign borrowing potential has allowed the country to draw more extensively on foreign
savings and thus pushed farther into the future the balance
of payments constraint.
The balance of payments projections in the National Industrial Development Plan forecast a modest current account surplus
of $477 million in 1981, dropping to $26 million in 1982, before
going increasingly into deficit, reaching -$5.3 billion in 1985
and -$26.4 billion in 1990. Petroleum exports are estimated to
be $7.4 billion in 1981, $8.4 billion in 1982, and $12.5 billion
in 1990. The petroleum exports thus are looked upon as keeping
the current deficit low enough to be easily financed by foreign
loans. Exports of manufactured products are estimated to grow
from $2.4 billion in 1979 to $3.6 billion in 1982, and to reach
$16.6 billion in 1990. They obviously also play an important
role in keeping the foreign account deficit down to manageable
proportions.

CONCLUSIONS

In summary, it is clear from the preceding commentary on the National Industrial Development Plan and the stated objectives of the Mexican government that the authorities are prepared to use available resources within whatever technical limits may be imposed in order to produce a high level of economic growth while keeping the country's total debt within reasonable limits.

From the National Industrial Development Plan published in 1979, it appeared that average annual growth rates of 6.5 percent could be maintained while raising oil exports to around one million bpd by 1982, compared with 543,000 bpd in 1979. If this were done, it was calculated that Mexico would be in a position to reverse its current account deficit position in the range of $1.6 to $4.2 billion over the period 1975-79, and to surpluses of the same order in the 1980s. Alternatively, with the same level of oil exports, much higher plan trajectories leading to 10.6 percent GDP growth could be maintained, but with deficits reemerging in the period from 1983 onwards, reaching -$5 billion by 1985 and -$26 billion by 1990, both figures being in current prices.

Other constraints were applied in order to produce these figures. It was assumed, for example, that Mexico would be able to expand its external borrowing without extending its overall level of indebtedness, provided that the current account deficit should not, in any year, be more than two percent of GDP, and that, in the medium term, net factor payments abroad, including current transfers, should represent an average of less than 15 percent of the export income from goods and services.

Observing these limits, the country would, in the opinion of the government, without compromising its economic independence, obtain external resources sufficient to generate additional internal resources to help meet its development objectives.

However, the logic behind these calculations is open to question on several grounds. Most importantly, both the investment requirements and inflationary impact of the plan are underestimated. Second, changes in the world oil situation to better (1979) then worse (1981) have altered the expected revenue stream from petroleum exports.

Taking all these points into consideration and using the National Industrial Development Plan as the basis, one can produce a revised and restructured outlook for Mexican development in the 1980s. This is based on the following assumptions:

1. that at least for the first part of the period Mexico will not be in a position to grow rapidly without incurring excessive or worsening current account deficits. To the extent the deficit can be financed, growth will be limited by:

    a. the amount by which oil output can be raised to provide for national consumption and exports

    b. the rate of inflation considered politically tolerable

    c. the extent to which private sector investment responds to the slowdown in the domestic economy in 1982-83

2. that significantly larger increases in investment will be required than foreseen in the plan if growth is to be accelerated

With these considerations in mind, it was possible to complete the design of the optimal control forecasting model.

NOTES

1. E. V. K. Fitzgerald, "Oil and Mexico's Industrial Development Plan," Texas Business Review, May-June 1980, p. 133. See also James Street, "Prospects for Mexico's Industrial Development Plan in the 1980s," Texas Business Review, May-June 1980, pp. 125-32, and Victor Urquidi, "Not by Oil Alone: The Outlook for Mexico," Current History, February 1982, pp. 28-81.

2. One might also argue that the overall orientation of the government has been to emphasize industry to the neglect of agriculture. See Sam Lanfranco, "Mexican Oil, Export-led Development and Agricultural Neglect," Journal of Economic Development, July 1981, pp. 125-51, for an articulation of this view.

3. As documented in John Evans, "The Evolution of the Mexican Tax System During the 1970s," paper presented at the Southern Economic Association Meetings, Washington, D.C., November 5, 1980.

4. Calvin P. Blair, Economic Development Policy in Mexico: A New Penchant for Planning, Technical Papers Series no. 26, (Austin: Office for Public Sector Studies, Institute of Latin American Studies, University of Texas, 1980), p. 15.

5. Ibid., pp. 15-16.

6. These patterns are common to oil exporters. See Alan Gelb, Capital-Importing Oil Exporters: Adjustment Issues and Policy Choices, World Bank Staff Working Paper no. 475 (New York: International Bank for Reconstruction and Development

[World Bank], August 1981) for a comparison of Mexico and other developing country oil exporters.

7. Calvin P. Blair, "Mexico's Economic Development and Relations with the United States," Texas Business Review, March-April 1979, p. 41. See also Stanley Ross, "Key Issues in Mexican-United States Relations," Texas Business Review, March-April 1979, pp. 51-53, and Richard Erband and Stanley Ross, eds., U.S. Policies Toward Mexico (Washington, D.C.: American Enterprise, 1979).

8. Ministry of National Properties and Industrial Development, Mexico Energy Program: Goals to 1990 and Projections to the Year 2000," Comercio Exterior de Mexico, December 1980, pp. 438-39.

9. Salvatore Bizzarro, "Mexico's Oil Boom," Current History, February 1981, p. 50.

10. Cf. George Grayson, The Politics of Mexican Oil (Pittsburgh, Pa.: University of Pittsburgh Press, 1980), Chap. 7 for an excellent account of the U.S.-Mexican gas negotiations.

11. Ibid. See also George Grayson, "Oil and Politics in Mexico," Current History, November 1981, pp. 379-83.

12. An interesting radical critique of the surplus and government corruption is given in Jim Cockcroft and Ross Gandy, "The Mexican Volcano," Monthly Review, May 1981, pp. 32-44.

7

OPTIMAL GROWTH PATHS TO 1995:
NUMERICAL SOLUTIONS

INTRODUCTION

The longer-term strategy of economic development most
likely over the next two decades in light of existing problems
will be a continuation of the patterns established in the National
Industrial Development Plan. In general, previous chapters
have concluded that given the alternatives this is a prudent
strategy. It is also a strategy that has certain technical limitations and is ambiguous concerning the levels certain economic
variables must attain or be constrained within before its eventual
success will be assured. The forecasts presented below are
intended to overcome these difficulties.

FORECASTING PROCEDURES

As noted above, the methodology used here to arrive at a
set of optimal forecasts of the economy and its macroeconomic
components consisted of—

1. estimating the structural equations (Table 5.1) that
depict the basic economic forces at work in the country
2. assigning instruments and objectives
3. specifying growth rates for the exogenous variables—
United States gross domestic product; world price levels, domestic oil production, etc.
4. running the model on a simultaneous equation basis to
account for the interrelationships between the endogenous variables

5. determining areas of performance deficiency—excessive government deficits, inflation, government-private sector imbalances

6. choosing and modifying the major policy variable—government investment

7. altering the level of crude oil production

8. rerunning the model with the new government investments and crude petroleum production levels

9. continuing the process until an equilibrium was reached, whereby the terminal capital stock was maximized and the domestic rate of inflation kept reasonably close to that of the United States (consistent with the assumed fixed U.S. dollar-peso exchange rate).

OBJECTIVES AND INSTRUMENTS

Solis has given the general guidelines followed in designing the objectives and instruments to be used in conjunction with the forecasting model presented in Chapter 5 (Table 5.1).[1] The objectives of Mexican policy in nonpriority order are that economic capacity must grow at a rate sufficient to absorb the growing labor force to improve unemployment; development must reach the most unfavored social groups; high GDP growth must be sustained; and balance of payments stability must be maintained.

Obviously, a high GDP growth rate is a necessary but not a sufficient condition for development. Again, following Solis, "Desarrollo Estabilizator can not be blamed for its growth; it can be blamed for not having grown more than it did. In a developing country growth is clearly a complement to achieving other objectives."[2]

The tools available to achieve these objectives consist of oil exports and crude oil production rates; the exchange rate (and trade policy); domestic savings (with emphasis on public domestic savings); and the structure of public expenditure (i.e., division between government consumption and investment expenditures).[3]

With these objectives and instruments defined, the conceptual policy design and optimum control forecasts attempt—

1. to find a transfer mechanism of petroleum scarcity rents from the oil sector to the rest of the economy (in such a way so as to allocate this income entirely to productive investment and to increase permanent income)

2. to find an optimal rate of extraction and exports consistent with economic restrictions and general economic objectives outlined above

3. to give policy alternatives if the optimal (or sub-optimal, second best) rate is not followed.

From recent Mexican history it is clear that—

1. if the composition of public investment is not strictly and successfully adjusted to development priorities, it will yield even more to political and economic winds. This is expedient only in a political short run. The effective use of a tool presupposes that the government has explicated development priorities and that it has at least a minimum power to affect trend directions.

2. if the public expenditure composition is to be effective in implementing economic policy, it is necessary that—
    a. the objectives are coherent within themselves
    b. the instruments are coherent within themselves
(or at least not operationally exclusive)
    c. a general compatibility exists between instruments and objectives.

In terms of this framework, it is fair to say that the stabilizing development strategy lacked condition a, while the shared development strategy ultimately lacked condition c; i.e., high economic growth with a fixed exchange rate was unattainable. In the first case, the economic objectives related to social aspects were constrained by poorly handled economic instruments, related to technical aspects. While in the latter case, the lack of congruence between instruments and objectives resulted in declining attainment of the government's overall objectives.

For the optimal control forecasts, the initial objective chosen was to maximize the terminal capital stock in each of the five-year intervals chosen: the historical period 1974-79, 1980-85, 1985-90, and 1990-95. The rationale for choosing the capital stock for optimization was discussed in the previous chapter. Suffice it to say that, given the nature of the production function, optimization of the capital stock is synonymous with maximizing the rate of growth of real gross domestic product.

The policy tool used in the optimization procedure was the level of real government investment, with the prime constraint one of restraining the rate of inflation in line with that of the United States.[4]

EXOGENOUS VARIABLES

For purposes of the forecasts, the exogenous variables
were set at their historical rates for 1980 and 1981. The variables and their rates consisted of:

1. the exchange rate (EX), 40 pesos per Special Drawing
Right (SDR), 1982-95
2. the U.S. export unit price (USEUV), 8.0 percent per
annum increase 1982-95
3. the rate of growth of real U.S. gross domestic product
(USYP), 3.0 percent per annum in 1982-95
4. the U.S. wholesale price (USWP), 8.0 percent increase
per annum, 1982-95
5. the growth in the export unit value of the industrialized
countries (WINF), 8 percent per annum, 1982-95
6. the U.S. consumer price index (INFUS), 8 percent
increase per annum, 1982-95
7. nominal U.S. gross domestic product (USGDP), 10
percent per annum, 1982-95
8. Mexican crude oil production (CPP), separate runs of
10 percent, 15 percent, and 20 percent average increase per
annum, 1982-95
9. the U.S. treasury bill rate (USTB), 10 percent, 1982-95

Of these, the rationale for the crude petroleum production
(CPP) and the exchange rate (EX) needs to be elaborated.

Crude Petroleum Production

The conceptual problem with this tool is to design a technique of utilization that will maximize economic wealth, i.e.,
maximize not only the current income growth but also economic
growth for the coming generations. In order to achieve this
general target, it is necessary to transform oil income into a
permanent source of income. To be able to do this, it is necessary to find an optimum rate of petroleum extraction and exports.
In this regard there are real and monetary restrictions to the
economy that have to be respected.

There is a maximum of oil income that the economy can
absorb productively; i.e., in the short run there are some
serious semi-structural bottlenecks that result in unacceptable
levels of inflation if expenditures exceed this limit. For sure,
additional investment in high priority areas is needed. But

additional investment beyond a limit is clearly self-defeating.
To exceed this level would counter the effort to transform oil
income into permanent income.

This problem stems in large part from the interdependence
between monetary and real restrictions; i.e., there is a maximum
of international reserves that the economy can monetize at a
time. International reserves affect the monetary base and thus
increase the money supply; undesired monetary balances are
translated into increased consumption of foreign goods and
domestic inflationary effects. Excessive oil revenue monetization
will, therefore, create price increases and an enlarged deficit
of nonpetroleum balance of payments. Thus the monetary restrictions would depend on the desired inflation targets and the
expected effects of money reserves on undesired money balances.

If oil reserve monetization exceeds the monetary maximum,
the options could be—

1. to simultaneously control other sources of monetary
growth, mainly domestic credit, through traditional monetary
tools
2. to reduce and/or pay public foreign debt through
diminishing net reserve increases. This implies a substitution
between oil reserves and public financing through foreign debt.
It might not be optimal on strictly financial grounds, but it
might be the better of two evils.
3. to buy foreign assets so as not to monetize currently
undesired rents
4. to increase expenditure on foreign consumption and
additional unwelcome investment, thus worsening current
account deficits. To the extent that this means rent use for
additional present consumption, it is undesirable.[5]

While these alternatives themselves are not optimum, the
issue is really whether or not they are worse than the consequences of excessive monetization.

In part these considerations explain the conservatism
associated with present production policies. With 33.4 billion
barrels of proven crude oil reserves and a 2.25 billion bpd
production target, the ratio of reserves to annual production
is 41 years in Mexico, whereas Saudi Arabia's ratio is around
33 years, Venezuela's is 17 years, and that of the United States
is 27 years.[6]

In addition, conservatism is based on the traditional
nationalism of Mexico, grounded in bad colonial memories of
fast exploitation of nonrenewable mineral resources for export.[7]

More important, however, is the awareness of the negative symptoms of fast oil exploitation. Lopez Portillo has repeatedly expressed the view that immoderate pumping of oil can create undesirable effects or "financial indigestion" and serious inflation. He is also on record against the use of oil to make Mexico a net exporter of capital.

Mexican officials have also expressed their mistrust of sudden oil riches by linking the Iranian revolution and the 1978 balance of payments problems of Venezuela to the increases generated by too rapid exploitation of the oil sector. [8]

The Rand Organization has identified major alternatives that appear open to the Mexican authorities in terms of the production rate for oil between 1980 and 2000. [9]

1. Low production option—oil production at 2.5 to 3.5 million bpd. Exports of oil would probably not exceed domestic consumption at this rate. Peak annual oil production would be only 1/75 to 1/90 of ultimate recoverable resources.

2. Moderate production option—with a production rate of 3.5 to 5.5 million bpd. Exports at this rate could be twice as great as internal oil consumption. Peak annual oil production would be 1/50 to 1/60 of ultimate recoverable resources.

3. High production option—5.0 to 7.5 million bpd. At this level, exports might be more than double internal oil consumption by the late 1980s. Annual oil production would be 1/40 of ultimate recoverable resources.

On the basis of the Rand analysis, rates of 10 percent, 15 percent, and 20 percent were initially chosen for the average annual rate of increase in crude petroleum production. Preliminary runs with the optimal control model developed here indicated quite clearly that the implications of runs below 10 or above 20 percent were unacceptable either in terms of inflation (above 20 percent) or employment creation (below 10 percent).

The Exchange Rate

The exchange policy to be adopted in the future is of course closely connected with the inflation objective of the government. A fixed exchange rate would require accepting the United States inflation rate. A gliding parity, on the other hand, would permit a domestic inflation rate exceeding that of the United States by the amount of the depreciation of the exchange rate, while a floating rate is in theory consistent with any inflation target. A basic question in the design of an appropriate combination of monetary and exchange policy is, How much inflation should the Mexican authorities accept?[10]

It is a truism that the optimal exchange rate policy is one that allows for the greatest increase in real output and maximizes short-term destabilizing capital flows and fluctuations in the domestic price level.[11] On the other hand, it is not clear which type of rate is capable of meeting these objectives simultaneously, for exchange rate measures aimed in one direction frequently produce undesired effects with respect to a second objective. The main challenge facing the Mexican authorities in the design of the current exchange rate policy is to reconcile the short-term objective, or exchange rate stability, with the long-run requirement of a realistically valued rate.[12]

It is difficult to exaggerate the importance of maintaining a correct alignment of the exchange rate. An overvalued exchange rate would lead to a reduction of the tradable goods sector of the economy, reducing exports, raising imports and augmenting the dependence of the economy on the petroleum industry. The affluence of financial resources resulting from oil revenues would only aggravate the problem since the necessary adjustments could be postponed indefinitely. At the same time, given that Mexico's manufacturing exports tend to be labor intensive, there would be a conflict between the goals of employment creation and the target rate of income growth.[13]

A flexible or semiflexible rate may not produce a satisfactory solution either. For example, after the devaluation of September 1976 and during the first few months of 1977, during which time the exchange rate showed substantial fluctuations, speculative short-run capital flows were quite large. When the Bank of Mexico followed a more active policy of intervention in the foreign exchange market, capital flows were considerably smoothed. Apparently, small unannounced depreciations of the exchange rate triggered destabilization capital flows.[14]

A related problem that seems to be associated with a fluctuating (and depreciating) exchange rate is that of dollarization, or a faster increase in deposits denominated in foreign currency—mostly the U.S. dollar—than in peso denominated deposits.

The problem is that, because currency substitution of this type is quantitatively quite important in Mexico, any attempt to achieve monetary independence through flexible or semiflexible rates may be quite futile; i.e., currency substitution or dollarization may undermine any advantage associated with floating rates.[15]

Some observers have gone so far as to argue that exchange rate uncertainty may be destabilizing in Mexico's case, i.e., that the problem might degenerate from simply one where individuals desired to hold a diversified currency portfolio (controlled shifts into dollars) to one that was of the all-or-nothing variety. If a decline in the value of the peso was anticipated, for example it is conceivable that massive shifts into dollars would completely destabilize the currency. 16

The problems presented by dollarization in Mexico are easy to illustrate. Probably the best measure of the degree of dollarization is the dollar to peso ratio of various money aggregates. By this indicator, the proportion of dollar denominated financial claims rose from 5.2 percent in 1975 to 19.4 percent in December 1976. The ratio of foreign to domestic currency deposits in Mexican banks in July 1979 was such that nearly 20 percent of the total deposits held by the public were in foreign currency.

In short, the real size of the banking system was reduced during this period because of a lack of confidence in the economy and the stability of the peso brought about by rising inflation. The result was that investment fell off drastically because peso credit was scarce while at the same time dollar credits were considered too risky. 17

Dollarization in Mexico is, therefore, clearly associated with exchange rate uncertainty. Apparently this problem cannot be overcome through forward markets because of their thinness and the high cost of transactions. Therefore, in the absence of working futures markets (and their ability to play a potentially stabilizing role), the peso would likely continue experiencing substantial fluctuations under a floating rate regime. The experience since 1976 indicates that the process of currency substitution can be traced directly to exchange rate uncertainty associated with government attempts at letting the peso exchange rate be determined by free market forces.

In any case, the managed float practice of the peso since late 1976 amounted to a de facto peg to the dollar, and it reinforced Mexico's tie to and dependence on the United States. Mexico cannot gain much short-run stimulus from any peso depreciation vis a vis Germany, Japan, or Switzerland, for example, because of her relatively small export markets in those countries. 18 Furthermore, since oil exports are denominated in dollars, at least one-half of the country's exports would not be affected in any case by a devaluation.

Because of these considerations, a fixed peso exchange rate (that of March 1982) was used in the forecasts. This required in addition, of course, that the Mexican inflation rate had to be held close to that of the United States to avoid overvaluation

OPTIMAL CONTROL SIMULATION

As a prelude to the forecasts to 1995, the model was tested to see, given the actual values of the exogenous variables in 1979, how close it would generate values for the endogenous variables to their actual 1979 magnitudes. The forecast period was the five years from 1974 to 1979, and in general (Table 7.1) estimated and actual values were quite close—most within one or two percent of the actual figures.

When the 1974-79 period was subjected to the control-optimization procedures—i.e., government investment used as a control variable with the maximization of the 1979 capital stock subject to inflation close to the U.S. rate—several interesting results were obtained:

1. While the optimum capital stock is lower than the estimated or actual values for 1979 (696.2 versus 766.4 and 727.8 billion 1975 pesos, respectively), only marginal declines in real gross domestic product occurred, with the optimum GDP equal to 1167.4 billion 1975 pesos, versus 1207.6 actual and 1181.3 estimated.

2. For a decline in the average rate of growth in real GDP of only 0.7 percent annual rate over the 1974-79 period (4.9 actual versus 4.2 optimum), the country would have been able to reduce the rate of inflation in terms of the wholesale price index from 14.1 to 9.1 percent (in the control program only one variable can be minimized). The rate of change in the wholesale price index was selected, accounting for its usually lower optimal value compared with the rate of increase in the consumer price and the GDP deflator.

3. The lower rate of inflation can be explained largely in terms of the lower rate of money growth (M2) in the optimal solution (37.1 average annual rate versus 45.8 actual).

4. The lower rate of monetary expansion is in turn related to the smaller government deficit (optimal average annual rate of increase of 2.0 percent versus 8.5 percent actual average annual increase.

The 1974-79 optimal control results show, therefore, that increased government deficits and money supply increases during the period produced only marginal gains in terms of real income gains, hardly worth the cost in terms of inflation.

In fact, as a result of the optimal control results, the standard of living might have been even higher (on the basis of the levels of real private consumption, which are somewhat higher in the optimal run than the actual figures for 1979).

TABLE 7.1

Mexico: Optimal Control Path, 1974-79
(maximize capital stock)

	Actual Values 1974	Actual Values 1979	Esti-mated Values 1979	Opti-mum Results 1979	Average Annual Growth 1974-79		
					Actual - Actual	Actual - Esti-mated	Actual - Opti-mal
Real Variables (billions of 1975 pesos)							
Gross Domestic Product (GDPNP)	949.6	1207.6	1181.3	1167.4	4.9	4.5	4.2
Government Consumption (GCNP)	90.6	138.3	130.2	130.1	8.8	7.5	7.5
Government Investment (GIP)	80.6	141.0	141.0	112.0	11.8	11.8	6.8
Total Government Expenditures (GENANP)	171.2	279.4	271.2	242.1	10.3	9.6	7.2
Private Consumption (PCNP)	635.8	752.8	784.2	786.1	3.4	4.3	4.3
Private Investment (PIP)	121.6	163.7	138.3	129.5	6.1	2.6	1.3
Total Private Expenditures (PENANP)	757.4	916.5	922.5	915.6	3.9	4.0	3.9
Capital Stock (KP)	544.6	766.4	727.8	696.2	7.1	6.0	5.0
Total Investment (TINP)	202.6	304.6	279.2	241.5	8.5	6.6	3.6
Exports (EP)	88.3	149.3	151.8	151.8	11.1	11.4	11.4
Imports (ZP)	-113.2	-170.4	-161.3	-150.6	8.5	7.3	5.9

Government Revenue (GREVP)	85.1	149.9	147.6	147.2	12.0	11.6	11.6
Government Deficit (GDEFP)	-86.1	-129.4	-123.7	-94.9	8.5	7.5	2.0
Growth in GDP (GGDPNP)	5.6	7.4	5.6	4.4	–	–	–
Monetary Variables (billions of pesos)							
Bank of Mexico Net Foreign Assets (BMFA)	18.2	72.5	74.4	74.4	31.8	32.5	32.5
Bank of Mexico Reserve Money (BMRM)	105.3	537.9	371.8	334.8	38.6	28.7	26.0
Narrow Money (M1)	100.8	383.1	336.1	332.5	30.6	27.2	27.0
Broad Money (M2)	139.2	917.9	705.5	673.9	45.8	38.3	37.1
Price Variables (average annual growth)							
Inflation - Wholesale Price Index (INFW)	18.3	15.5	14.1	9.1	–	–	–
Inflation - Consumer Price Index (INFC)	23.6	18.2	17.0	15.1	–	–	–
Inflation - Gross Domestic Product							
Deflator (INF)	19.3	17.1	17.7	13.1	–	–	–
Wholesale Price Deflator (WPI)	90.5	236.4	214.5	178.7	21.2	18.8	14.6
(1975 = 100.0)							
Interest Rates (percent)							
Nominal Rate of Interest	10.2	16.0	11.4	11.4	–	–	–
Real Rate of Interest	-12.3	-2.3	1.4	5.6	–	–	–

Source: Compiled by the author.

OPTIMAL CONTROL FORECASTS 1980-85

Four forecasts (models I through IV) were made for the 1980-85 period under different sets of constraints. Starting with Model I successive constraints were added to correct for undesired trends in several of the variables (the exogenous variables were, of course, assuming the same values in each of the runs).

Model I

Model I results (Table 7.2) indicate that the simple maximization of the capital stock, given crude petroleum rates of increase of 10, 15, and 20 percent, would yield an acceptable rate of inflation at the 10 percent crude petroleum production rate. The major problems with higher rates of petroleum output are excessive increases in government expenditures (14.0 average annual rate for 10 percent increase versus 18.5 percent and 23.3 percent for the 15 and 20 percent increases, respectively).

Since the econometric model upon which the results are ultimately dependent was based on historical data, the tendency of government expenditure to outrun its revenue base was magnified at higher rates of oil production.

Ironically, at higher levels of revenue the government expenditure response tends to be so strong that its deficit actually increases (18.7 percent average annual increase at 10 percent oil production versus 23.1 and 28.3 percent at 15 and 20 percent, respectively).

Since the model links the rate of inflation to the government deficit, the end result is that, with only marginal gains in the growth of real GDP (5.9 at 10 percent versus 6.6 and 7.6 at 15 and 20 percent crude petroleum production rates, respectively), inflation in terms of the wholesale price increase rises from the 9.6 percent of the 10 percent oil increase to 15.2 and 24.8 percent when oil production is increased to annual rates of 15 and 20 percent, respectively.

The rest of the inflation stems from the excessive monetization of the oil revenues, with M2 increasing at average annual rates of 14.8, 21.4, and 28.6 percent per annum as crude oil production increases from 10 to 15 and 20 percent, respectively.

Because of the crowding out of private consumption by government expenditure, it is conceivable that real standards of living might be lower at higher rates of oil production. In

TABLE 7.2

Mexico: Optimal Control Forecast I, 1980-85
(maximize capital stock, government consumption unconstrained)

	1979 Optimal Base	1985 Optimum Values with Oil Production Average Annual Increase			Average Annual Rate of Growth 1979-85 with Oil Production		
		10%	15%	20%	10%	15%	20%
Real Variables (billions of 1975 pesos)							
Gross Domestic Product (GDPNP)	1167.4	1642.3	1712.1	1808.5	5.9	6.6	7.6
Government Consumption (GCNP)	130.1	294.7	383.0	489.7	14.6	19.7	24.7
Government Investment (GIP)	112.0	237.9	286.2	363.0	13.4	16.9	21.7
Total Government Expenditures (GENANP)	242.1	532.6	669.2	852.7	14.0	18.5	23.3
Private Consumption (PCNP)	786.1	876.7	802.4	713.7	1.8	0.3	-3.4
Private Investment (PIP)	129.5	208.9	227.6	257.3	8.3	9.9	12.1
Total Private Expenditures (PENANP)	915.6	1085.6	1030.0	971.0	2.9	2.0	1.0
Capital Stock (KP)	696.2	1205.5	1364.0	1583.2	9.6	11.9	14.7
Total Investment (TINP)	241.5	446.8	513.7	620.3	10.8	13.4	17.0
Exports (EP)	151.8	250.3	286.7	330.7	8.7	11.2	13.9
Imports (ZP)	-150.6	-237.9	-252.0	-277.6	7.9	9.0	10.7
Government Revenue (GREVP)	147.2	267.4	339.7	429.9	10.5	15.0	19.6

(continued)

Table 7.2 (continued)

	1979 Optimal Base	1985 Optimum Values with Oil Production Average Annual Increase			Average Annual Rate of Growth 1979-85 with Oil Production		
		10%	15%	20%	10%	15%	20%
Government Deficit (GDEFP)	-94.9	-265.2	-329.5	-422.8	18.7	23.1	28.3
Growth in GDP (GGDPNP)	5.6	6.6	7.3	9.3	—	—	—
Monetary Variables (billions of pesos)							
Bank of Mexico Reserve Money (BMRM)	334.8	831.8	1228.5	1849.2	16.4	24.2	33.0
Narrow Money (M1)	332.5	936.0	1082.3	1269.4	18.8	21.7	25.0
Broad Money (M2)	674.0	1541.6	2154.6	3049.7	14.8	21.4	28.6
Price Variables (average annual growth)							
Inflation—Wholesale Price Index (INFW)	9.1	9.6	15.2	24.8	—	—	—
Inflation—Consumer Price Index (INFC)	13.1	12.4	18.0	27.1	—	—	—
Inflation—Gross Domestic Product Deflator (INF)	15.1	11.6	14.8	20.0	—	—	—
Gross Domestic Product Deflator (GDPDF) (1975 = 1.00)	2.04	4.04	4.75	5.74	12.0	15.1	18.8

Source: Compiled by the author.

fact, private consumption actually declines at an average rate of -3.4 percent for the 20 percent crude petroleum production run.

Model II

To see if it was possible to improve on Model I results, Model II was run on the same assumptions except that in this case government consumption was constrained to grow at a rate equal to 0.75 percent of the increase in government investment.

This is a realistic assumption, and there has certainly been precedent for it in the Middle East, where Iran and Saudi Arabia, for example, found that government consumption expenditures exploded soon after the 1973 OPEC price increases. Eventually, to control inflation, each country placed severe restraints on consumption expenditures while moving ahead in their development plans with much less of a proportional cut in their investment programs.

This run (Table 7.3) is much superior to Model I in that growth in real GDP is higher for each level of oil production while inflation is more or less the same.

Private consumption no longer declines and in fact maintains a fairly respectable increase of 3.8, 3.8, and 3.7, respectively, with the 10, 15, and 20 percent oil production rates. The government deficit is down considerably, 14.5 versus 18.7 average annual rate of growth at 10 percent oil production. In an attempt to see if inflation could not be reduced to more acceptable levels, Model III was designed.

Model III

Model III is identical to Model II with the added constraint that the government deficit must stay in the range of 10 to 12 percent of GDP. This level of deficit was more or less the range in the late 1970s and similar to that anticipated in the National Industrial Development Plan.

The results indicate that the 15 percent rate of oil expansion may now be realistic since the corresponding inflation rate would only be 12.9 percent (Table 7.4). By 1985, this would increase the growth of GDP to 7.0 percent (over 5.9 for the 10 percent rate).

What all three models show is that the 10 percent rates of growth forecast by the plan are quite unrealistic given the politi-

TABLE 7.3

Mexico: Optimal Control Forecast II, 1980-85
(maximize capital stock, government consumption constrained)

Real Variables (billions of 1975 pesos)	1979 Optimal Base	1985 Optimum Values with Oil Production Average Annual Increase			Average Annual Rate of Growth 1979-85 with Oil Production		
		10%	15%	20%	10%	15%	20%
Gross Domestic Product (GDPNP)	1167.4	1662.4	1746.9	1847.2	6.1	6.9	8.0
Government Consumption (GCNP)	130.1	236.5	276.9	326.4	10.5	13.4	16.6
Government Investment (GIP)	112.0	245.4	300.4	370.7	14.0	17.9	22.1
Total Government Expenditures (GENANP)	242.1	481.9	577.3	697.1	12.2	15.6	19.3
Private Consumption (PCNP)	786.1	981.3	982.9	977.0	3.8	3.8	3.7
Private Investment (PIP)	129.5	221.1	249.1	283.6	9.3	11.5	14.0
Total Private Expenditures (PENANP)	915.6	1202.4	1232.0	1260.6	4.6	5.1	5.5
Capital Stock (KP)	696.2	1251.0	1443.0	1671.0	10.3	12.9	15.7
Total Investment (TINP)	241.5	466.5	549.5	654.3	11.6	14.7	18.1
Exports (EP)	151.8	250.4	286.7	330.7	8.7	11.2	13.9
Imports (Z)	-150.6	-243.9	-262.5	-286.1	8.4	9.7	11.3

Government Revenue (GREVP)	147.2	268.1	340.9	431.2	10.5	15.0	19.6
Government Deficit (GDEFP)	-94.9	-213.9	-236.4	-265.9	14.5	16.4	18.7
Growth in GDP (GGDPNP)	5.6	6.8	7.9	9.5	—	—	—
Monetary Variables (billions of pesos)							
Bank of Mexico Reserve Money (BMRM)	334.8	886.3	1351.2	2001.9	17.6	26.2	34.7
Narrow Money (M1)	332.5	958.3	1126.8	1328.8	19.3	22.6	26.0
Broad Money (M2)	674.0	1628.6	2343.9	3296.4	15.8	23.1	30.3
Price Variables (average annual growth)							
Inflation—Wholesale Price Index (INFW)	9.1	10.4	16.7	24.8	—	—	—
Inflation—Consumer Price Index (INFC)	13.1	13.3	19.5	27.3	—	—	—
Inflation—Gross Domestic Product Deflator (INF)	15.1	12.0	15.5	20.0	—	—	—
Gross Domestic Product Deflator (GDPDF) (1975 = 1.00)	2.04	4.14	4.98	6.04	12.5	16.0	19.8

Note: Real government consumption constrained to 0.75 average annual increase in government investment.

Source: Compiled by the author.

TABLE 7.4

Mexico: Optimal Control Forecast III, 1980-85
(maximize capital stock, government consumption, deficit constrained)

	1979 Optimal Base	1985 Optimum Values with Oil Production Average Annual Increase			Average Annual Rate of Growth 1979-85 with Oil Production		
		10%	15%	20%	10%	15%	20%
Real Variables (billions of 1975 pesos)							
Gross Domestic Product (GDPNP)	1167.4	1625.1	1693.6	1767.2	5.7	6.4	7.2
Government Consumption (GCNP)	130.1	213.9	247.7	288.4	8.6	11.3	14.2
Government Investment (GIP)	112.0	215.3	260.3	316.5	11.5	15.1	18.9
Total Government Expenditures (GENANP)	242.1	429.2	507.9	604.9	10.0	13.1	16.5
Private Consumption (PCNP)	786.1	989.5	982.0	977.2	3.9	3.8	3.7
Private Investment (PIP)	129.5	208.2	232.6	257.1	8.2	10.3	12.1
Total Private Expenditures (PENANP)	915.6	1197.7	1214.6	1234.3	4.6	4.8	5.1
Capital Stock (KP)	696.2	1166.4	1320.0	1489.3	9.0	11.3	13.5
Total Investment (TINP)	241.5	423.5	492.9	573.6	9.8	12.6	15.5
Exports (EP)	151.8	250.4	287.7	330.7	8.7	11.2	13.9
Imports (Z)	-150.6	-231.5	-248.4	-268.6	7.4	8.7	10.1

Government Revenue (GREVP)	147.2	266.8	339.0	428.4	10.4	14.9	19.5
Government Deficit (GDEFP)	-94.9	-162.3	-169.0	-176.4	9.4	10.1	10.9
Growth in GDP (GGDPNP)	4.4	5.9	7.0	8.3	—	—	—
Monetary Variables (billions of pesos)							
Bank of Mexico Reserve Money (BMRM)	334.8	715.8	1071.4	1482.4	13.5	21.4	28.1
Narrow Money (M1)	332.5	908.1	1035.0	1167.6	18.2	20.8	23.3
Broad Money (M2)	673.9	1382.2	1917.6	2528.6	12.7	19.0	24.7
Price Variables (average annual growth)							
Inflation—Wholesale Price Index (INFW)	9.1	5.5	12.9	19.2	—	—	—
Inflation—Consumer Price Index (INFC)	13.1	8.7	15.5	21.7	—	—	—
Inflation—Gross Domestic Product Deflator (INF)	15.1	9.3	13.5	16.9	—	—	—
Gross Domestic Product Deflator (GDPDF) (1975 = 1.00)	2.04	3.87	4.48	5.18	11.3	14.0	16.8

Note: Government consumption constrained to 0.75 average annual increase in government investment. Government deficit constrained to equal or less than 0.10 gross domestic product.

Source: Compiled by the author.

cal limitations that would probably prevent petroleum rates of increase over 20 percent and/or inflation rates below 20 percent.

They also show that the plan was undermined by 1981 by its underestimation of the deficits that would develop at the high rates of crude production together with uncontrolled government expenditures. Undoubtedly, the actual rates of real GDP obtained during this period were only marginal in terms of their inflationary cost. This conclusion is supported by a comparison of the various structural changes that occur over time in the models (Table 7.5). In the unconstrained version, Model I, the government deficit rises to 23.4 percent of GDP at 20 percent rate of oil production, while for the same run private consumption decreases from 62.3 percent of GDP in 1979 (67.3 percent optimal) to 39.5 percent, clearly an unacceptable result.

These trends are not as severe in Model II.

Model IV

To see if the objective function could be improved upon, Model IV was run with total consumption (government plus private) maximized instead of the capital stock in 1985. (The condition that increases in government consumption be limited to 0.75 percent of government investment and that the government deficit be constrained within 10 to 12 percent of real GDP still applied.)

The results (Table 7.6) were quite interesting in that inflation was reduced while the rates of growth in real GDP were down only marginally over Model III (Table 7.7). All things considered, the higher levels of private consumption, 994.8 billion pesos at 15 percent oil production versus 982.0 for model III, and rates of inflation of 8.7 versus 12.9 for model III (again at crude production rates of 15 percent), maximization of consumption would appear to be the best objective function for the authorities to pursue.

As a basis of comparison, the Wharton-DIEMEX model[19] antiinflationary plan moderate deceleration (Tables 7.8, 7.9, 7.10) forecasts real GDP at 7.17 percent with the rate of change in the wholesale price index at 17.18 given a crude petroleum production rate of 12.70 for the same period. Clearly, the Wharton results can be improved upon through a structural control of government expenditures. In the Wharton model real government expenditures increase at 10.32 percent; however, its movement is more erratic than in the optimal control path.

TABLE 7.5

Mexico: Patterns of Growth, Models I and II, 1980-85
(1985 values)

	Actual 1979	1979 Optimal	Model I			Model II		
			10%	15%	20%	10%	15%	20%
Real variables (percent real Gross Domestic Product)								
Government Consumption	11.5	11.1	17.9	22.4	45.3	14.2	15.9	17.7
Government Investment	11.7	9.6	14.5	16.7	27.1	14.8	17.2	20.1
Total Government Expenditure	23.1	20.7	32.4	39.1	47.1	29.0	33.0	37.7
Private Consumption	62.3	67.3	53.4	46.9	39.5	59.0	56.3	52.9
Private Investment	13.6	11.1	12.7	13.3	14.2	13.3	14.3	15.4
Private Expenditures	75.9	78.4	66.1	60.2	53.7	72.3	70.5	68.2
Capital Stock	63.4	59.6	73.4	79.7	87.5	75.3	82.6	90.5
Total Investment	25.2	20.7	27.2	30.0	34.3	28.1	31.4	35.4
Exports	12.4	13.0	15.2	16.7	18.3	15.1	16.4	17.9
Imports	14.1	12.9	14.5	14.7	15.3	14.7	15.0	15.5
Government Revenue	12.4	12.6	16.3	19.8	23.8	16.1	19.5	23.3
Government Deficit	10.7	8.1	16.1	19.2	23.4	12.9	13.5	14.4
Monetary Variables (percent nominal Gross Domestic Product)								
Bank of Mexico Reserve Money	19.4	14.0	12.5	15.1	17.8	12.9	15.5	17.9
Narrow Money	13.8	13.9	14.1	13.3	12.2	13.9	13.0	11.9
Broad Money	33.2	28.1	23.2	26.5	29.4	23.7	26.9	29.6

Source: Compiled by the author.

TABLE 7.6

Mexico: Optimal Control Forecast IV, 1980-85
(maximize consumption, government consumption, deficit constrained)

	1979 Optimal Base	Optimal Values with Oil Production Average Annual Increase			Average Annual Rate of Growth 1979-85 with Oil Production		
		10%	15%	20%	10%	15%	20%
Real Variables (billions of 1975 pesos)							
Gross Domestic Product (GDPNP)	1167.4	1623.3	1680.1	1780.0	5.6	6.3	7.3
Government Consumption (GCNP)	130.1	213.5	247.9	297.9	8.6	11.3	14.8
Government Investment (GIP)	112.0	214.8	259.2	329.8	11.5	15.0	19.7
Total Government Expenditures (GENANP)	242.1	428.3	506.2	627.7	10.0	13.1	17.2
Private Consumption (PCNP)	786.1	991.4	994.8	984.6	3.9	4.0	3.8
Private Investment (PIP)	129.5	206.8	223.3	259.1	8.1	9.5	9.5
Total Private Expenditures (PENANP)	915.6	1198.2	1218.1	1243.7	4.6	4.9	5.2
Capital Stock (KP)	696.2	1162.1	1291.4	1518.4	8.9	11.0	13.9
Total Investment (TINP)	241.5	421.6	482.5	588.9	9.7	12.2	16.0
Exports (EP)	151.8	250.4	286.7	330.7	8.7	11.2	13.8
Imports (Z)	-150.6	-231.1	-248.4	-272.1	7.4	8.7	10.4
Government Revenue (GREVP)	147.2	266.8	338.6	428.9	10.4	14.9	19.5

Government Deficit (GDEFP)	-94.9	-161.6	-167.6	-198.9	9.3	9.9	13.1
Growth in GDP (GGDPNP)	4.4	5.8	6.7	8.4	—	—	—
Monetary Variables (billions of pesos)							
Bank of Mexico Reserve Money (BMRM)	334.8	700.6	955.5	1550.1	13.1	19.1	29.1
Narrow Money (M1)	332.5	904.7	1009.0	1204.2	18.2	20.3	23.9
Broad Money (M2)	673.9	1363.3	1771.8	2648.0	12.5	17.5	25.6
Price Variables (average annual growth)							
Inflation—Wholesale Price Index (INFW)	9.1	4.8	8.7	18.7	—	—	—
Inflation—Consumer Price Index (INFC)	13.1	8.1	12.1	21.2	—	—	—
Inflation—Gross Domestic Product Deflator (INF)	15.1	8.9	11.0	16.6	—	—	—
Gross Domestic Product Deflator (GDPDF) (1975 = 1.00)	2.04	3.85	4.34	5.34	11.2	13.4	17.4

Note: Government consumption constrained to 0.75 average annual increase in government investment. Government deficit constrained to equal or less than 0.10 gross domestic product.
Source: Compiled by the author.

217

TABLE 7.7

Mexico: Patterns of Growth, Models III and IV
(1985 values)

	Actual 1979	1979 Optimal	Model III 10%	Model III 15%	Model III 20%	Model IV 10%	Model IV 15%	Model IV 20%
Real Variables								
Government Consumption	11.5	11.6	13.2	14.6	16.3	13.2	14.8	16.7
Government Investment	11.7	9.6	13.2	15.4	17.9	13.2	15.4	18.5
Government Expenditure	23.1	20.7	26.4	30.0	34.2	26.4	30.1	35.3
Private Consumption	62.3	67.3	60.9	58.0	55.3	61.1	59.2	55.3
Private Investment	13.6	11.1	12.8	13.7	14.5	12.7	13.3	14.6
Private Expenditures	75.9	78.4	73.7	71.7	69.8	73.8	72.5	69.9
Capital Stock	63.4	59.6	71.8	77.9	84.3	71.6	76.9	85.3
Total Investment	25.2	20.7	26.1	29.1	32.5	26.0	28.7	33.1
Exports	12.4	13.0	15.4	17.0	18.7	15.4	17.1	18.6
Imports	14.1	12.9	14.2	14.7	15.2	14.2	14.8	15.3
Government Revenue	12.4	12.6	16.4	20.0	24.2	16.4	20.2	24.1
Government Deficit	10.7	8.1	10.0	10.0	10.0	10.0	10.0	11.2
Monetary Variables								
Bank of Mexico Reserve Money	19.4	14.0	11.4	14.1	16.2	11.2	13.1	16.3
Narrow Money	13.8	13.9	14.4	13.6	12.8	14.5	13.8	12.7
Broad Money	33.2	28.1	22.0	25.3	27.6	21.8	24.3	27.9

Source: Compiled by the author.

218

TABLE 7.8

Mexico: Continuation of the Antiinflationary Plan
(moderate decelerations in 1980, higher crude oil export prices)

Main Economic Indicators	1980	1981	1982	1983	1984	1985
Gross domestic product (billion pesos 1960)	508.02	551.42	595.85	623.13	667.36	718.30
Change (%)	7.1	8.5	8.1	4.6	7.1	7.6
Gross domestic product (billion pesos)	3,512.32	4,601.93	5,973.16	7,315.24	9,098.81	11,342.35
Change (%)	30.7	31.0	29.8	22.5	24.4	24.7
Sectoral output						
Primary sector (billion pesos 1960)	43.00	44.38	45.84	47.40	49.06	50.83
Change (%)	3.5	3.2	3.3	3.4	3.5	3.6
Secondary sector (billion pesos 1960)	200.91	222.88	245.94	260.62	284.51	310.60
Change (%)	9.1	10.9	10.3	6.0	9.2	9.2
Tertiary sector (billion pesos 1960)	264.11	284.17	304.06	315.11	333.79	356.88
Change (%)	6.2	7.6	7.0	3.6	5.9	6.9
Prices and wages						
Implicit price deflator—GDP (1960=1.0)	6.914	8.346	10.025	11.740	13.634	15.790
Change (%)	22.0	20.7	20.1	17.1	16.1	15.8
Consumers' price index—National (1960=1.0)	5.979	7.282	8.796	10.342	12.035	13.958
Change (%)	23.1	21.8	20.8	17.6	16.4	16.0
Wholesale price index (1960=1.0)	6.024	7.227	8.613	10.029	11.567	13.309
Change (%)	20.5	20.0	19.2	16.4	15.3	15.1
Average annual wage rate (thousands pesos)	49.901	63.162	78.563	93.407	113.301	135.977
Change (%)	22.9	26.6	24.4	18.9	21.3	20.0
Average annual wage rate (thousand pesos 1960)	7.218	7.568	7.837	7.957	8.310	8.611
Change (%)	0.7	4.9	3.5	1.5	4.4	3.6

(continued)

219

Table 7.8 (continued)

Main Economic Indicators	1980	1981	1982	1983	1984	1985
Exchange rate (pesos per dollar)						
Average for the year	22.87	24.86	26.85	26.85	26.85	26.85
Change (%)	0.2	8.7	8.0	0.0	0.0	0.0
Value at the end of the year	22.87	26.85	26.85	26.85	26.85	26.85
Change (%)	0.0	17.4	0.0	0.0	0.0	0.0
Balance on current account (billion dollars)	-3.197	-1.377	1.233	1.612	1.388	0.205
Exports ($ billion)	21.920	29.232	37.956	44.250	51.218	58.999
Imports ($ billion)	25.117	30.609	36.723	42.638	49.830	58.794
Long-term capital account ($ billion)						
Long-term capital inflows	5.019	4.781	2.043	1.199	2.096	3.736
Public sector	3.736	3.418	1.403	0.473	1.024	2.333
Private sector and others	1.284	1.362	0.641	0.727	1.072	1.404
Total long-term public external debt ($ billion)	31.080	34.499	35.901	36.374	37.398	39.731
Public external debt/GDP ratio	0.20	0.20	0.16	0.13	0.11	0.09
Money supply—M1 (billion pesos)	458.90	606.76	799.82	993.61	1,261.19	1,608.70
Change (%)	32.5	32.2	31.8	24.2	26.9	27.6
Govt. total expenditures (billion pesos 1960)	110.60	123.64	137.39	145.23	162.34	180.76
Change (%)	12.1	11.8	11.1	5.7	11.8	11.3
Total gross fixed investment (billion pesos 1960)	126.81	144.79	161.65	167.27	186.77	208.11
Change (%)	16.7	14.2	11.7	3.5	11.7	11.4
Employment (million of workers)	19.072	19.804	20.642	21.400	21.997	22.792
Change (%)	3.9	3.8	4.2	3.7	2.8	3.67

Source: Abel Beltram del Rio, "The Mexican Oil Syndrome: Early Symptoms, Preventive Efforts, and Prognosis," Quarterly Review of Economics and Business (Summer 1981), p. 126.

TABLE 7.9

Mexico: Continuation of the Antiinflationary Plan
(moderate deceleration in 1980, higher crude oil export prices)

Hydrocarbon Sector	1980	1981	1982	1983	1984	1985
Pemex production						
Crude oil, condens. & liqs. (billions bbls/day)						
Total production	1.977	2.353	2.793	3.000	3.276	3.594
Change (%)	20.8	19.0	18.7	7.4	9.2	9.7
Exports	0.775	1.025	1.332	1.457	1.605	1.769
Change (%)	45.1	32.3	30.0	9.4	10.2	10.2
Domestic consumption	1.104	1.210	1.322	1.393	1.507	1.645
Change (%)	8.0	9.7	9.2	5.4	8.2	9.1
Gas (billions cu. ft./day)						
Total production	3.780	4.748	5.679	6.336	6.990	7.658
Change (%)	28.9	25.6	19.6	11.6	10.3	9.5
Exports	0.350	0.750	1.100	1.270	1.350	1.420
Change (%)		114.3	46.7	15.5	6.3	5.2
Domestic consumption	3.241	3.760	4.295	4.749	5.291	5.855
Change (%)	16.4	16.0	14.2	10.6	11.4	10.7

(continued)

221

Table 7.9 (continued)

Hydrocarbons Sector	1980	1981	1982	1983	1984	1985
Export prices (annual average)						
Avg. price of Mex. oil exports ($/bl)	32.50	37.05	41.00	44.89	48.71	52.36
Change (%)	62.5	14.0	10.7	9.5	8.5	7.5
Avg. price of Mex. gas exports ($/TCF)	4.50	4.98	5.49	6.01	6.53	7.02
Change (%)	24.1	10.2	10.8	9.5	8.5	7.5
Total value of hydrocarbon exports ($ billions)	9.768	15.219	22.139	26.663	31.752	37.447
Crude oil	9.193	13.861	19.933	23.875	28.536	33.811
Gas	0.575	1.358	2.205	2.788	3.216	3.636
Ratio: hydcrb. exp./exp. gds. svcs. & facs.	0.446	0.521	0.583	0.603	0.620	0.635
Public investments in pet. & gas (billion pesos)						
Nominal	91.81	103.82	115.28	125.61	177.11	212.27
Change (%)	27.1	13.1	11.0	9.0	41.0	19.9
Real (1960 pesos)	13.28	12.44	11.50	10.70	12.99	13.44
Change (%)	4.2	-6.3	-7.6	-7.0	21.4	3.5

Source: Abel Beltram del Rio, "The Mexican Oil Syndrome: Early Symptoms, Preventive Efforts, and Prognosis," Quarterly Review of Economics and Business (Summer 1981), p. 125.

TABLE 7.10

Projection of the Primary and Secondary Oil Indicators of
Mexico 1985 and 1990
(percentages)

	1979	1985	1990
Primary indicators			
Share of crude oil			
in merchandise exports	45.2%	74.0%	76.5%
Share of crude and gas			
in merchandise exports	45.2	82.0	86.4
Share of petroleum			
in GDP	6.5	8.6	9.6
Crude oil production			
per capita			
(barrels per inhabitant)	8.7	16.1	22.3
Secondary: composition of GDP			
Exports	11.3	11.5	11.1
Government consumption	10.7	11.2	11.8
Gross fixed investment	22.9	29.0	31.8
Public	10.1	14.0	16.6
Private	12.8	15.0	15.2
Increase in stocks	2.7	2.8	2.9
Private consumption	66.3	63.8	62.3
Imports	-13.9	-18.3	-19.9
GDP	100.0	100.0	100.0
Government expenditure	18.8	25.2	28.4

Source: Abel Beltram del Rio, "The Mexican Oil Syndrome:
Early Symptoms, Preventive Efforts, and Prognosis," Quarterly
Review of Economics and Business (Summer 1981), p. 127.

OPTIMAL CONTROL FORECAST, 1985-90

For the 1985-90 period, the model was run with a 10 percent rate of crude petroleum production level. This is not only in line with the National Industrial Development Plan (although a bit high) but also based on the fact that higher rates were inconsistent with the imposed inflation barrier. One run maximized the capital stock in 1990 and the other the level of total consumption (again with the restrictions on government consumption and the government deficit).

The consumption oriented run is clearly superior, yielding an inflation rate of only 4.8 percent versus 9.6 percent for the optimal capital stock, while at the same time reaching a higher rate of real GDP and private consumption (Table 7.11).

The government deficit rises to 12.6 percent (versus 6.8 for the maximization of the capital stock), but this is still within acceptable levels and a small price to pay for the overall economic improvement.

OPTIMAL CONTROL FORECAST, 1990-95

For the period past 1990, the model was set to maximize total consumption. Here the main interest in light of the deceleration of inflation in the late 1980s was whether or not crude oil production (political considerations aside) could be increased without setting off another inflationary spiral.

Two runs were made—one with crude petroleum production at 10 percent and another at 12 percent. Interestingly enough there was little difference in the runs (Table 7.12). By this time, GDP will (if the 1980s optimal path is approximated) have settled into a stable expansion at about 6.5 percent in real terms, but one where any shock will result in another sharp increase in inflationary pressure. The risk associated with increased oil production levels would be too great in this regard, particularly in terms of the marginal gains in real GDP and consumption, to warrant anything over around 8 percent maximum. The same, of course, holds for 1995-2000.

Despite several marked differences—anticipated inflation rates and the size of the government deficits—a number of areas of common ground exist between the optimal control forecasts developed here and the Wharton model.

1. With the rapid development of its oil sector during the recent past, 1978-79, Mexico has shown clear evidence of the

TABLE 7.11

Mexico: Optimal Control Forecast, 1985-90

	1985 Optimal: Capital Stock Maximized	1985 Optimal: Consumption Maximized	Maximizing Capital Stock 1990 Optimal	Maximizing Consumption 1990 Optimal	Average Annual Growth 1985-90 Maximizing Capital Stock	Average Annual Growth 1985-90 Maximizing Consumption
Real Variables (billions of 1975 pesos)						
Gross Domestic Product	1642.3	1623.3	2255.1	2250.2	6.5	6.7
Government Consumption	294.3	213.5	418.7	333.6	7.3	9.3
Government Investment	237.9	206.8	378.6	340.2	9.8	10.5
Total Government Expenditures	532.6	428.3	797.2	719.6	8.4	10.9
Private Consumption	876.7	991.4	1124.1	1295.6	5.1	5.5
Private Investment	208.9	206.8	337.0	339.3	10.0	10.4
Total Private Expenditures	1085.6	1198.2	1461.1	1634.9	6.1	6.4
Capital Stock	1205.5	1162.1	1981.2	1942.7	10.4	10.8
Total Investment	446.8	421.6	715.6	725.4	9.9	11.5
Exports	250.3	250.3	346.1	346.1	6.7	6.7
Imports	-237.9	-233.1	-289.5	-317.9	4.0	6.4
Government Revenue	267.4	266.8	428.0	427.9	9.9	9.9
Government Deficit	-265.2	-161.5	-369.2	-291.7	6.8	12.6
Growth in GDP	6.6	5.9	6.3	6.8		

(continued)

Table 7.11 (continued)

	1985 Optimal: Capital Stock Maximized	1985 Optimal: Consumption Maximized	Maximizing Capital Stock 1990 Optimal	Maximizing Consumption 1990 Optimal	Average Annual Growth 1985-90 Maximizing Capital Stock	Average Annual Growth 1985-90 Maximizing Consumption
Monetary Variables (billions of pesos)						
Bank of Mexico Reserve Money	831.8	700.6	2019.3	1317.5	19.4	13.5
Narrow Money	936.0	904.7	2093.1	1725.0	17.5	13.8
Broad Money	1541.6	1363.3	3579.1	2437.9	18.3	12.3
Price Variables (average annual rate)						
Inflation—Wholesale Price Index	9.6	4.8	11.2	7.5	—	—
Inflation—Consumer Price Index	12.4	8.1	13.9	10.8	—	—
Inflation—Gross Domestic Product Deflator	11.6	8.9	12.7	10.1	—	—
Gross Domestic Product Deflator (1975 = 1.00)	4.04	3.85	7.71	6.28	13.8	10.3

Note: 1985 base year for optimizing capital stock run for 1985-90 derived from 1975-85 run with capital stock optimized, constrained government consumption at 0.75 growth in government investment and an unconstrained government deficit; 1985 base year for maximization of consumption for 1985-90 derived from 1979-85 run assuming constrained government consumption, constrained deficit and optimization of consumption. Crude oil production increasing at an annual average rate of 10 percent in each of the 1985-90 runs. Government deficit not constrained in maximization of capital stock run, but constrained in consumption maximization run; government consumption constrained at 0.75 growth in government investment in both 1985-90 runs. In all cases, government deficits are constrained in the range of 10-12% of GDP

Source: Compiled by the author.

TABLE 7.12

Mexico: Optimal Control Forecast, 1990-95

	1990 Optimal Solution	Optimal 1995 Oil Production = 10%	Optimal 1995 Oil Production = 12%	Average Annual Growth with Oil Production = 10%	Percent of Gross Domestic Product 1990	Percent of Gross Domestic Product 1995
Real Variables (billions of 1975 pesos)						
Gross Domestic Product (GDPNP)	2250.2	3099.5	3098.9	6.6	—	15.0
Government Consumption (GCNP)	333.6	465.8	465.4	6.9	14.8	19.3
Government Investment (GIP)	386.1	599.4	598.9	9.2	17.2	
Total Government Expenditures (GENANP)	719.6	1065.2	1064.4	8.2	32.0	34.4
Private Consumption (PCNP)	1295.6	1773.6	1774.2	6.5	57.6	57.2
Private Investment (PIP)	339.3	518.1	517.8	8.8	15.1	16.7
Total Private Expenditures (PENANP)	1634.9	2291.7	2292.0	7.0	72.7	73.9
Capital Stock (KP)	1970.0	3069.9	3068.5	9.3	87.6	99.0
Total Investment (TINP)	725.4	1117.5	1116.8	9.0	32.2	36.1
Exports (EP)	346.1	493.4	521.7	7.3	15.4	15.9
Imports (Z)	-317.9	-361.7	-360.3	2.6	14.1	11.7
Government Revenue (GREVP)	427.9	681.8	737.7	9.8	19.0	22.0
Government Deficit (GDEFP)	-291.8	-383.4	-326.7	5.6	13.0	12.4
Growth in GDP (GGDPNP)	6.8	6.5	6.5	—	—	—

(continued)

Table 7.12 (continued)

Monetary Variables (billions of pesos)	1990 Optimal Solution	Optimal 1995 Oil Production		Average Annual Growth with Oil Production = 10%	Percent of Gross Domestic Product	
		= 10%	= 12%		1990	1995
Bank of Mexico Reserve Money (BMRM)	1317.5	4053.8	4085.9	25.2	9.3	9.7
Narrow Money (M1)	1725.0	3835.4	3851.3	17.3	12.2	9.2
Broad Money (M2)	2437.9	6959.6	7013.5	23.3	17.2	16.7
Price Variables (average annual rate)						
Inflation—Wholesale Price Index (INFW)	7.5	14.2	14.2	—	—	—
Inflation—Consumer Price Index (INFC)	10.8	16.8	16.8	—	—	—
Inflation—Gross Domestic Product Deflator (INF)	10.2	14.5	14.5	—	—	—
Gross Domestic Product Deflator (GDPDF) (1975 = 1.00)	6.29	13.49	13.56	1.65	—	—

Note: Percent of Gross Domestic Product for 1995 based on 10% crude oil production run; total consumption maximized in both runs.
Source: Compiled by the author.

early signs of the oil syndrome, as found in the Persian Gulf countries, although in a milder form, given Mexico's size and economic diversification.

2. Unplanned rapid growth weakened Lopez Portillo's antiinflationary effort. As a result, his fundamental aim of eliminating the inflationary gap (mainly with the United States) before entering the oil based expansionary phase did not materialize.

3. The long (and hard to control) northern border makes Mexico a very open economy. Consequently, a chronic inflationary gap cannot be allowed if a weakening of the financial system and a strengthening of the income protection demands are to be avoided.

4. The prognosis for most of the 1980s is a continuation of a tug-of-war between Lopez Portillo's antiinflationary standard and the oil boom.

5. In the prognosis, a prudent oil policy is assumed. It reaches 2.8 million bpd of crude output and doubles by 1990.

MEXICO IN THE 1990s

Mexico's medium-term development potential thus appears to be assured. This means that, until the mid-1980s, almost irrespective of external factors such as a possible stagnation or collapse in the price of crude oil, the country should be able to sustain a relatively noninflationary expansion of 6.5 to 7 percent per annum in real terms. Furthermore, this is possible well within the capacity of Mexico's oil reserves and at rates that are considered acceptable in both political terms and in terms of exploitation in relation to reserves within the oil industry.

It also appears that this is possible without making Mexico nearly as dependent on oil exports for its economic survival as is the case with many of the OPEC countries. Provided that the government deficits can be kept in the 10 to 12 percent of GDP range used in the forecasts above, the country would be able to tap the international capital markets on good terms if temporary difficulties arose.

For the second half of the 1980s, it would be possible, all other things being equal, for these trends to continue. However, several problems could develop. First, serious collapse could occur in real oil prices. If this took place, then Mexico might have to increase its oil exports to high levels (i.e., 6 to 7 million bpd in order to continue to fund GNP growth at 6.5 to 7 percent per annum on a steady basis. Second, politics could become a destabilizing force with the opening of the recent political process A backlash from conservatives insisting on the preservation of power of the PRI could result in declining investor confidence both domestic and foreign. The result would likely be a slow-down in the rate of funding of expansion and hence of expansion itself. As seen from the spring of 1982, neither of these events appears highly likely, but the possibility that they could occur cannot be easily ruled out.

The 1990s are even more uncertain largely because of external factors over which Mexico has little influence. The optimal control forecasts have assumed a relatively stable international system in terms of the U.S. economy and international prices through this period. Under these circumstances, Mexico's growth prospects are quite favorable in what must be considered the most probable environment. Clearly, if external conditions deteriorate, Mexico's prospects would be much less favorable.

Assuming that neither external or internal factors divert the path of Mexican development in the 1980s, some speculation about the 1990s is possible.

It is reasonable to assume that, after a decade of relatively rapid growth, Mexico would find it expedient to consolidate its investments and perhaps opt for a greater domestic utilization of its oil wealth or at least pursue increasingly conservative production rates. The result is likely to be a slowdown in the rate of growth of output to 5 percent per annum or so in the 1990s compared with 6.5 or 7 percent in the 1980s.

In terms of per capita income, the picture of course is less bright. By the end of the century, the Mexican population will be around 40 percent of the size of the U.S. population (compared with 27 percent in 1975). Given that the income gap between Mexico and the United States should be slowly reduced over the next two decades, pressures will gradually lessen for Mexicans to emigrate to the United States. It is unlikely, however, that the gaps will be narrowed sufficiently to halt migration.

NOTES

1. Leopoldo Solís, Economic Policy Reform in Mexico (Elmsford, N.Y.: Pergamon Press, 1981), p. 116.
2. Ibid.
3. Ibid., pp. 116-17.

4. A similar approach was used by C. H. Wong and O. Pettersen, "Financial Programming in the Framework of Optimal Control," Weltwirtschaftliches Archiv no. 1, 1979, pp. 20-37, for a short-run analysis of the Philippine economy.

5. Solis, Economic Policy Reform in Mexico, p. 118.

6. Abel Beltran del Rio, "The Mexican Oil Syndrome: Early Symptoms, Preventive Efforts and Prognosis," Quarterly Review of Economics and Business, Summer 1981, p. 124.

7. Jesus-Augustin Velasco, Mexico in the World Oil Market: Opportunities and Dangers for Mexican Development, John F. Kennedy School of Government Discussion Paper E-80-07, Cambridge, Mass.: Harvard University, October 1980, pp. 31-32.

8. Beltran del Rio, "Mexican Oil Syndrome," p. 124.

9. David Ronfeldt, Richard Nehring, Arturo Gandara, Mexico's Petroleum and U.S. Policy: Implications for the 1980s (Santa Monica, Calif.: Rand Corporation, 1980), p. 81.

10. Guillermo Ortiz and Leopoldo Solis, "Financial Structure and Exchange Rate Experience," Journal of Development Economics, 1979, p. 538.

11. A stable rate is also said to reduce investor uncertainty and facilitate investment and trade. Cf. James R. Dempsey, "Pesos or Dollars in Mexico?" Euromoney, June 1978, pp. 147-64; and James R. Dempsey, "The Mexican Back to Back Loan," Euromoney, May 1978, pp. 69-75, for an excellent account of how fluctuating rates complicate business decision making.

12. Abel Beltran del Rio, "Mexico's Troubled Economy: Peso Prognosis," Wharton Magazine, Winter 1977, p. 56.

13. Leroy O. Laney, "Oil Inflation and the Mexican Peso," Voice of the Federal Reserve Bank of Dallas, September 1979, p. 3.

14. Solis, Economic Policy Reform in Mexico, p. 119.

15. Cf. Guillermo Calvo and Carlos Alfredo Rodriguez, "A Model of Exchange Rate Determination under Currency Substitution and Rational Expectations," Journal of Political Economy, June 1977; and Arturo Brillenbourg and Susan Schadler, "A Model of Currency Substitution in Exchange Rate Determination, 1973-78," International Monetary Fund Staff Papers, September 1979.

16. Leroy O. Laney, "Currency Substitution: The Mexican Case," Voice of the Federal Reserve Bank of Dallas, January 1981, p. 8.

17. Solis, Economic Policy Reform in Mexico, pp. 119-20.

18. Calvin Blair, Economic Development Policy in Mexico: A New Penchant for Planning, Technical Papers Series no. 26,

(Austin: Office for Public Sector Studies, Institute of Latin American Studies, University of Texas at Austin, 1980), p. 15.

19. Summarized in Beltran del Rio, "The Mexican Oil Syndrome," pp. 124-28.

8

SUMMARY, CONCLUSIONS, AND
IMPLICATIONS FOR
THE UNITED STATES

INTRODUCTION

The oil discoveries and expanded production levels have
and will continue to have several important impacts on Mexico.
Firstly, they have provided the country with the means to
change fundamentally the status quo between itself and the
United States. Secondly, Mexico's economic power was suddenly
increased, but its vulnerability also rapidly increased as the
government became accustomed to a larger source of revenues.
Thirdly, the interdependence between the government, the
private sector, and various groups within the country has become more unstable in both the political and economic senses as
frictions developed between these groups.[1] And fourthly, for
all these reasons, the government has sought a development
strategy that would enable it to achieve a viable interdependence
between internal groups and between itself and the United
States.

Several possible strategies were both logical and feasible:

1. a rapid increase in the production of crude oil
2. expanded crude oil production, but based largely on
domestic needs
3. a policy of diversified industrialization
4. a policy mix consisting of moderate industrialization
and development of service sectors and government employment
5. a high growth strategy of petroleum based industrialization combined with high and steady levels of oil exports.

Each of these strategies has certain advantages and disadvantages. Clearly, the strategy of expanding the production and export of crude would increase revenues, but at the same time it would also increase the country's external vulnerability and risk, increasing internal friction between the government and various conservationist-nationalistic groups. Likewise, a stabilization of output levels for domestic needs and supplemental foreign exchange earnings would minimize dislocations and inflationary pressures, but would not permit the government to address the country's growing unemployment problem.

Ultimately, of course, the country adopted the National Industrial Development Plan with its orientation toward some sort of viable interdependences between the United States and Mexico together with its implicit compromise between nationalistic and high growth oriented domestic groups. Viable interdependence with domestic investment of oil revenues in heavy industries (made possible by high levels of export) was seen as the best means of achieving some sort of balance between efficiency and vulnerability.[2] Through government investment of oil revenues, the authorities sought structural change capable of (1) increasing the ability of the country to utilize more of its oil and gas resources domestically (so that the country's dependence on hydrocarbon exports could be curtailed); (2) increasing the country's ability to produce and trade products derived from hydrocarbons; (3) enabling the country to trade and bargain on relatively equal technological and economic ground; and (4) making the country less vulnerable to the effects of severe market fluctuations or sudden changes in the politics and trade policies of the United States and other developed countries.

UNITED STATES-MEXICAN RELATIONS

The forecasts in the previous chapter have a number of implications for the United States. U.S. energy difficulties have more or less coincided with: (1) the large oil discoveries in Mexico, (2) sharply rising Mexican exports of other products, e.g., agricultural items, to the United States, and (3) an awareness that approximately six million Mexicans are living in the United States, many of them illegally.

It is clear from the forecasts and in light of (2) and (3) above that the scope for Mexican discretionary action in oil production and export rates is rather limited, particularly in terms of the recent fall in oil prices. The forecasts indicate that it will take increases in crude oil production rates of at

least 10 percent per annum through the 1980s and into the 1990s
if Mexico is to create the number of jobs sufficient to reduce and
eventually eliminate the need for Mexicans to migrate to the
United States in search of work.

Mutual interest over the long term is thus likely to bring
an increase of pragmatism in Mexican/U.S. relations, with an
eventual reduction in dogmatism on the Mexican side, though
this will presumably be provided by the politicians as long as
their domestic audiences require it.

Present Mexican policy appears committed to maintain existing Mexican markets in the United States and open up new ones.
Faced with the benefits of this increased exchange in terms of
industrial and agricultural employment, any future Mexican
government would have to consider carefully the implications
of embarking on policies that might prove damaging to U.S.
interests.

As oil wealth brings average Mexican income levels closer
to those of the United States, pressures to migrate from Mexico
to the United States should lessen. By that time the Mexican
American community in the United States will have become that
much larger, wealthier, more respected and a more permanent
feature of U.S. life. These tendencies cannot but more closely
link the two countries and increase their mutual interests.

However, despite movements toward closer identity of
interests, it would be erroneous for Americans to believe that
increased wealth will make the Mexicans more "reasonable."
They will continue to wish to preserve and develop their own
very distinct traditions and institutions, many of which they
consider superior to those of the United States.

POTENTIAL DEVELOPMENT PROBLEMS

While the econometric model in the previous chapter indicated this strategy to be optimal and feasible, albeit at 6 or 7
percent real growth rather than the 10 percent envisaged by
the plan, it is still true that—

1. the country is becoming more and more dependent on
oil exports and on the impact of these oil revenues on the domestic
economy
2. the strategy is largely a resource based, capital intensive process of industrialization, with agriculture playing a
largely passive role of maintaining structural balance, and the
noneconomic one of enduring some level of food self-reliance

3. the strategy requires careful preplanning and identification of profitable investments (particularly since the break with past patterns of growth has been so radical)

4. the strategy has been deficient in assessing realistically the manpower and education requirements of such industries

5. little attention has been given to the identification of operational means of shifting from essentially an import substitution development strategy to one more viable in terms of the country's comparative advantage.

There are several problems that are potentially serious enough to warrant government action. It is difficult to assign priority to these possible problems in terms of relative importance for concern. A tentative ranking based on factors discussed in the previous chapters would be: (1) a worsening of the world food situation, (2) deterioration of the income distribution, (3) sector uncertainty as to the role of the government in the economy, and (4) those problems requiring reforms in planning procedures.

These factors are capable of creating a number of potential problems, which, if left unattended, could undermine the country's whole development effort.

Worsening of the World Food Situation

The world food situation will likely continue to deteriorate over the next 20 years as population pressures begin to make themselves felt and the amount of usable land per capita declines.[3] While existing technology should be able to offset this trend, the inability of many developing countries to implement productivity increases (largely for political reasons) will mean lagging output. The result will be increases in scarcity whereby food, even if available, will sell for much higher prices, causing Mexico's balance of payments to deteriorate drastically.

Agriculture is surely the weak link in any chain of integrated development policies in Mexico. The National Industrial Development Plan itself points out that a doubling of public investment in the sector between 1977 and 1982 will barely arrest the decline in agricultural output, and if that output grows no faster than the 3 percent minimum rate projected in the plan, food imports will require 21 percent of petroleum export revenues in 1982 and 54 percent in 1990.[4]

Facing increased food imports and declining agricultural growth, Mexico can pursue one of two options. It can finance

necessary food imports out of export revenues and take the
chance that the world food situation will not deteriorate, or it
can redirect food crop production and processing to better
serve domestic needs. The first path leads to increased food
dependency and the second to increased food self-reliance.
Both paths will influence the long-term structure of the Mexican
economy and its comparative advantage in the world market.

In a major effort at modeling the overall Mexican agricultural sector, Goreoux and Manne identify the slow growth of
demand (domestic and export) and a serious constraint of agricultural growth contributing to low rural incomes and adverse
changes in the agricultural terms of trade.[5] Rural incomes
could be increased by higher support prices, administered by
the state enterprise Compania Nacional de Subsistencias Popu-
lares (CONASUPO), at the cost of the welfare of the consumers
and growing food stockpiles, unless Conasupo also subsidized
domestic sales, which it does. Such funding, if not offset by
tax revenues, would however contribute to inflation. Oil as a
source of foreign exchange offers subsidized imported food as
a noninflationary option, but this increases dependence and
vulnerability toward price movements.[6]

Given the possibility of a dismal worldwide agricultural
performance and the seriousness of the problem, several more
direct actions should be undertaken. These include:

1. improving the productivity of traditional agriculture.
This will require a much higher level of support services and
easier access to financial aid. Policies along these lines could
substantially increase the production of corn and beans in the
higher rainfall areas (where most of the traditional agriculture
is located)

2. bringing more land under cultivation, particularly in
the southeast, which possesses water resources but is underpopulated

3. improving transportation.[7]

The government appears to be moving in these directions.
In April 1980, it announced a whole series of new measures
directed toward the improvement of agriculture within the context of the Overall Development Plan, 1980-82 and under the
Mexican Food System. Some of the measures included under
these plans are:

1. encouragement of producers' cooperatives for the sale
of produce and the purchasing of materials

    2. increases in research and development directed toward rain dependent agriculture

    3. improvement of water resource infrastructure in rain dependent areas

    4. concentration of cattle breeding in order to bring more grazing land under cultivation

    5. promotion of colonization of new agricultural areas

    6. improved credit and insurance facilities for producers of essential commodities. [8]

These measures seem long overdue. They are in a large part directed toward areas where rainfall is adequate, to areas where the poorest traditional farmers work the land, and to regions to be opened up for further development.

These measures are designed to raise the rate of growth of agricultural production to 4.1 percent in real terms by 1982 (at which point self-sufficiency in maize and beans would be assured). Self-sufficiency in rice, wheat, sesame, soybeans, and sorghum is sought by 1985.

To achieve these objectives, it is planned to increase goverr ment investment connected with agriculture by over 20 percent per annum in real terms during the period. The total expenditure earmarked for agricultural development in 1980 as a result of these plans approaches $6 billion. This compares with a total investment in the sector of around $1 billion in the mid-1970s. [9]

Despite the encouraging directions of these changes, considerable organizational difficulties are developing, not the least of which are corruption at the local level and mistrust of administrators of the programs by the traditional farming community. Despite these reservations, a significant increase in the resources reaching the farmers is to be expected, and, with this, corresponding increases in output and productivity should come if not by the target dates, at least by 1990.

Deterioration in Income Distribution

There is evidence that in Mexico (as in many other developing countries) rapid growth is resulting in a worsening of the already highly unequal distribution of income. [10] Unless action is taken soon, the deterioration may become even more severe in the 1980s as industrialization speeds up. As is typically the case in countries at this stage of development, gaps are appearing between various income groups and regions in the country as well as between the country's urban and rural population. [11]

The main problems preventing a better distribution of wealth appear to be the inability of the rural sector to generate sufficient wealth for its population, and excessive concentration of population in the largest cities, making it difficult to provide adequate levels of services and to satisfy aspirations, particularly of the lowest earning categories.

Whether these shortcomings are likely to be solved by the implementation of the government's policy in relation to urban and industrial development (which aims at spreading growth more evenly around the country) is certainly problematical. Other moves, such as the Mexican Food System and the intention to provide a higher proportion of agricultural workers with regular wages, appear more promising, at least in the near term.

There is no reason why a conflict between equity and efficiency has to arise[12] even though, in its eagerness to promote growth, the government has tended to allocate oil revenues to capital intensive industrial development capable of creating (at least directly) only a limited number of jobs. These investments have prevailed at the expense of more potentially labor intensive investments located in the more populous areas. While it is highly inefficient to counter the forces of economic efficiency completely and solely on the basis of social efficiency criteria, it is clear in light of the Iranian experience that a balance must soon be struck on both human and political grounds so as to prevent a disruption of the social fabric.

In this regard Mexico is somewhat fortunate that, by developing later, it can avoid many of the mistakes made by Iran. There is no question that a major lesson to be learned from Iran's development strategy is that, even though the level of income for most of the population may be increasing fairly rapidly, discontent is likely to arise if the gap between regions, urban and rural, or even particular groups continues to widen.[13] Adverse income distributional patterns of this sort ordinarily will not cause a problem if corrected fairly early. Increasing income disparity can, however, cause mass alienation, as in the case of Iran. This is most likely to occur during periods such as the present when expectations of future living standards are accelerating (because of the knowledge of increased wealth and its accumulation in relatively few hands).

Income distributional considerations translate themselves into the setting of targets to minimize the urban/rural income gap and the achievement of better interregional balances. Investments along these lines can be easily justified given the potential social strains associated with the country's present strategy. This conclusion holds even though the resulting investment pattern might reduce the country's overall economic growth potential.

Role of the Government

In order to implement its long-run development strategy efficiently, it will be necessary for the authorities to define more precisely than they have so far the role of government in the economy. To be sure, the existence of a large influx of oil based revenues implies an increasing role for the public sector. On the other hand, it is not clear what will happen when the oil revenues level off (perhaps as early as 1990). Unless there is some sort of tax reform, the role of the public sector may have to decrease rapidly relative to that of the private sector.

The forecasts of the previous chapter indicate, however, that the private sector may not be in a position to generate the type of demand needed to maintain the growth rates capable of being attained in the country. This is particularly true of private investment, whose rate of growth was positively affected by government investment in the forecasts.

In principle, therefore, while the government's intention of encouraging the private sector to assume wide responsibility for production is a wise one given the inefficiencies usually associated with public sector involvement, reduction of government activities should not proceed too rapidly; there is a real risk of deflation if the government contracts its investment too rapidly. This problem is reinforced by the apparent accelerator mechanism underlying private investments; i.e., a reduction in the rate of growth would have a compound contracting effect on private investment.

While it is clear, therefore, that the government's overall industrial development strategy is a sound way of spending the oil revenues, this strategy must eventually rest on the abilities and dynamism of the private sector. The government must, therefore, clearly convey to the private sector that its continued activity in the economy is necessary for stabilization purposes. Otherwise, there may be a number of misunderstandings over the true scope of the government's economic involvement that would cause the private sector to be even more reluctant to undertake investments in manufacturing than it has been at times in the past when there was uncertainty over its role.

In any case the government should have little trouble finding areas in which to spend money in order to direct the path of the economy toward the creation of a normal balance with the private sector. These include:

1. investing in health and education necessary to maintain and increase the human element in the development process (while at the same time contributing to improvements in labor and managerial quality)

2. participating initially in heavy industries where the private sector may be reluctant to venture

3. subsidizing regional investments in backward areas to mold the future spatial configuration of population and economic activity in a manner more compatible with existing sociocultural factors.

Planning Reforms

There is a great need to revise the country's system of planning[14] in order to fill the current gap in decision making that exists not only between the various ministries in Mexico City but also between the decision makers in the capital and those in the provinces. Again, the Iranian experience illustrates the ramifications of overcentralized decision making. Thus qualified individuals at the regional and city level presumably well acquainted with local problems must be drawn into the decision-making process to an extent much greater than has been the case in the past.

The major institutional problems in this area that need to be examined by the authorities include the scope and capability of the planning system, the implementation of decentralization policies involving decisions designed to increase participation of more individuals in the development process, and the necessity of administrative reforms.

In view of the very high goals set for Mexico's social and economic system over the longer term and the pressures associated with reaching these goals, it is clear that not only private sector efficiency, but also increases in public sector efficiency, are of paramount importance. Despite some recent reforms along these lines, the country's overly bureaucratic planning procedures must be streamlined in order to reduce the time delays in project identification and the subsequent awarding of contracts. Reforms should also help reduce the duplication of effort and the numerous cost overruns that currently characterize the Mexican development effort. Better coordination of expenditure plans between ministries would also help (through stricter budgetary control) to reduce inflationary pressures.

The question of reforming the public administrative apparatus is an efficiency question that needs to be examined on a longer-term basis. Eliminating red tape is important as a complementary factor in the strategy of development outlined above, especially with respect to creating private sector enthusiasm and dynamism. Within the public sector, there should also be a reform in the incentive system for public employees. If the government is forced to increase its scope in the activity of the economy because of the natural conservatism of the private sector, then it must be able to attract and retain highly qualified managers. Clearly, for the government to expand its capability in the economy, it must revise its incentive system to reward individuals more on the basis of ability and performance.

CONCLUSIONS

On the basis of the above considerations, recent trends in the economy, and the experience of other oil exporting countries, two eventualities seem likely.[15] Firstly, despite recent political difficulties with the United States, Mexico will increase its crude oil and natural gas exports to this country as the most readily accessible market. The ease of making delivery and the high costs of processing gas and shipping oil to other markets will make contractual agreements mutually attractive, and balance of payments considerations will also encourage exports to the United States. The Mexican government's desire to eliminate the vestiges of the 1976 crisis and the evident expansionist leadership of PEMEX reinforce a tendency to accelerate petroleum production despite lingering efforts by some groups to return to a conservationist policy.

Secondly, unless measures are taken, the increased foreign exchange flow into Mexico will continue to create strong inflationary pressures. Although Mexican economists are well aware of the problem, the experience of other oil exporting countries in handling such difficulties has not been particularly encouraging. Leopoldo Solis, subdirector general of the Bank of Mexico, has noted:

Two dilemmas are apparent. Firstly, the petroleum income has a huge inflationary potential, which would jeopardize Mexico's import substitution policy and the creation of jobs through it. Therefore, aggregate demand should be tempered by controlling PEMEX's expenditures. And, since not all of the petroleum income may be spent, because of its inflationary pressure, it will be necessary to increase the price of oil and derivatives sold domestically to complement this frozen income.

The second dilemma also proceeds from the inflationary pressure of petroleum income which would cause a deterioration of the exchange rate of the Mexican peso. This, in its turn, would reflect unfavorably on Mexico's import substitution policy, its capacity to export, and therefore diversify production and employment. The example of Iran is evident: petroleum has provoked a decline in the production of Persian carpets, which require a large amount of labor and a favorable exchange rate.[16]

While overall Mexico's economic future seems assured, the Iranian experience has demonstrated how fragile oil based economies really are. A charting of the country's likely growth path is quite pretentious and should be done only in the context of the caviats discussed above (plus, or course, all the political, social, and military ones so often seen in the popular press).

NOTES

1. Cf. Pablo Gonzalez Casanova, "Mexico, The Most Probable Course of Development," Latin American Perspectives, Winter 1982, pp. 78-88.

2. A model along these lines is developed in Elias Tuma, "Strategic Resources and Viable Interdependence: The Case of Middle Eastern Oil," The Middle East Journal, Summer 1979, pp. 269-87.

3. Radha Sinha, "The World Food Problem: Consensus and Conflict," World Development, May-June 1977, pp. 371-82.

4. Arthur Silvers and Pierre Crossin, Rural Development and Urban-bound Migration in Mexico (Washington, D.C.: Resources for the Future, 1980) pp. 53-54.

5. J. H. Duloy and R. D. Norton, "CHAC Results: Economic Alternatives for Mexican Agriculture," in Multilevel Planning: Case Studies in Mexico, ed. L. M. Goreux and A. S. Manne (New York: North Holland, 1973).

6. Sam Lanfranco, "Mexican Oil, Export-led Development and Agricultural Neglect," Journal of Economic Development, July 1981, p. 138.

7. Along similar lines see Carlos Benito, "Policies for Food Production and Consumption in Underdevelopment: The Case of Mexico," Journal of Policy Modeling, September 1979, pp. 383-98.

8. "SAM, the Beginnings of Strategy," Comercio Exterior de Mexico, July 1980, pp. 243-49.

9. Ibid., p. 248.

10. Salvatore Bizzarro, "Mexico's Poor," Current History, November 1981, pp. 370-73.

11. John Bailey, "Agrarian Reform in Mexico," Current History, November 1981, pp. 357-60.

12. See Montek Ahluwalia and Hollis B. Chenery, "A Model of Distribution and Growth," in Redistribution with Growth, ed. H. Chenery (London: Oxford University Press, 1974), pp. 209-35, for a proof of this proposition.

13. Robert Looney, Economic Origins of the Iranian Revolution (New York: Pergamon Press, 1982), Chap. 14.

14. Given Lopez Portillo's background, a number of constructive administrative reforms have been carried out since 1976. He summarizes the scope of the problem in "Improving the Planning Process: An Imperative for Mexico at This Time," Comercio Exterior de Mexico, May 1978, pp. 191-96.

15. Cf. James Street, "Prospects for Mexico's Industrial Development Plan in the 1980s," Texas Business Review, May-June 1980, p. 129.

16. Leopoldo Solis, "The Petroleum Boom in Mexico: An Opportunity for Correcting the Pattern of Economic Development," paper presented at the North American Economic Studies Association Meetings, Mexico City, December 28, 1978, p. 1.

VARIABLES AND THEIR PROPERTIES

The variables listed below (Table A.1) were used in the analysis and forecast of the economy. They cover the period 1951 to 1979 or 1980 and are based on annual data. To make the listing briefer, the following conventions were used in the presentation of the equations in the main body of the study:

1. Constant prices are of variables deflated with the GDP deflator, 1975 = 100.0, and are represented by P at the end of the variable; i.e., GDPNP is real or constant gross domestic product, whereas GDPN is nominal or gross domestic product at current prices.

2. Δ is an operator, referring to the difference between two successive time periods, e.g., 1970 minus 1969.

3. L at the end of a variable means it is lagged one year, while L2 at the end refers to a lag of two years.

4. Either a dot over the variable, e.g., $\dot{M2}$, or a G preceding the variable (GM2) indicates the percentage rate of growth.

5. Symbols beginning with L (as LGDPNP) refer to the natural log of the variable.

TABLE A.1

Variables and Their Properties

Symbol	Variable Name	Character-istic	Possible Policy Variable
PEN	Nominal private consumption	endogenous	no
PCNP	Real private consumption	endogenous	no
PC	nominal private credit	endogenous	no
PCP	real private credit	endogenous	yes
GCN	nominal government consumption	endogenous	yes
GCNP	real government consumption	endogenous	yes
TIN	total investment	endogenous	no
PENAN	total nominal private expenditure	endogenous	no
PENANP	total real private expenditure	endogenous	no
GIN	nominal government expenditure	exogenous	yes
GINP	real government expenditure	exogenous	yes
EXPTNA	nominal exports	endogenous	no
EP	real exports (deflated GDP deflator)	endogenous	no
EW	real exports deflated world price index (IMF)	endogenous	no
ZNAN (or Z)	nominal imports	endogenous	no
ZNAN (or ZP)	real imports	endogenous	no
CPP	crude petroleum production	exogenous	yes
K	nominal capital stock	endogenous	no
KP	real capital stock	endogenous	no
EX	exchange rate	exogenous	yes
USEUV	U.S. export unit price	exogenous	no
USYP	real U.S. gross domestic product	exogenous	no
USWP	U.S. wholesale price index	exogenous	no

Symbol	Variable Name	Character-istic	Possible Policy Variable
WINF	rate of change industrial countries export unit price = world inflation	exogenous	no
INFUS	rate of change U.S. wholesale price index	exogenous	no
USGDP	U.S. nominal gross domestic product	exogenous	no
USTB	U.S. treasury bill rate	exogenous	no
BMRM	Bank of Mexico reserve money	endogenous	no
BMFA	Bank of Mexico net foreign assets	endogenous	no
BMGC	Bank of Mexico government credit	endogenous	yes
TIME	time	exogenous	no
M1	narrow money	endogenous	no
M2	broad money	endogenous	no
PENAN	nominal private expenditures	endogenous	no
GENAN	nominal government expenditures	endogenous	yes
PENANP	real private expenditures	endogenous	yes
GENANP	real government expenditures	endogenous	yes
IP	nominal private investment	endogenous	no
IPP	real private investment	endogenous	no
WPI	wholesale price index	endogenous	no
CIP	consumer price index	endogenous	no
GDPDF	gross domestic product deflator	endogenous	no
INFW	rate of change wholesale price index	endogenous	no
INFC	rate of change consumer price index	endogenous	no
INF	rate of change GDP deflator	endogenous	no
INFWE	expected rate of inflation (wholesale price index)	endogenous	no
INFCE	expected rate of inflation (consumer price index)	endogenous	no
EXCESSA	M1/GDPNP	endogenous	no

(continued)

Table A.1 (continued)

Symbol	Variable Name	Character-istic	Possible Policy Variable
EXCESSB	M2/GDPNP	endogenous	no
GREV	nominal government reve-nue	endogenous	yes
GREUP	real government revenue	endogenous	yes
MI	nominal interest rate	endogenous	yes
MRI	real interest rate	endogenous	yes
PC	nominal private credit	endogenous	yes
PCP	real private credit	endogenous	yes
GDPN	nominal gross domestic product	endogenous	no
GDPNP	real gross domestic product	endogenous	no
BOPE	balance of payments—exports	endogenous	no
BOPZ	balance of payments—imports	endogenous	no
BOP	balance of payments current account	endogenous	no
BOPC	balance of payments long term capital account	endogenous	no
BOPST	balance of payments short term capital account	endogenous	yes
BOPR	balance of payments change in reserves	endogenous	no
DUMEX	dummy variable: 0, 1951-75 1, 1976-80	exogenous	no
DUMDV	dummy variable: 0, 1951-75 0, 1977-80 1, 1976	exogenous	no
DUMTDV	dummy variable: 0, 1951-53 1, 1954-75 2, 1976-80	exogenous	no
INFD	difference Mexican-U.S. inflation rate	exogenous	no
GAP	TINP - SNP	endogenous	no
GAPA	ZP - EP	endogenous	no
TT	terms of trade (USEUV / WPI)	exogenous	no

Source: Compiled by the author.

BIBLIOGRAPHY

Ahking, Francis W. "Mexico: The Open Economy—A Note." Review of Business and Economic Research, Fall 1978, pp. 103-07.

Ahluwalia, Montek, and Chenery, Hollis B. "A Model of Distribution and Growth." In H. Chenery, Redistribution with Growth. London: Oxford University Press, 1974.

Akhtar, M. A. "An Empirical Note on Inflation and Openness in Less Developed Economies." Philippine Economic Journal, no. 4, 1976, pp. 636-49.

Alisky, Marvin. "Population and Migration Problems in Mexico." Current History, November 1981, pp. 365-69.

Almon, S. "The Distributed Lag Between Capital Appropriations and Expenditures." Econometrica, January 1965, pp. 178-96.

Ando, A., and Polash, C. "Some Stabilization Problems of 1971-1975 with an Application of Optimum Control Algorithms." American Economic Review, May 1976, pp. 346-48.

Arronte, R. Carrillo. An Empirical Test on Interregional Planning: A Linear Programming Model for Mexico. Rotterdam: Rotterdam University Press, 1970.

Aspra, L. Antonio. "Import Substitution in Mexico: Past and Present." World Development, January-February 1977, pp. 111-24.

Bailey, John. "Agrarian Reform in Mexico." Current History, November 1981, pp. 357-60.

Bank of Mexico. Informe Anual, various issues.

Baranson, Jack. North-South Technology Transfer: Financing and Institution Building. Mt. Airy, Md.: Lomond Publications, 1981.

Barkely, Sylvia. "Oil for Technology: Blueprint for Mexico's Development." Fusion, July 1981, pp. 26-30.

Barkin, David, and Esteva, Gustavo. Inflacion y Democracia: el Caso de Mexico. Mexico, D.F.: Siglo XXI, 1979.

____. "Social Conflict and Inflation in Mexico." Latin American Perspectives, Winter 1982, pp. 48-64.

Bath, C. Richard, Evans, John, and James, Dilmus. "Dependency, Inflation and the Allocation of Mexico's Petroleum Reserves." Texas Business Review, September-October 1981, pp. 196-202.

Beeker, C. "A Theory of the Allocation of Time." Economic Journal, September 1965, pp. 493-517.

Behrman, Jere, and Klein, L. "Econometric Growth Models for the Developing Economy." In Induction, Growth and Trade, Essays in Honour of Sir Roy Harrod, edited by W. A. Eltis. London: Oxford University Press, 1970.

Beltran del Rio, Abel. "The Mexican Oil Syndrome: Early Symptoms, Preventive Efforts and Prognosis." Quarterly Review of Economics and Business, Summer 1981, pp. 115-30.

____. "Mexico's Troubled Economy: Peso Prognosis." Wharton Magazine, Winter 1977, pp. 55-56.

Benito, Carlos. "Policies for Food Production and Consumption in Underdevelopment: The Case of Mexico." Journal of Policy Modeling, September 1979, pp. 383-98.

Benoit, Emile. Defense and Economic Growth in Developing Countries. Lexington, Mass.: Lexington Books, 1973.

____. "Growth and Defense in Developing Countries." Economic Development and Cultural Change, January 1978, pp. 271-80.

Bergsman, Joel. Income Distribution and Poverty in Mexico. World Bank Staff Working Paper No. 395. New York: International Bank for Reconstruction and Development (World Bank), June 1980.

Bertram, G. W. "The Relevance of the Canadian Wheat Boom in Canadian Economic Growth." Canadian Journal of Economics, November 1973, pp. 545-66.

Bhalla, Surjit. "The Transmission of Inflation into Developing Economies." In World Inflation and the Developing Countries, edited by William Cline. Washington, D.C.: Brookings Institution, 1981.

Bizzarro, Salvatore. "Mexico's Oil Boom." Current History, February 1981, pp. 49-52.

_____. "Mexico's Poor." Current History, November 1981, pp. 370-73.

Blair, Calvin P. Economic Development Policy in Mexico: A New Penchant for Planning. Technical Papers Series no. 26. Austin: Office for Public Sector Studies, Institute of Latin American Studies, University of Texas, 1980.

_____. "Mexico's Economic Development and Relations with the United States." Texas Business Review, March-April 1979, pp. 39-42.

Brillenbourg, Arturo, and Schadler, Susan. "A Model of Currency Substitution in Exchange Rate Determination, 1973-78." International Monetary Fund Staff Papers, September 1979, pp. 513-42.

Bruton, Henry J. "Productivity Growth in Latin America." American Economic Review, December 1967, pp. 1109-16.

Bueno, Geraldo M. "Desarrollo y Petroleo: La Experiencia de los Paises Exportadores." Trimestre Economico, April-June 1980, pp. 256-81.

_____. "The Structure of Protection in Mexico." In The Structure of Protection in Developing Countries, edited by Bela Balassa. Baltimore, Md.: Johns Hopkins University Press, 1973.

Caiden, Naomi, and Wildavsky, Aaron. Planning and Budgeting in Poor Countries. New York: John Wiley, 1974.

Calvo, Guillermo, and Alfredo Rodriguez, Carlos. "A Model of Exchange Rate Determination under Currency Substitution and Rational Expectations." Journal of Political Economy, June 1977, pp. 617-26.

Carbajal, Carlos Vidali. "Politica Tributaria." In Politica Hacendaria y Financiera en Mexico, 1971-1976. Suplemento de Comercio Exterior, August 1976, pp. 72-85.

Casanova, Pablo Gonzalez. "Mexico, The Most Probable Course of Development." Latin American Perspectives, Winter 1982, pp. 78-88.

Caves, R. E. "Export Lead Growth and the New Economic History." In Trade, Balance of Payments and Growth, Essays in Honor of Charles Kindleberger, edited by J. Bhagwati. Amsterdam: North Holland, 1971.

Centro de Investigacion y Docencia Economicas. Economia Mexicana. Mexico, D.F., 1979.

____. "The Mexican Economy: Recent Development and Future Prospects." Cambridge Journal of Economics, June 1980.

Chislett, William. "Critical Year for Economy after Peso Devaluation." Financial Times, March 22, 1982, p. 2.

____. "Lopez Portillo Plays for High Economic Stakes." Financial Times, February 23, 1982, p. 3.

____. "Mexico Faces Crucial Economic Decisions," p. 4 Financial Times, December 10, 1981, p. 2.

____. "Military Eye on Central America." Financial Times, March 22, 1982, p. 3.

____. "U.S.-Mexico Friendship Dogged by Growing Policy Differences." Financial Times, February 12, 1982, p. 5.

Chenery, H. "The Structuralist Approach to Development Policy." American Economic Review, May 1975.

Chow, Gregory C. Analysis and Control of Dynamic Economic Systems. New York: McGraw Hill, 1975, pp. 310-16.

____. "Control Methods for Macroeconomic Policy Analysis." American Economic Review, May 1976, pp. 340-45.

Coale, Ansley. "Population and Growth and Economic Development: The Case of Mexico." Foreign Affairs, January 1978, p. 415-29.

Cockcroft, Jim, and Gandy, Ross. "The Mexican Volcano." Monthly Review, May 1981, pp. 32-44.

Comercio Exterior de Mexico, September 1979.

Crockett, Andrew, and Evans, Owen. "Demand for Money in Middle Eastern Countries." International Monetary Fund Staff Papers, September 1980, pp. 543-77.

Dasgupta, P., and Heal, G. M. "The Optimal Depletion of Exhaustible Resources." Review of Economic Studies, October 1974, pp. 1-29.

Dempsey, James R. "The Mexican Back to Back Loan." Euromoney, May 1978, pp. 69-75.

____. "Pesos or Dollars in Mexico?" Euromoney, June 1978, pp. 147-64.

Dominquez, Jorge. Introduction to Mexico's Political Economy: Challenges at Home and Abroad, edited by Jorge Dominquez. Beverly Hills, Calif.: Sage Publications, 1982.

____, ed. Mexico's Political Economy: Challenges at Home and Abroad, Beverly Hills, Calif.: Sage Publications, 1982.

Duloy, J. H., and Norton, R. D. "CHAC Results: Economic Alternatives for Mexican Agriculture." In Multilevel Planning: Case Studies in Mexico, edited by L. M. Goreux and A. S. Manne. Amsterdam: North Holland, 1973.

La Economia Mexicana. Mexico City: Publicaciones Ejecutivas de Mexico, 1976-1980.

Erband, Richard, and Ross, Stanley, eds. U.S. Policies Toward Mexico. Washington, D.C.: American Enterprise, Institute for Public Policy Research, 1979.

Escobedo, Gilberto. "Formulating a Model of the Mexican Economy." Federal Reserve Bank of St. Louis Review, July 1973, pp. 8-19.

____. "The Response of the Mexican Economy to Policy Actions." Federal Reserve Bank of St. Louis Review, June 1973, pp. 15-23.

Estados Unidos Mexicanos. Poder Ejecutivo Federal. Secretaria de Programacion y Presupuesto. Plan Global de Desarrollo, 1980-82. Mexico, D.F., 1980.

____. Secretaria de Patrimonio y Fomerto Industrial. Plan Nacional de Desarrollo Industrial, 1979-82. Mexico, D.F., March 1979.

Evans, John. "The Evolution of the Mexican Tax System During the 1970s." Paper presented at the Southern Economic Association Meetings, Washington, D.C., November 5, 1980.

Evans, Michael. Macroeconomic Activity: Theory, Forecasting and Control. New York: Harper & Row, 1969.

Felix, David. "Income Inequality in Mexico." Current History, March, 1977, pp. 111-14.

Ferber, Robert. "Consumer Economics: A Survey." Journal of Economic Literature, December 1973, pp. 1303-42.

Fitzgerald, E. V. K. "Capital Accumulation in Mexico." Development and Change, July 1980, pp. 391-418.

____. The Fiscal Deficit and Development Finance: A Note on the Accumulation Balance in Mexico. Center of Latin American Studies Working Papers No. 35. Cambridge, England: University of Cambridge, 1979.

____. "Mexico: A New Direction in Economic Policy?" Bank of London and South America Review, October 1978, pp. 528-38.

____. "Oil and Mexico's Industrial Development Plan." Texas Business Review, May-June 1980, pp. 133-37.

____. Patterns of Public Sector Income and Expenditure in Mexico. Technical Paper Series No. 17. Austin: Institute of Latin American Studies, University of Texas, 1978.

____. "Recent Writing on the Mexican Economy." Latin American Research Review, no. 3, 1981, pp. 236-44.

___. "Stabilization Policy in Mexico: The Fiscal Deficit and Macroeconomic Equilibrium 1960-77. In Inflation and Stabilization in Latin America, edited by Rosemary Thorp and Laurence Whitehead. New York: Holmes and Meier, 1979.

___. "The State and Capital Accumulation in Mexico." Journal of Latin American Studies, November 1978, pp. 263-82.

Frenkel, Jacob, and Johnson, Harry. "The Money Approach to the Balance of Payments: Essential Concepts and Historical Origins." In The Monetary Approach to the Balance of Payments, edited by Jacob Frenkel and Harry Johnson. London: George Allen and Unwin, 1976.

Friedmann, John. Urban and Regional Development in Chile: A Case Study of Innovative Planning. Santiago: The Ford Foundation Urban Regional Development Advisory Program, Chile, 1969.

Friedman, M. A Theory of the Consumption Function. Princeton, N.J.: National Bureau of Economic Research, 1957.

Gallagher, Charles F. Population, Petroleum and Politics: Mexico at the Crossroads. Parts I and II. Hanover, N.H.: American Universities Field Staff Reports Nos. 19 and 42, 1980.

Gannage, Elias. "The Distribution of Income in Underdeveloped Countries." In The Distribution of Income, edited by Jean Marchal and Bernard Ducros. New York: St. Martin's Press, 1968.

Gelb, Alan. Capital-Importing Oil Exporters: Adjustment Issues and Policy Choices. World Bank Staff Working Paper No. 475. New York: International Bank for Reconstruction and Development (World Bank), August 1981.

___. "Optimal Control and Stabilization Policy: An Application to the Coffee Economy." Review of Economic Studies, no. 1 1977, pp. 39-52.

Gonzalez, P., and Florescano, E., eds. Mexico Hoy. Mexico, D.F.: Siglo XXI, 1979.

Gordon, David. "Mexico: A Survey." Economist, April 22, 1978, pp. 32-76.

Grayson, George. "Oil and Politics in Mexico." Current History November 1981, pp. 379-83.

____. The Politics of Mexican Oil. Pittsburgh, Pa.: University of Pittsburgh Press, 1980.

Greenberg, E. "Fixed Investment." In David Heathfield, Topics in Applied Macroeconomics. New York: Academic Press, 1976.

Greenwood, Michael. "An Econometric Model of Internal Migration and Regional Economic Growth in Mexico." Journal of Regional Science, April 1978, pp. 1-32.

Griffiths, Brian. Inflation: The Price of Prosperity. New York: Holmes & Meier, 1976.

____. Mexican Monetary Policy and Economic Development. New York: Praeger, 1972.

Hall, Bronwyn, and Hall, Robert E. Time Series Processor, Version 3.5. Stanford, Calif., April 6, 1980.

Hansen, Niles. "Unbalanced Growth and Regional Development." Western Economic Journal, September 1965, pp. 3-14.

Hansen, Rodger D. The Politics of Mexican Development. Baltimore, Md.: Johns Hopkins University Press, 1971.

Harberger, Arnold. "The Dynamics of Inflation in Chile." In Measurement in Economics, edited by C. Christ. Stanford, Calif.: Stanford University Press, 1963.

Heal, G. M. "The Depletion of Exhaustible Resources: Some Theoretical Issues." In Issues in Contemporary Economics, edited by M. Parkin and R. Nobay. Manchester: Manchester University Press, 1974.

El Heraldo. Mexico City, November 21, 1977.

Higgins, Benjamin. Economic Development. New York: Norton, 1968.

_____. World Development Report, 1980. New York: Oxford University Press, 1980.

_____, World Development Report, 1981. New York: Oxford University Press, 1981.

Iyoha, Milton. "Inflation and Openness in Less Developed Economies: A Cross Country Analysis." Economic Development and Cultural Change, October 1973, pp. 31-38.

James, Preston E. Latin America. 4th ed. New York: Odyssey Press, 1972.

Johnson, Harry. "The Monetary Approach to the Balance of Payments Theory." In H. Johnson, Further Essays in Monetary Economics. Cambridge, Mass.: Harvard University Press, 1973.

Jolly, Richard. "Objectives and Means for Linking Disarmament and Development." In Disarmament and World Development, edited by Richard Jolly. London: Pergamon Press, 1978.

Kaldor, Mary. "The Military in Development," World Development, June 1976, pp. 459-82.

Kaldor, Nicholas. "Inflation and Recession in the World Economy." Economic Journal, December 1976, pp. 703-14.

Kennedy, G. The Military in the Third World. London: Duckworth, 1974.

Kirkpatrick, C. H., and Nixson, F. I. "The Origins of Inflation in Less Developed Countries: A Selective Review." In Inflation in Open Economies, edited by Michael Parkin and George Zis. Manchester: Manchester University Press, 1976.

Kitamura, H. "Trade and Capital Needs of Developing Countries and Foreign Assistance." Weltwirtschaftliches Archiv, no. 2 1966, pp. 303-24.

Klein, L. R. "Political Aspects of Economic Control." In Theory of Economic Efficiency: Essays in Honor of Abba Lerner, edited by H. Greenfield. Cambridge, Mass.: MIT Press, 1979.

Koehler, John. Economic Policy Making with Limited Information The Process of Macro Control in Mexico. Santa Monica, Calif. Rand Corporation, 1968.

Krause, Lawrence, and Salant, Walter, eds. Worldwide Inflation Theory and Recent Experience. Washington, D.C.: Brooking Institution, 1977.

Kuhand, Edwin, and Schmalensee, Richard. An Introduction to Applied Macroeconomics. Amsterdam: North Holland, 1973.

Kuznets, Simon. "Economic Growth and Income Inequality." American Economic Review, March 1955, pp. 1-28.

____. "Quantitative Aspects of the Economic Growth of Nations: Part IV, Distribution of National Income by Factor Shares." Economic Development and Cultural Change, April 1959, pp. 1-97.

Lamadrid, A. "Industrial Location Policy in Mexico." In United Nations Industrial Development Association, Industrial Location and Regional Development—Proceedings of an Inter-regional Seminar. New York: United Nations, 1971.

Landau, Luis. "Saving Functions in Latin America." In Studies in Development Planning, edited by Hollis Chenery. Cambridge, Mass.: Harvard University Press, 1971.

Laney, Leroy O. "Currency Substitution: The Mexican Case." Voice of the Federal Reserve Bank of Dallas, January 1981, pp. 1-10.

____. "How Contagious is 'Dutch Disease'?" Federal Reserve Bank of Dallas Economic Review, March 1982, pp. 3-12.

____. "Oil, Inflation and the Mexican Peso." Voice of the Federal Reserve Bank of Dallas, September 1979, pp. 1-8.

Lanfranco, Sam. "Mexican Oil Export-led Development and Agricultural Neglect." Journal of Economic Development, July 1981, pp. 125-51.

Lavell, A. M. "Regional Industrialization in Mexico: Some Policy Considerations." Regional Studies, August 1972, pp. 343-63.

Lazar, Arpad von, "Development Planning in Mexico: Case Study of an Oil-Rich Economy." Resources Policy, September 1979, pp. 198-210.

Lecaillon, Jacques. "Changes in the Distribution of Income in the French Economy." In The Distribution of National Income, edited by Jean Marchal and Bernard Ducros. New York: St. Martin's Press, 1968.

Lees, Francis, and Eng, Maximo. International Financial Markets: Development of the Present System and Future Prospects. New York: Praeger, 1975.

Leff, N., and Sato, K. "Macroeconomic Adjustment in Developing Countries: Instability, Short-run Growth and External Dependency." Review of Economics and Statistics, May 1980, pp. 170-79.

Looney, Robert E. The Economic Consequences of World Inflation on Semi-dependent Countries. Washington, D.C.: University Press of America, 1979.

_____. Economic Origins of the Iranian Revolution. New York: Pergamon Press, 1982.

_____. Mexico's Economy: A Policy Analysis with Forecasts to 1990. Boulder, Colo.: Westview Press, 1978.

_____. "Mexico's Fiscal Crisis: A Critique of the Fitzgerald Thesis." Paper presented at the Eastern Economic Association Meetings, Philadelphia, April 9-11, 1981.

_____ and Frederiksen, Peter. "The Regional Impact of Infrastructure investment in Mexico." Regional Studies, July 1981, pp. 285-96.

Lopez Portillo, Jose. "Improving the Planning Process: An Imperative for Mexico at This Time." Comercio Exterior de Mexico, May 1978, pp. 191-96.

Luis, Luis R. "Stabilization Policy, Employment and the Balance of Payments: The Recent Mexican Experience." Paper presented at the Eastern Economic Association Meetings, Philadelphia, April 9-11, 1981.

McClelland, Edward. "U.S.-Mexico Border Industry Back on Fast Growth Track." Voice of the Federal Reserve Bank of Dallas, July 1979, pp. 3-9.

McGee, Mary. "Social and Economic Factors in the Differential Growth of Mexican States." Regional Sciences, September 1961, pp. 114-79.

McNown, Robert, and Wallace, Myles. "International Reserve Flows to OPEC States: A Monetary Approach." Journal of Energy and Development, Spring 1977, pp. 267-78.

Mancke, Richard. Mexican Oil and Natural Gas. New York: Praeger, 1979.

Marcos, Ernesto. "Design of a Development Policy for Mexico: Industry and Oil." In Public and Private Enterprise in a Mixed Economy, edited by William Baumol. New York: St. Martin's Press, 1980.

Marquez, Travier. "La Economia Mexicana en 1977 y su Futuro. Madrid, October 28, 1977 (mimeo).

Mayer, Thomas. "Plant and Equipment Lead Times." Journal of Business, April 1960, pp. 127-32.

_____. "The Structure of Monetarism (I)." In Thomas Mayer, The Structure of Monetarism. New York: Norton, 1978.

_____ and Sonenblum, S. "Lead Times for Fixed Investment." Review of Economics and Statistics, August 1955, pp. 300-30.

Meiselman, David, and Laffer, Arthur, eds. The Phenomenon of Worldwide Inflation. Washington, D.C.: American Enterprise Institute for Public Policy Research, 1975.

Mendoze-Berrueto, Eliseo. "Regional Implications of Mexico's Economic Growth." Weltwirtschaftliches Archiv, no. 1, 1968, pp. 87-123.

Metwally, M. M., and Tamaschke, H. V. "Oil Exports and Economic Growth in the Middle East." Kyklos, no. 3, 1980, pp. 499-521.

Mexico: National Industrial Development Plan. Vol. 1. London: Graham & Trotman, 1979.

"Mexico's Reluctant Oil Boom: A Tight Rein on Development to Promote Balanced Growth," Business Week, January 15, 1979, p. 74.

Mikesell, Raymond. "The Contribution of Petroleum and Mineral Resources to Economic Development." In Foreign Investment in the Petroleum and Mineral Industries, edited by Raymond Mikesell. Baltimore, Md.: Johns Hopkins University Press, 1972.

Ministry of National Properties and Industrial Development, "Mexico Energy Program: Goals to 1990 and Projections to the Year 2000," Comercio Exterior de Mexico, December 1980, pp. 436-61.

Morgan, David. "Fiscal Policy in Oil Exporting Countries, 1972-1978." International Monetary Fund Staff Papers, March 1979, pp. 55-86.

Mueller, Marnie. "Structural Inflation and the Mexican Experience." Yale Economic Essays, Spring 1965, pp. 162-90.

Mussa, M. "A Monetary Approach to Balance of Payments Analysis." Journal of Money, Credit and Banking, August 1974, pp. 333-52.

Nankani, G. Development Problems of Mineral-Exporting Countries. World Bank Staff Working Paper No. 354. New York: International Bank for Reconstruction and Development (World Bank), August 1979.

Navarette, A. "El Sector Publico en el Desarrollo Economica." Investigacion Economica, January 1957, pp. 43-61.

Niering, Frank E., Jr. "Mexico: A New Force in World Oil." Petroleum Economist, March 1979, pp. 109-15.

Nowick, A., ed., Mexico: Manufacturing Sector, Situation, Prospects and Policies. Washington, D.C.: International Bank for Reconstruction and Development (World Bank), 1979.

Nugent, Jeffrey. "Momentum for Development and Development Disequilibria." Journal of Economic Development, July 1977, pp. 31-52.

_____ and Tarawneh, Fayez. "The Anatomy of Changes in Income Distribution and Poverty Among Mexico's Economically Active Population Between 1950 and 1970." Paper presented at the Eastern Economic Association Meetings, Philadelphia, April 9-11, 1981.

Opie, Redvers. Mexican Industrialization and Petroleum. Mexico, D.F.: ECANAL, 1979.

_____. The Overall Development Plan 1980-1982: An Appraisal, Mexico, D.F.: ECANAL, 1980.

Organization of American States. General Secretariat. Short Term Economic Reports—Mexico. Washington, D.C., 1980.

Ortiz, Guillermo, and Solis, Leopoldo. "Financial Structure and Exchange Rate Experience." Journal of Development Economics, December 1979, pp. 515-48.

Otani, Ichiro. "Inflation in an Open Economy: A Case Study of the Philippines." International Monetary Fund, Staff Papers, November 1975, pp. 750-74.

Parkin, Michael. "A Monetarist Analysis of the Generation and Transmission of World Inflation: 1958-1971." American Economic Review, February 1977, pp. 164-71.

_____, and Zis, George, eds. Inflation in Open Economies. Manchester: Manchester University Press, 1976.

Perez Mendoze, Vincente Ernesto. The Role of the Armed Forces in the Mexican Economy in the 1980s. M.A. thesis, Naval Postgraduate School, June 1981.

Petroleos Mexicanos. Report Delivered by the Director General, 1978. Mexico, D.F., 1978.

Polster, T. H. Public Program Analysis. Baltimore, Md.: University Park Press, 1978.

Putnam, Bluford, and Wilford, D. Sykes. The Monetary Approach to International Adjustment. New York: Praeger, 1978.

Rao, Potluri, and Miller, Roger. Applied Econometrics. Belmont, Calif.: Wadsworth, 1971.

Rawls, J. A Theory of Social Justice. Cambridge, Mass.: Harvard University Press, 1971.

Reyes, Saul Trejo. "Comments." In Economic Stabilization in Developing Countries, edited by William Cline and Sidney Weintraub. Washington, D.C.: Brookings Institution, 1981.

Reynolds, Clark. "Labor Market Projections for the United States and Mexico and Current Migration Controversies." Food Research Institute Studies, no. 2, 1979, pp. 121-56.

_____. The Mexican Economy. New Haven, Conn.: Yale University Press, 1970.

_____. A Shift Share Analysis of Regional and Sectoral Productivity Growth in Contemporary Mexico. International Institute for Applied Systems Analysis Research Report-80-41. Laxenberg, Austria, November 1980.

_____. "Review. Mexico's Economy: A Policy Analysis with Forecasts to 1990 by Robert E. Looney," Journal of Economic Literature, June 1980, pp. 608-10.

_____. "Why Mexico's 'Stabilizing Development' was Actually Destabilizing." World Development, July-August 1978, pp. 1005-18.

Riding, Alan. "Mexico's Mood is Pessimistic." San Francisco Chronicle, February 15, 1982, p. 23.

_____. "Mexico's Road to Trouble is Coated with Oil." New York Times, February 21, 1982, p. 17.

_____. "Oil Glut Threatens Mexico's Economy." New York Times, July 6, 1981, p. 9.

Roberts, Robert, and McBee, George. "Modernization and Economic Development in Mexico: A Factor Analytic Approach."

Economic Development and Cultural Change, July 1968, pp. 603-12.

Ronfeldt, David, Nehring, Richard, and Gandara, Arturo. _Mexico's Petroleum and U.S. Policy: Implications for the 1980s._ Santa Monica, Calif.: Rand Corporation, 1980.

Ros, Jaime. "Pricing in the Mexican Manufacturing Sector." _Cambridge Journal of Economics_, September 1980, pp. 211-32.

Ross, Stanley. "Key Issues in Mexican-United States Relations." _Texas Business Review_, March-April 1979,

"SAM, the Beginnings of Strategy." _Comercio Exterior de Mexico_, July 1980, pp. 243-49.

Sanders, Thomas. _Mexico in 1975._ American Universities Field Staff Reports North America Series, Vol. III, no. 4, September 1975.

Sargent, Thomas, and Wallace, Neil. "Rational Expectations and the Theory of Economic Policy." _Journal of Monetary Economics_, April 1976, pp. 169-85.

Schlagheck, James. _The Political, Economic and Labor Climate in Mexico._ Rev. ed. Philadelphia, Pa.: Wharton School, University of Pennsylvania, Industrial Research Unit, 1980.

Serrano, Diaz. "Petroleos Mexicanos: Activities in 1980," _Comercio Exterior de Mexico_, April 1981, pp. 134-42.

Sheehey, E. J. "On the Measurement of Imported Inflation in Developing Countries." _Weltwirtschaftliches Archiv_, no. 1, 1979, pp. 68-79.

Shourie, Aron. "The Use of Macroeconomic Regression Models of Developing Countries for Forecasts and Policy Prescription." _Oxford Economic Papers_, March 1972, pp. 1-35.

Silvers, Arthur, and Crossin, Pierre. _Rural Development and Urban-bound Migration in Mexico._ Washington, D.C.: Resources for the Future, 1980.

Simon, H. A. "Dynamic Programming Under Uncertainty with a Quadratic Criterion." _Econometrica_, January 1956, pp. 74-81.

Sinha, Radha. "The World Food Problem: Consensus and Conflict." World Development, May-June 1977, pp. 371-82.

Smithies, Arthur. The Economic Potential of the Arab Countries. Santa Monica, Calif.: Rand Corporation, 1978.

Solis, Leopoldo. Economic Policy Reform in Mexico. Elmsford, N.Y.: Pergamon Press, 1981.

_____. "The Financial System in the Economic Development of Mexico." Weltwirtschaftliches Archiv, no. 1 1968, pp. 36-68.

_____. "Industrial Priorities in Mexico." In United Nations Industrial Development Organization, Industrial Priorities in Developing Countries. New York: United Nations, 1979.

_____. "The Petroleum Boom in Mexico: An Opportunity for Correcting the Pattern of Economic Development." Paper presented at the North American Economic Studies Association Meetings, Mexico City, December 28, 1978.

Solow, R. M. "Intergenerational Equity and Exhaustible Resources." Review of Economic Studies, October 1974, pp. 29-47.

Statistical Analysis System (SAS). User's Guide, 1979. Cary, N.C.: SAS Institute, 1979.

Stiglitz, J. E. "Growth with Exhaustible Natural Resources: Efficient Optimal Growth Paths." Review of Economic Studies, October 1974, pp. 23-49.

Stohr, Walter. Regional Development Experiences and Prospects in Latin America. The Hague: Mouton, 1975.

Street, James. "Prospects for Mexico's Industrial Development Plan in the 1980s." Texas Business Review, May-June 1980, pp. 125-32.

Tello, C. La Politica Economica en Mexico, 1970-1976. Mexico, D.F.: Siglo XXI, 1979.

ten Kate, Adriaan, and Wallace, Robert Bruce. Protection and Economic Development in Mexico. New York: St. Martin's Press, 1980.

Theil, H. "A Note on Certainty Equivalence in Dynamic Planning." Econometrica, April 1957, pp. 346-49.

____. "On the Theory of Economic Policy." American Economic Review, May 1956, pp. 49-60.

Timbergen, J. On the Theory of Economic Policy. Amsterdam: North Holland, 1952.

Torres, Olga E. "Regional Development." In Banco Nacional de Comercio Exterior, S.A., Mexico 1976. Mexico, D.F.: 1976.

Tuma, Elias. "Strategic Resources and Viable Interdependence: The Case of Middle Eastern Oil." Middle East Journal, Summer 1979, pp. 269-87.

Twomey, Michael. "Exchange Rate Devaluations and Income Distribution in Latin America." Paper presented at the Western Economics Association Meetings, San Francisco, Calif., July 2, 1981.

Urguidi, Victor. "Not by Oil Alone: The Outlook for Mexico." Current History, February 1982, pp. 78-81.

____. "An Overview of Mexican Economic Development." Weltwirtschaftliches Archiv, no. 1, 1968, pp. 2-20.

U.S. Arms Control and Disarmament Agency. World Military Expenditures and Arms Transfers: 1967-1976. Washington, D.C., 1978.

Vakil, F. Estimating Iran's Financial Surplus 1352-1371. Tehran: Economic Research Institute, 1975.

Vanek, J. Estimating Foreign Resource Needs for Economic Development. New York: McGraw-Hill, 1967.

van Ginneken, Wouter. Socio-economic Groups and Income Distribution in Mexico. London: Croom Helm, 1980.

Velasco, Jesus-Agustin. Mexico in the World Oil Market: Opportunities and Dangers for Mexican Development. John F. Kennedy School of Government Discussion Paper E-80-07. Cambridge, Mass.: Harvard University, October 1980.

Venezian, Eduardo, and Gamble, William. The Agricultural Development of Mexico. New York: Praeger, 1969.

Vernon, Raymond. "Comprehensive Model Building in the Planning Process: The Case of Less Developed Economies." Economic Journal, March 1966, pp. 57-69.

Villarreal, Rene, and de Villarreal, Rocio. "Mexico's Development Strategy." In Susan Purcell, Mexico-United States Relations. New York: Praeger, 1981.

Vogel, R. "The Dynamics of Inflation in Latin America, 1950-1969." American Economic Review, March 1974, pp. 102-14.

Wacher, Susan. Latin American Inflation. Lexington, Mass.: Lexington Books, 1976.

Weinstein, M. C., and Zeckhauser, R. J. "The Optimum Consumption of Depletable Natural Resources." Quarterly Journal of Economics, August 1975, pp. 371-92.

Weintraub, Sidney. "Case Study of Economic Stabilization: Mexico." In Economic Stabilization in Developing Countries, edited by William Sline and Sidney Weintraub. Washington, D.C.: Brookings Institution, 1981.

Whitehead, Laurence. "Mexico from Bust to Boom: A Political Evaluation of the 1976-79 Stabilization Programme." World Development, November 1980, pp. 843-64.

Whynes, David. The Economics of Third World Military Expenditures. Austin: University of Texas Press, 1979.

Wilford, D. Sykes. Monetary Policy and the Open Economy: Mexico's Experience. New York: Praeger, 1977.

_____. "Price Levels, Interest Rates, Open Economies and a Fixed Exchange: The Mexican Case 1954-1974." Review of Business and Economic Research, Spring 1977, pp. 52-65.

_____ and Wilford, W. T. "The Revenue-Income Elasticity Coefficient: Performance and Stability Criteria." Review of Business and Economic Research, Winter 1976, pp. 23-34.

_____ and Zecher, J. Richard. "Monetary Policy and the Balance of Payments in Mexico, 1955-1975." Journal of Money, Credit and Banking, August 1979, pp. 340-48.

Wilke, James. The Mexican Revolution: Federal Expenditure and Social Change Since 1910. Berkeley: University of California Press, 1970

_____. Statistics and National Policy Supplement 3: Statistical Abstract of Latin America. Los Angeles: University of California at Los Angeles Latin America Center, 1974.

Williams, Edward. "Petroleum and Political Change." In Mexico's Political Economy, edited by Jorge Dominquez. Beverly Hills, Calif.: Sage Publications, 1982.

_____. The Rebirth of the Mexican Petroleum Industry. Lexington, Mass.: Lexington Books, 1979.

Wionczek, Miguel. "Incomplete Formal Planning: Mexico." In Planning Economic Development, edited by Everett Hagen. Homewood, Ill.: Richard D. Irwin, 1963.

Wong, Chorng-huey. "Demand for Money in Developing Countries." Journal of Monetary Economics, January 1977, pp. 59-86.

_____ and Pettersen, O. "Financial Programming in the Framework of Optimal Control." Weltwirtschaftliches Archiv, no. 1 1979, pp. 20-37.

Yates, P. Lamartine. Mexico's Agricultural Dilemma. Tucson: University of Arizona Press, 1981.

Young, Frank, "The Structural Context of Rural Poverty in Mexico: A Cross-state Comparison." Economic Development and Cultural Change, October 1979, pp. 669-87.

ABOUT THE AUTHOR

ROBERT E. LOONEY is associate professor of national security affairs at the Naval Postgraduate School, Monterey, California. He has been a faculty member of the University of California at Davis, the University of Santa Clara, and the Monterey Institute of International Studies. He has also been a development economist at the Stanford Research Institute, and has been a consultant to the International Labor Office, the Inter-American Development Bank, the International Bank for Reconstruction and Development (World Bank) and the governments of Iran, Saudi Arabia, Mexico, and Panama.

Dr. Looney has published numerous articles in professional journals and is the author of: The Economic Development of Iran (1973), Income Distribution Policies and Economic Growth in Semi-industrialized Countries (1975), The Economic Development of Panama (1976), Iran at the End of the Century (1977), A Development Strategy for Iran Through the 1980s (1977), Mexico's Economy: A Policy Analysis with Forecasts to 1990 (1978), The Economic Consequences of World Inflation on Semi-dependent Countries (1979), Saudi Arabia's Growth Potential (1981). His most recent book is The Economic Origins of the Iranian Revolution.